Alexandria
A Cultural and Religious
Melting Pot

Aarhus Studies in Mediterranean Antiquity (ASMA)

IX

ASMA is a series which will be published approximately once a year by The Centre for the Study of Antiquity, University of Aarhus, Denmark.

The Centre is a network of cooperating departments: Greek and Latin, Classical Archaeology, History, and the Faculty of Theology. The objective of the series is to advance the interdisciplinary study of Antiquity by publishing articles, e.g., conference papers, or independent monographs, which among other things reflect the current activities of the centre.

Alexandria
A Cultural and
Religious Melting Pot

Edited by George Hinge and Jens A. Krasilnikoff

Aarhus University Press |

Alexandria. A Cultural and Religious Melting Pot
© Aarhus University Press and the authors 2009

Cover by Jørgen Sparre
Illustration: Roman mosaic from Palestrina. Archaeological Museum
© 1990. Photo Scala, Florence – courtesy of the Ministero Beni e Att. Culturali
Typeset with Minion
and printed by Narayana Press
Printed in Denmark, 2009

ISBN 978 87 7934 491 4
ISSN 1399 2686

Aarhus University Press
Langelandsgade 177
DK-8200 Aarhus N
www.unipress.dk

White Cross Mills
Hightown, Lancaster, LA1 4XS
United Kingdom
www.gazellebookservices.co.uk

PO Box 511
Oakville, CT 06779
www.oxbowbooks.com

Published with the financial support of
The Aarhus University Research Foundation
The Danish Research Council for the Humanities

The Centre for the Study of Mediterranean Antiquity at the University of Aarhus is a research forum for the advancement of interdisciplinary studies of Antiquity. The dominant activity of the Centre is to arrange seminars and conferences and to publish the contributions from these events in monographs. Additionally, several individual monographs have been published in the Centres series, Aarhus Studies in Mediterranean Antiquity (ASMA). The Centres seminars and conferences are devoted to the study of such significant fields and topics that will benefit from an interdisciplinary approach. The publications of the Centre is therefore reflections of the ongoing process, which binds the various fields of activity together at the University of Aarhus, and between our university and the international scholarly community.

In May 2004 the Centre hosted an international seminar on Alexandria. Several distinguished colleagues from different countries contributed to this seminar, both as givers of papers and as discussants. Some of these papers have been included in this volume, while other contributions have been added later. First of all, our warmest thanks to the contributors for their professional and scholarly approach and their patience regarding the preparation of this volume. The distinguished Members of the Board of the Centre for the Study of Mediterranean Antiquity, deserves our gratitude because of their never failing enthusiasm and encouragement and Aarhus University Research Foundation for making the necessary donations available in the first place; and the Danish Research Council for Culture and Communication for financial support of the publication. Last but not least we extend our gratitude to the research assistants and secretaries, without whose help and support none of this would have happened.

Aarhus, December 2008
George Hinge and Jens A. Krasilnikoff

CONTENTS

INTRODUCTION

George Hinge and Jens A. Krasilnikoff

The appreciation amongst the international host of scholars of ancient Alexandria as a field of research has been growing these recent years and one can even suggest that it has been accelerating within the past three decades or more. The continued interest is manifested in increased knowledge of the material culture of Ptolemaic and Roman Alexandria, and the increase in the publication rate of papyri manuscripts and other evidence from Egypt continues to fuel scholarly debate. Moreover, the growing interest among scholars of the humanities worldwide in the mental aspects of past societies invites to develop the tenets of cultural history, language and religion within the wider frame of ancient Alexandria.

This project was conceived in 2002 as part of the continued discussion and charting of the current and future activities of Centre for the Study of Mediterranean Antiquity. The Centre board agreed to the simple observation that most of the partakers of the Centre were all somehow researching aspects of Egypt's culture, history, or religions of the Graeco-Roman period. Further pondering suggested that this rather board scope should be narrowed down to just "Alexandria," in particular those aspects of the Alexandrine past, which encompassed the aforementioned aspects of cultural history, history and religion. Thus, although previous research projects have successfully navigated the difficult waters of interdisciplinary research much reward was to be expected from the insistence upon the combination of a wide thematic scope examined within the confines of the wide chronological spectrum. Consequently, as several contributions demonstrate and observe, the Alexandrine past is notoriously marked by meeting of cultures and frequent and rapid development, which is quite difficult to grasp in its totality if the longer perspective is ignored. Additionally, the long-held insistence of the "fact" that Alexandria represented a world totally different from the parallel cultural and political construct of traditional Egyptian culture is also being challenged. And so are different aspects of the religious and philosophical milieus, which developed almost from the foundation of the city to Late Antiquity and the beginning of the Middle Ages.

As the title of this volume suggests, throughout the entire span of Graeco-Roman antiquity Alexandria represented a meeting place for many ethnic cultures and the city itself was subject to a wide range of local developments, which created and formatted a distinct Alexandrine "culture" as well as several distinct "cultures". Ancient Greek, Roman and Jewish observers communicated or held claim to that particular message. Hence, Arrian, Theocritus, Strabo, and Athenaeus reported their fascination of the Alexandrine melting pot to the wider world and so did Philo, Josephus and Clement.

As some of the reviewers observed one is in serious danger of being trounced by the sheer amount of information, life, abundance, ingenuity and vigour, which for some time became "Alexandria" by the accomplishment of Fraser's monolithic *Ptolemaic Alexandria* from 1972. Fraser's "antiquarian" (if this word has a positive connotation) reconstruction and "compilation" of Alexandria until the coming of Rome continue to leave us in the state of Strabo, slightly bewildered and overwhelmed. We shall, nonetheless, insist that the Alexandrine melting pot made up a distinct order, one of different not always corresponding, abiding and enduring elements of cultural amalgamations.

Recently, the German professor Christian Meier argued for the existence of "Europe's special path," in order to explain the relative success of Europe in dominating the remainder of the world in the courses of the nineteenth and twentieth centuries. Meier anchors the beginning of Europe in Greece, more accurately in Athens of the fifth century BCE, where he focuses on the democratic institutions, citizenship, freedom to debate and a firm belief in the positive effect of "the debate" for a positive future development. Multiple objections and corrections can be made against Meier's hypothesis. One is the fact that Europe would not have been what it became without an Alexandria to take in and further develop what it inherited from the Greek and Near Eastern worlds.

Time, acceleration and volume are features that dominated the development of Alexandrine history, but also paucity, contemplation and stability. The mildly stressed Strabo would have acknowledged both the ambiguities and the "beat" of Alexandria. Here, in the largest city known to mankind – later only surpassed by Rome – the multi-ethnic and internationalised community insisted upon setting the standards in and of a globalised world. Alexandria thus became the centre for communication of scientific and scholarly achievements as well as religious novelties, digression and development. Alexandrine "culture" came to signify novelty and speed, but also degeneration and the target of the special versions of early "Orientalism'.

In various fashions, the four papers of Part I of the monograph, **Alexandria from Greece and Egypt,** deals with the relationship between Ptolemaic Alexandria and its Greek past. However, the Egyptian origin and heritage also plays important roles for the arguments. In the first contribution of the volume, Jens A. Krasilnikoff discusses and explores the potentials of humanistic geography as a theoretical tools and approach for the study of the earliest Alexandrine history. Thus, with examples of how Alexandria was created as *place*, Krasilnikoff argues that the city of Alexander differed fundamentally form the majority of classical and Hellenistic cities. The evidence suggests that the rulers of Alexandria were soon to create their own standards of urbanism, conspicuous consumption and cultural amalgamation in close resonance with a profound exclusiveness of its royal ideology. Undoubtedly, the heirs of Alexander exercised great impact upon the religions and cultural amalgams of the city. Concurrently, however, they also subscribed to the institutions and traditions of the classical Greek *polis*, a dominant feature in the ancient literary tradition on and about Alexandria. Paradoxically, the acute need of the first Ptolemaic rulers to create Alexandria into a distinct, unique and self-preserving urban entity in its own right demanded that the city of Alexander was made exactly that by the creation of Alexandria as a distinct Greek *place*. This was achieved partially by exploitation of the logics of earlier Greek colony foundations, a process which allows for the newly founded city to become its own, to win its independence. Secondly, the Ptolemies, by claim of ancestry to Alexander's project and by exploitation of the relationship between the *oikist*, Alexander and his city, created a *place* for royal ideology, which was not dependent on either a Graeco-Macedonian or an Egyptian political or cultural-religious dependency but uniquely Ptolemaic.

In "Theatrical Fiction and Visual Bilingualism in the Monumental Tombs of Ptolemaic Alexandria" Marjorie Susan Venit displays and discusses the contents, contexts as well as the implications of the unique tombs of Ptolemaic Alexandria. Two distinct elements are peculiar to these Alexandrian tombs: the first, Venit finds, is their amalgamation of Egyptian elements into a genuinely Hellenically-inspired monument and the second is their inclusion of the theatrical element. Thus two architectural traditions and two ethnically discrete visual systems are mixed to produce a unique expression, which creates a distinct frame of the performance of ritual drama. However, Venit takes this observation further and argues that this new mortuary building type, "independent of place and time and so ideational in its goals, must have served to encourage in the polyglot population of Alexandria an identity as Alexandrians as it also concretised their eschatological ideals." Certainly, Venit argues, one shall not presuppose that each Alexandrian individual saw his or her own relation with the afterlife as identical with that of his (or her) neighbour. Individual Alexandrians may have been associated with a number of different cults. However, the (potential) discrepancy between individual or group differences one might anticipate "… and despite the ethnically distinct divisions that current thought imposes on the population of Ptolemaic Alexandria (and that may have well existed in everyday affairs), the city's monumental tombs suggest an inclusiveness and a commonality of purpose within the rite of burial." Thus Venit arrives at the important conclusion that the tombs, so to speak, reflect that the mode of burial stressed both the tombs' performative-embracing function and its Egypto-Hellenic intellectual content. Venit concludes to the effect that Alexandrian tomb-culture represented a unique expression of the Ptolemaic-period and that the establishment of the mortuary buildings as bi-cultural monuments can only have had their genesis in the peculiar construct that was ancient Alexandria.

The argument of George Hinge's contribution "Language and Race: Theocritus and the Koine Identity of Ptolemaic Egypt," is that "…language played a major role in the ancient concept of ethnicity; and that linguistic differences and similarities were, to a certain extent, shaped by the ethnic divisions and groupings". Hinge sets off his argument from the observation that Herodotus in his famous passage 8.144.2 operates language to the effect that it helps define ethnicity – it supports the important point that language is fundamental to Herodotus' concept of ethnicity. Accordingly, Hinge disputes Jonathan Hall's contention (*Ethnic identity in Greek Antiquity*, 1997) that language played only a minor role in the formation of ethnic groups, amongst various arguments by the presentation of a different understanding of the role of isoglosses. Hinge's preliminary conclusion is that it cannot "be stressed often enough that this identity is not natural *per se*, but a cultural construction. The linguistic, cultural and religious similarity of the future Greeks, which already existed as a consequence of the cultural convergence in the Mycenaean Age, was an impetus to this construction." Thus, the construction of Hellenic identity that emphasised these parallels would, Hinge argues, naturally minimise the differences and maximise the similarities. Thus, the creation of the *koine* is to Hinge a clear indication of the importance of language to the contemporary ponderings about Greek ethnicity.

The connection and relevance of Alexandria to the theme of Hinge's paper is therefore obvious. In the Alexandrine context, Hinge examines the question of the development of *koine* and concludes that "the Koineisation is therefore better described as a gradual convergence of related linguistic norms towards an imagined super regional standard ("dialect levelling")." Finally, Theocritus' 15th idyll is analysed as an example of how linguistic and ethnic consciousness was formulated in the time of Ptolemy Philadelphus. Although Hinge does not find the 15th idyll to testify to "the spoken language of the streets of Ptolemaic Alexandria," it is, nonetheless, important evidence of the *attitudes* towards language. Clearly, the population expresses their cultural meeting linguistically, new-comers become Alexandrines by acknowledgement of *koine* and Alexandria is rightfully declared a "melting-pot." Hence, some degree of bilingualism is discussed in two variants: first, Egyptian interference in Greek and secondly Greek interference in Egyptian. Hinge finds that Greek interference is quite widespread in the Coptic language, while Egyptian interference in Greek is more ambiguous. However, when the local dialects are replaced by *koine*, we are facing the symptom of a new identity, and not only a symptom, but also a most powerful contribution to that identity.

One of the institutions to dominate and secure the Greek influence on Alexandria was the Library and the Museum, and here Homer continued to play a dominant role as subject of scholarly scrutiny. The paper by Minna Skafte Jensen focuses on the organisation of the great Alexandrian Museum. Here, "The best Greek scholars in both the humanities and the sciences – to use modern terminology – were invited to the Museum, where they had free board and lodging and access to the books, and during the Hellenistic period this "centre for advanced study" achieved brilliant results in the full spectrum of research fields known to the ancient world." The focal point of Jensen's paper is, however, the research that was conducted there on language and philology. The Alexandrine philologists performed what is acknowledged as the first, fundamental studies of Homer and produced the versions of the *Iliad* and the *Odyssey* as we know them today. Besides the achievements of the Alexandrine scholars extended to studies of Hesiod, Pindar and other early poets as well as of Athenian drama, and they worked on orthographic and prosodic problems. Additionally, the complexities of ancient as well as modern scrutiny into the Homeric Question and the *scholia* are presented. The final part of the paper is devoted to a discussion of scholarly achievements, including textual criticism, interpretation and finally how the activities of the Museum contributed to the development of multicultural Alexandria. Jensen focuses on the systematic criticisms of the Homeric text that was conducted at the Museum including the vexed questions of the meaning of the terms *ekdosis* and *diorthōsis*, that is, the question of whether scholars edited the texts. Jensen opts for a process where scholars presented their personal commentaries to other scholars for further discussion. As for the question on interpretation, Jensen discusses the criteria applied by the scholars including athetising and observes the fact that the criterion for a verse or passage to be considered spurious was just stated and the reasons not given. Jensen argues that the Alexandrines had a more or less precise idea of a Homeric linguistic form, which was "not only viewed as more elevated and poetic than prosaic Greek of their own day, but was competently analysed as an older stage of the language." Additionally, the Alexandrines were critical towards Atticising elements as well as passages with a "political" content, inconsistencies and blasphemous content. In their literary criticism, Jensen observes that the Alexandrians adopted the general principle of interpreting Homer from Homer, *Homēron ex Homērou saphēnizein*. They seem to have accepted the *Iliad* and the *Odyssey* as fictional entities with their own logic and universe. Both in this and in their careful "close reading" of the poems they might be considered ancient forerunners of 20th century New Criticism. In conclusion Jensen finds that "the impression we get in the sources does not confirm the picture of the Library as an important participant in the great interaction of cultures and religions. On the contrary, the philologists of the Library appear to have been concerned with Greek literature and nothing else." On the basis of the evidence it seems as if the Macedonian rulers established a centre of Greek learning, for which Greek books were acquired and made an institution where Greek scholars were invited to study.

The contributions to the second part of the book are devoted to discussions of various aspects of contact and development between **Rome, Judaism and Christianity**. The first of the papers in Part II is Per Bilde's study of Philo as a polemist and a political apologist. Philo, who is the author of the two books to be discussed by Bilde, belonged to the most influential Jewish family in Alexandria. He played a significant political role in the years 38-41, a period of great importance in the history of the Jewish people in the ancient world. Thus, scholarly discussions of his literary produce continue to shed light on the development of the international politics during the early Principate as well as adding significant information and detail to the further development of Alexandria as a multi-ethnic and cultural entity. The aim of Bilde's analysis is to present and examine the two treatises as evidence indicating that Philo worked as a polemist and political apologist. First, Bilde presents a historical reconstruction of the course of events in Alexandria in the year 38. Secondly, based on this, Bilde presents the main purpose of this investigation, which is a close analysis and interpretation of the two historical treatises *Against Flaccus* and *The Embassy to Gaius*. Finally, Bilde discusses the literary genre and the aim, dating and intended readers of the two writings; and he presents a discussion of the question whether these writings of Philo could be perceived as a threat to Rome. Presumably, according to Philo, the Jewish population in Alexandria continued to thrive well over the first year of Caligula's rule (37-38 CE). Then, Philo informs, the Roman prefect in Alexandria (and Egypt) for reasons that are not evident, seems to have cancelled the Jewish population's established right to live in Alexandria according to the customs of their fathers and under internal self-government. Anti-Jewish riots ensued where the Roman authorities chose to follow the "Greeks" denouncing the Jews as "foreigners and newcomers" (*xenous kai epēludas*) in Alexandria and massive prosecutions followed. Bilde infers that the Jews in Alexandria were subjected to widespread cruel and violent persecutions in the summer of 38, but he cautions, however, against too rigid conclusions regarding the actual historical circumstances, which cannot be established directly on the basis of Philo's very committed descriptions. We should refrain, Bilde insert, "when reconstructing historical circumstances in Antiquity, from using terms related to the European persecutions of Jews in the Middle Ages and in recent times." However, the peace was restored when the Emperor Claudius ascended the throne in 41 CE.

In respect to the chain of incidents and actions that commenced during the turbulent years of Gaius Caligula, Bilde concludes that Philo took an active part in politics, including the leadership of the Alexandrian-Jewish delegation of five representatives to plead for the Alexandrian Jews with the Emperor Caligula. Bilde agrees with Goodenough that the political activity of Philo "does not contrast with, but is in continuation of his exegetic and philosophical activity." To this, Bilde adds, it can be surmised that Philo's significant political effort should also be considered in relation to his family background (close relations with the Roman imperial family of the Julians), which made him able to communicate directly with both Caligula and Agrippa I.

Moreover Bilde holds that we can conclude that Philo, during and immediately after this critical period, probably in the year 41, wrote the two historical books analysed here. These, Bilde argues, should rightfully be characterised as political-apologetic and theological-apologetic writings aimed at Jewish as well as non-Jewish, especially Roman, readers. The theological-apologetic character of these writings places them alongside the works of Josephus.

Finally, Bilde demonstrates a contrast in these two writings between Philo's "pacifist" ideology and his barely disguised military threat to Rome. Finally, on the basis of this analysis, Bilde concludes that Philo was solidly anchored within the mainstream of Jewish literature in Antiquity.

Anders Klostergaard Petersen's paper, "Alexandrian Judaism: Rethinking a Problematic Cultural Category," focuses on the theoretical aspects of how to reconstruct past cultural entities, though it is not concerned with the empirical subject matter of Alexandrian Jewry. First, Petersen presents a survey of some of the most important stages in the history of Alexandrian Jewry; and secondly, he discusses "Alexandrian Judaism with close attention to a number of theoretical problems that are infrequently mentioned in the predominant strands of scholarship." Additionally, his ambition is to contribute to the continuous research on Alexandrian Jewry; but also to increase the scholarly awareness of some fundamental theoretical problems that pertain to the understanding of culture within the academic fields studying antiquity. Hence, Petersen develops a series of arguments by first discussing some of the involved theoretical issues, which are reflected upon by previous scholarship only to a limited extent. In particular, this involves the constrained nature of the sources, the fact that they seldom are reflected upon, and finally the lack of reflection upon the applied as well as the potential definitions of culture and cultural categories.

Throughout the many examples and discussions, Petersen arrives at the important observation that the constrained nature of the sources should not only be acknowledged but also paid close heed to in the conclusions drawn from them. Though not necessarily in disagreement with the arguments of Per Bilde, Petersen argues that Philo "most certainly did not embody Alexandrian Judaism in its cultural and social breadth as is often the impression one gets from studies on Alexandrian Jewry." And he ponders that "Like other writers, Philo's writings should be interpreted as the creations of a composite being who under particular circumstances and with particular aims and situations in mind attempts to conquer the cultural battlefield of his time. That, of course, applies to all other antique writers as well." Petersen argues as well, that several sources speaking of the Jewish *politeuma* do not, in fact, say much about the impact of these institutions on the legal and social life of Alexandrian Jews. Additionally, lack of information on Jewish jurisprudence, inferences about the lower social segments of Alexandrian Jewry as well as the elite strands of Alexandrian Jewry severe the prospect of detailed and sound assessments. Moreover, Petersen opts for caution when cultural dualisms like the Hellenism-Judaism dichotomy is extrapolated from the evidence. Petersen makes the important observation: "In so far as the dichotomy has a bearing on the primary sources and is not exclusively the reflection of the taxonomising practices of modern scholarship, it is urgent to distinguish between actual ancient antique social reality and its imagined reality."

Samuel Rubenson's paper "From School to Patriarchate. Aspects on the Christianisation of Alexandria" addresses the transformation of the classical heritage into an early medieval Christian culture and the role played by the city of Alexandria in that respect.

It was only the combined efforts of the emperor and the bishops of Rome and Constantinople that finally ended Alexandrian ecclesiastical power by means of the council of Chalcedon in 451 CE. However, because of the nature of evidence, the development of Christianity in Alexandria and the Christianisation of the city is poorly documented and analysed. In contrast to the dominant interpretations of Bauer and others who have mainly seen the early developments of Christianity in Alexandria as a matter of doctrinal change, the author suggests that one should consider the changes from a social point of view. Accordingly, Rubenson suggests that the significant move was not made from Gnostic heterodoxy to Ecclesial orthodoxy, but was constituted by a movement from a school of philosophy to a powerful communal institution supplanting traditional forms of imperial as well as local power.

In conclusion, Rubenson observes that the early phase of Christianity in Alexandria is primarily known to us through the presence of a number of Christian teachers during the second century CE. Thus, a strong tradition was established and associated with the Christian schools and the prominent philosophers associated with these schools gaining recognition in the city as well as in the wider Christian community. Consequently, their success as teachers resulted in the growth of a Christian community, which in the third century was led by a series of Christian philosophers. The severe and prolonged persecutions of the Christian leadership of Alexandria in 303-11 resulted in schisms as well as a rift between the leadership of the church and the school. The recognition of the position of the bishop of Alexandria by Emperor Constantine and his successors provided the bishops of the fourth century with a completely new official position and responsibility. In their efforts to unite the Christians under their control they encountered opposition from groups of intellectuals who had settled on the fringes of the desert. With support from the local authorities the bishops were able to defeat the opposition and with the support of the imperial power they could unite the Christians against the continued pagan tradition of parts of the Alexandrian elite.

In the final paper of the monograph, "Religious Conflict in Late Antique Alexandria," Troels Myrup Kristensen discusses the attitude of the early Christians towards pagan sculpture work. Statues of men and gods were an important part of the public space in Graeco-Roman antiquity. Most of these statues survive to the present age only in a fragmentary state. The question is to which decree the Christians were responsible for this destruction. Literary sources refer to Christian mobs and clergy being responsible for violent attacks on pagan institutions and deliberate destructions of pagan sculpture work. Yet, as Kristensen emphasises, these sources are strongly biased: Christian church historians present the incidents as the triumph of the Living God over pagan idols housed in the dead statues. The radical wing of early Christendom detested cult images of any kind and of course even more so when those images were of a pagan kind. At the same time, however, other literary sources bear witness to a widespread continuity in the tradition of ornamenting the public space with sculpture work.

A closer reading of the literary sources and a more scrupulous interpretation of the material record demonstrate that the reality was more complicated than it would seem at first sight. Kristensen discusses different sites in Alexandria and its hinterland: the Serapeum did witness a systematic destruction, and statues were either broken into pieces or removed for mockery in other contexts. In other sites, however, there are examples of crosses having been carved into older statues, which may interpreted either as a neutralising of the pagan powers inside the page or as some kind of ritual baptism of the pagan symbol. Once reinterpreted as Christian figures, pagan sculpture work might survive in their original location for centuries, as in the case of the Tychaeum.

In a Temple of Isis in Menouthis, east of Alexandria, the Patriarch Peter, we are told, discovered in the 480s a secret collection of pagan idols and clear signs of worship. This led to a public trial against the priest conducting the worship. The wooden idols were burnt, but apparently the more valuable statues were catalogued for the purpose of sale. Another Isis temple, in Ras el-Souda, on the other hand, has been preserved with its status in perfect condition, only covered by sand. Finally, in the Temple of Isis at Taposiris, which was converted into a Roman fortress and later served as a Coptic monastery, fragments of the cult status have been found all over the site. However, it is impossible to tell whether the status has been destroyed for religious or for practical purposes, i.e. as pivotal stones.

Even though it cannot be denied that Alexandria witnessed several outbreaks of religious violence directed against the pagan minorities, matters were more complicated, and destructions were never carried systematically all over the region, but were limited to certain contexts and situations.

PART I

ALEXANDRIA FROM GREECE AND EGYPT

Alexandria as *Place*: Tempo-Spatial Traits of Royal Ideology in Early Ptolemaic Egypt

Jens A. Krasilnikoff

The founding of Alexandria – the narrative of the transformation of the Canopus vicinity as *space* to the city of Alexandria as *place* – was a dominant and powerful ingredient of the city's mythology. According to the traditions of the Hellenistic and Roman periods, the foundation of Alexandria originated in Alexander's ability to see in the *space* of the Canopus region and the northern Lake Mareotis environs the potential of a *place* to be. Alexander was, however, aided in the process. Plutarch's well-known account of the founding (subscribing to a local tradition by Heraclides) attributes great importance to the alleged intellectual and spiritual partnership between Alexander and Homer.[1] Unmistakably, the highlighting of this prominent connection fixes the event in a profoundly Greek context:

> If what the Alexandrians say on the authority of Heracleides is true, then it seems that Homer was no idle or useless companion to him on his expedition. They say that after his conquest of Egypt he resolved to found and leave behind him a large and populous Greek city which would bear his name.[2]

Among modern scholars of Antiquity, Alexandria is often associated with achievement and grandeur, scholarly endeavour, culture, royal self-representation and spiritualism. However, besides its Greek ancestry, Alexandria displayed as important ingredients of its distinguished urban conglomerate, a wide range of well-known features and elements normally associated with the classical Greek *polis*. The evidence clarifies the existence

---

1   The Homeric "blue print" of city founding is treated in Malkin 1987, see esp. 68, 138-41 (*Od.* 6.7-19). On Alexander's association with Homer and other Greek "celebrities" see further Mossman 1988, 83-93.
2   Translation from Austin 1981, no. 7.

of civic and religious institutions and the physical hallmarks of Greek urbanity such as monuments, the application of the Hippodamian grid and the harbour complex. Thus, in short, and subscribing to the tenets of the geographer Yi-Fu Tuan, Alexandria emerges as a Greek *location* – or rather as a number of *spatial locations* that constituted a coherent and intelligible *place*.[3] Two fundamental questions emerge as the basis of a profitable historical project: how was *place* manifest in Ptolemaic Alexandria; and which purposes and functions did the places of Alexandria fulfil in the early phase of the city's history?

Obviously, the description and discussion of all the many-faceted political, religious and cultural complexities, and their developments during the long history of Ptolemaic Alexandria, form a very large project. This is also the case with respect to their relevance to an accurate spatial characterisation of the city in a historical perspective. Although some of these themes and aspects have been dealt with before a lot more could be said on the matter. This is especially true when certain recent approaches and theories on the relationship involving identity and space, place and location are brought into play. I shall therefore confine this paper to the discussion of some aspects of how later narratives of the development of early Alexandria reflected the need to create Alexandria as *place*. Thus, first, I discuss how the components of the foundation myth worked to explain the creation of Alexandria in a *space-place* continuum. Jean Bingen once posed the question of how Ptolemy Soter

> ... a self-made man, needed and tried to justify the royal power he had seized. Indeed such an inquiry may reveal the values by which the new king felt, consciously or not, that he was able to create those ties between ruler and the ruled which are the real sanctions of a new power.[4]

Thus, secondly, in reverberation with Bingen's remark I shall make some observations regarding how the first Ptolemies, especially Ptolemy Soter and Ptolemy Philadelphus, dealt with Alexandria as *place*. First, however, a short introduction to the concepts of space and place, and their relevance to our understanding of Greek and Hellenistic antiquity, is in order.

1. Space, Place and Identity

Modern theories on identity groups and their relationships to landscapes and places are pivotal to this area of research.[5] The recent decades of identity studies have fostered

---

3   Tuan 1974; 1977.
4   Bingen 2007, 15.
5   Barth 1969; Bourdieu 1977; Anderson 1991. The tenets of the two frequently cited monographs by Tuan 1974 and 1977 are highly relevant points of departure for reflections on the relationship between location and identity construction in ancient as well as modern societies. Creswell 2004 is a good introduction to place including a survey of potential fields of research exploiting place as a category of analysis.

a number of energetic, dynamic and operational tools, which invite the inclusion of initiatives beyond the traditional confines of Alexandrian and Ptolemaic history. In particular, Benedict Anderson's notion of the imagined society and Barth and Bourdieu's studies of the boundaries between ethnic groups represent attractive methodologies for further studies of Alexandria's cultural interactions. However, in this piece, I confine myself to exploiting the potential of the notion of space and place initially advocated and utilised in numerous publications by Yi-Fu Tuan (while paying due attention to the aspect of historical development, which is not a particularly strong aspect of Tuan's tenets). These modern anthropologists and geographers can widen our perspective and perhaps help us rethink the approach to the many paradoxes and vexed questions of Alexandrine history.

In his renowned treatment of the relationship between space and place, Tuan observed that:

> ...the meaning of space often merges with that of place. "Space" is more abstract than "place". What begins as undifferentiated space becomes place as we get to know it better and endow it with value ... The ideas "space" and "place" require each other for definition. From the security and stability of place we are aware of the openness, freedom, and threat of space, and vice versa. Furthermore, if we think of space as that which allows movement, then place is pause; each pause in movement makes it possible for location to be transformed into place.[6]

Thus, on the one hand, Tuan indicated the close interdependency of the two levels of spatial perception, space and place, while on the other hand insisting on the experiential quality and sense of history, which are involved in connection and attachment to different levels of human geography. Subsequently, numerous scholars have pondered and exploited the potential of Tuan's tenets and those of other scholars to formulate some fundamental opinions about how *space* and *place* are connected and determine the formation of different kinds of identity. Hence, it is possible to distinguish between *identity of place* and *place identity*, where the first category includes the identity markers that constitute a particular *place*, and the latter involves those qualities of a *place* that helps generate identities of individuals or groups. For obvious reasons, the two kinds of relationships between *place* and identity are often interchangeable, transposable, and supplementary. One example is to understand the scholarly institutions of Alexandria as powerful identity markers of the city as *place* (that is, "*identity of place*"), and the scholars who worked within the scholarly institutions to derive their individual and group identities from their engagement and employment at the very *place* (that is, "*place identity*").

When it comes to discussions of how these tenets apply to different types of states – most importantly the ancient Greek "city-state" in comparison to the modern nation-state, Tuan and others are less convincing. In the case of the ancient Greek city-state

---

6   Tuan 1977, 6.

it seems as if Tuan subscribed to the mainstream opinion that the *polis* territory was a confined *space* wherein the limited number of citizens would know one another and the entire *space* of which each and every citizen would be able to traverse in a matter of two days. Here, the Aristotelian characteristics of the "standard model" *polis* are somehow extrapolated into the fifth century example of Athens, leaving Sparta as the exception to the rule.[7] At least in the case of Athens one would suspect that the demands and requirements fulfilled by identity and ideology constructions, compared to those of the modern nation-state.

Essentially, at one level, humanistic geographers suggest that transformation of *space* into *place* involves the attachment and connection of identity to a location or the locale.[8] However, academic treatments of the relationship between identity and *place* commonly tend to focus on the beginnings of the nation-state in the nineteenth century. Subscribing to the tenets of Peter Taylor Tim Creswell recently observed that "A nation-state … combines the abstraction of space with the deeply-felt emotions of place." Creswell further quotes Taylor: "Nations have been constructed as imagined communities each with their own place in the world, their own homeland, some as "fatherland," others as "motherland." By combining state and nation in nation-state, sovereign territory has been merged with sacred homeland to convert a space into a place".[9] Generally, however, it is now a widely shared opinion that *place* as well as identity is a fluid entity, a construction in constant development and progress, and that *place* can be perceived rather differently according to each and every observer.[10] This observation also supports the idea that *places* can be shared by different identity groups, a condition which is, I believe, fundamental to our means of understanding the Alexandrian complex of *place* and identity. The approaches in the paradigmatic studies of Greek identities by Jonathan Hall and Greg Anderson, and the studies by Clarysse and Goudriaan on Ptolemaic Egypt could thus be further enriched by the chords introduced by scholars of modern cultural studies and humanistic geography.[11]

2. The Founding: from Egypt as *Space* to Alexandria as *Place*

Due to the nature of the evidence, scholars often lament the insurmountable problems associated with the reconstruction of Alexandria's earliest history. The problems are great indeed. The evidence is notoriously unreliable, and in many cases raises more question

---

7   Tuan 1977, 175-6.

8   For instance Agnew 1987 (on definition of place as location, the locale and sense of place).

9   Cresswell 2004, 99 citing Taylor 1999, 102.

10 A good survey is to be found in Creswell 2004, 53-79; *ibid.* 81-123 on different approaches to working with place.

11 Hall 1997 on ethnic identity in Greece, with special address to the complex of the Heraclids and Argos; Anderson 2003 on the creation of Athens as an imagined community in the early fifth century BCE; Clarysse (1985; 1998; 2000) and Goudriaan (1988) have addressed various aspects of identity in Ptolemaic Egypt. See also Bagnall 1997 and the many relevant contributions in Bilde, Engberg-Pedersen, Hannestad & Zahle 1992.

than it answers. Most scholars dismiss the later accounts of Alexandria as being profoundly mythical in character.[12] The narratives of Arrian, Plutarch, Pseudo-Callisthenes and others are, however, fundamental to understanding the character of Alexandria as *place*; in fact what these mythologies do, and do well, are to establish Alexandria as *place*. What is more, the fact that they circulated in the first and second centuries CE, more than suggests that the dominant role of Alexander and the Ptolemies had no negative impact in the Roman period, regarding the validity of these narratives for the continuance of the city's foundation mythology and early history.

According to Plutarch's well-known narrative on Alexandria's founding, special observance was paid to the economic and religious aspects of the first city "founded and left behind" by Alexander. For the sharpened minds of earlier Greek history, these allusions would probably signal the founding of a Greek *polis*. However, one peculiarity dominates the first and second century CE narratives of Alexandria's founding, that being the absence of the population and colonists normally associated with city life and founding of Greek cities. The *synoikia* of the indigenous populations of the villages around Canopus did not qualify as "Greeks" on the look-out for virgin land or as *politai* of a future citizen-state à la contemporary Athens.[13] First and foremost Alexandria's beginnings features elements that identify the city as an urban entity – not exclusively "Greek" but also universally "urban" in its nature.

However, the circumstances and the process by which this end was achieved were those things which brought Alexandria into contact with "Greekness" and the traditions of how Greek *places* were created. Something extraordinary was, however, at work in the case of Alexandria. First, although the partnership of Alexander and Homer brings the founding of Alexandria into contact with the wider Greek context, this strange alliance acts instead of the normal Archaic-Classical mother city-colony interdependence and thus disconnects the *oikist* and his fellow "colonists" from a clearly defined original and local Greek context. Homer's role is then the projector of tradition, a personified sense of renowned and revered acquaintance with the sublime aspect of being Greek as well as being the initiator of something distinguished as "Greek" beyond the confines of the "present". The choice of Homer as companion and inspiration would also set Alexander's city free to meet any future demands, claims and debts from a mother-city. Thus, Homer was the safe choice for a less troublesome future.

Secondly, Plutarch's narrative, as well as those of other authorities such as Arrian and Pseudo-Callisthenes, presented the distinctively Greek ethnicity of Alexandria's origins by describing the conduct and behaviour of its *oikist*. This acts as a somewhat

---

12 On the sources for the study of early Alexandrine history see Powell 1939; Tatum 1996; Hammond 1983 on the vulgate Authors; a good survey in Shipley 2000, 235-70. On the general problems associated with the study of Alexander's city founding see Fraser 1996, especially the first two chapters.

13 Plutarch and Arrian display little interest in the population of newly founded Alexandria, whereas Pseudo-Callisthenes developed some speculations as to the ethnicity of the indigenous populations of the region. Cf. Pseudo-Callisthenes 1.31.

subtle (but not necessary consciously conceived) supplement to the general portrait of Alexander as a Macedonian monarch and conqueror – and as *pharaoh* as well as Darius' successor as the new Great King of the Persian Empire.[14] Thus, on the one hand the distinct casting of its founder places Alexandria within the Greek tradition of colonisation and city founding, and the juxtaposition by Arrian of these general elements with those of economy and religion creates newly founded Alexandria as a distinctly Greek *place*. On the other hand, the way in which Alexander is cast as *oikist* establishes a mythology, which ensures the independence and exclusiveness of Alexandria:

> Alexander came to Kanobos, sailed round the Lake Mareotis, and landed on the site of the present city of Alexandria, which is called after himself. The site seemed to him to be a most favourable one for the foundation of a city, and he thought that it would be prosperous. He was therefore seized with a longing for the task, and marked out himself the main parts of the city, the location of the Agora, how many sanctuaries there should be and of which gods, those of Greek gods and of Egyptian Isis, and the course of the city-wall. He offered sacrifice over the plan, and the omens appeared favourable. The following story is also told, and I do not disbelieve it. It is said that Alexander wanted to indicate to the builders the line of the city-wall, but had nothing to mark the ground with. One of the builders suggested making use of the meal which the soldiers carried in vessels, and dropping it on the ground where the king indicated. In this way the circumference of the city-wall was marked out according to his wishes. The seers, and especially Aristander of Telmesus, who had made many correct prophecies to Alexander, reflected on this and declared that the city would be prosperous in every way, particularly as regards agricultural produce.[15]

Alexander in the role of *oikist* echoes a number of well-known themes from the narratives of Herodotus and other classical Greek authorities writing on Archaic history. First, however, Arrian does not directly associate Alexander's enigmatic journey to the Oracle of Zeus-Ammon at the Siwah Oasis in the Libyan Desert prior to the founding of Alexandria, with the founding itself. It is, however, explicitly mirrored in the narrative of Pseudo-Callisthenes:

> He demanded also to receive an oracle from the god as to where he should found a city bearing his name. And he beheld in his sleep the god who said to him:
> "King, to you I speak. <Behold> the god of the ram's horn.
> If you wish forever to flourish in youth eternal,

---

14 Already Préaux 1939 saw the distinct partition between the allocation of "Greek" religious elements to Alexandria and those of traditional Egyptian religion to Memphis. See further Clarysse 1985; 1998; 2000; Shipley 2000, 60-72, 213-23; Hölbl 2001, 77-98.

15 Arr, *Anab.* 3.1.5-2.2. Translation Austin 1981, no. 7.

Build an illustrious city above the island of Proteus
Where once Aion Plutonius first took his throne as ruler,
Lord of the boundless kingdom, over the five spreading mountains".[16]

However, prior to the founding of the city, Pseudo-Callisthenes sends Alexander on a "Pyrrhic" walk-about to Southern Italy and Sicily, before setting out for Northern Africa. This altogether untrustworthy relation creates, nonetheless, a more logical series of events than the ones known from Arrian and Plutarch. Thereby, Pseudo-Callisthenes brings Alexander's project into direct contact with the Libyans and most importantly with Cyrene whose founding (in Herodotus' two versions) almost stands as a *leitmotif* and as a reliable design for Greek colonisation in the Archaic Age. Thus, in comparison the acts that constituted the founding of Alexandria by Alexander halfway resemble the process brought about by the *oikist* of Cyrene, Battus. This founder of the royal house of Cyrene, acting on the orders of the Delphic oracle, probably marked out the sacred precincts, established cults and rites, and erected temples.[17] The relationship between Cyrene and the outer world, especially Egypt and the island *polis* of Thera was, however, complex and very much dependent on the elaborate traditions of how Cyrene was founded in the first place.[18]

Arrian and Pseudo-Callisthenes claim that Alexander founded a city protected by Greek as well as Egyptian deities. This suggests that the city's *pantheon* was explained and understood as a balanced construct by those non-contemporary ancient authorities who were engaged in the study of the city's history. The alleged assemblage of Greek and Egyptian divinities echoes cases from the Archaic and Classical Greek experience, where colonists pooled divine assets in order to strengthen religious support and the community's ability to deal with conflicts. We should probably understand this as a reflection of how a newly founded society dealt with the difficulties of the world in the most potent manner, as well as met the acute problems posed by potential opposition by local divinities to the new-comers. Malkin's observation that the *oikist* of the archaic age was forced to cope with the divinities of the locale is echoed in the accounts of how Alexander acted upon his arrival at the location of the city-to-be.[19] However, whereas Arrian and Plutarch simply note the outcome of the process of religious authorisation

---

16 Pseudo-Callisthenes 1.30. Translation Haight 1955. A short and synchronic reading is found in Hölbl 2001, 10.

17 See Malkin 1987, 68.

18 Hdt. 4.150-9. For the complex historicity see further Malkin 1987, 60-9 and Osborne 1996, 8-17. Robin Osborne gives an excellent analysis of how different narratives of Cyrene's founding were exploited by the Battiad family and the less fortunate mother city of Thera to further various goals. See also the recent discussion in Mitchell 2000 on the paradigmatic status of the political system of Cyrene when compared to the civic systems of other Greek colonies. Ogden 1997, 53-61, delves into the complex figure of Battus whose extraordinary powers and appeal eventually led him to found Cyrene. Earliest Ptolemaic involment with Cyrene, see *SEG* IX.I.

19 Malkin 1987, 147-60; on the activities of the *oikist*, see esp. 68, 138-141. For further discussions of hero and tomb cults see Malkin 1987, 189-240; Morris 1987; Whitley 1988; 1995; Hall 1997, 138-40.

and construction by reference to "Greek deities and Egyptian Isis," Pseudo-Callisthenes goes further. He gives an account of Alexander's observances to the aforementioned chthonic divinity in the guise of a snake, explores the divine "antiquities" of the *place* (that was), and sets the scene for the "revival" of Serapis.[20]

By these acts Alexander comes to terms with the past and anchors his city in the future. The element of "crisis-management" was always an important ingredient in religious innovation in traditional Greek religion. Another element of great importance is the profound insecurity and lack of knowledge which determined man's relationship with the divine. Thus, as Rudhardt suggested, gods had different names in different places and man would continue to acknowledge "new" gods, rather than merely recognise known ones.[21] This somewhat awkward way of dealing with unknown divine manifestations occurred simply because the discovery of divinities demands either the rare ability to acknowledge and recognise a divine presence or partaking, or for a set of special circumstances to occur, such as natural disasters, warfare or the founding of a city. Thus, the Greeks did not distinguish between Greek and foreign gods, but simply acknowledged that names and *nomoi* associated with them changed from one culture to another.

Some time ago Buxton pondered, "…what of myths invent a past, deploying themes and patterns which echo or contrast with the emphases of other narratives told in Greece?" Thus, in this sweeping statement, Buxton turned the tables by illustrating the Alexandrine example amongst others and suggested that we should reverse the per-spective and instead focus on the strong influence of "first order" founding – such as Thebes – on those of the second order, such as Cyrene.[22] In so doing, Buxton opts for the recycling of literary and poetic themes and elements exploited in the narrative of Cadmus and its efficacy as an example to be used in other foundation myths.[23] As in the founding of Thebes and other cities, Buxton observed that in the process of preparing and securing the place for the founding, a fierce animal had to be dealt with and the water supply for hygienic as well as religious purposes had to be secured. In the case of Alexandria, Alexander dealt with a snake (although clearly benign ones), subduing it in order to "bring luck and prosperity to the new city".[24]

---

20 On snakes and *Agathos Daimōn* in the Alexandrian context see Fraser 1972, 209; Pseudo-Callisthenes 1.32.

21 Rudhardt 1992, 219-38.

22 Buxton 1994, 189, 190 on the likeness between the founder mythologies of Thebes and Alexandria.

23 On poetry associated with the founding of Greek cities – *ktisis* poetry – see further Dougherty 1994. By this argument, Buxton is also presenting yet another critique of Bernal's *Black Athena* and his argument for an Egyptian and near-eastern origin of Greek civilisation and the "kernel-of-truth" and "no-smoke-without-fire" approach to myths and mythology.

24 Pseudo-Callisthenes 1.32. Buxton subscribes to Vian's analysis 1963, 76-82. See Kühr 2007, esp. 199-256, ch. 4 on Thebes as "Erinnerungslandschaft". Although not an explicit tenet, the theoreti-cal basis of Kühr's synthesis includes challenging parallels and examples of how the relationship of history and space can be conceived; in this case Thebes is presented almost as an archetype or model of a Greek city creation and contemplation. Snakes seems to play many and different roles in the subsequent history of Alexandria. Diodorus related Ptolemy Philadelphus' great interest in

The foundation–markers of Thebes, as Buxton saw them have further relevance in the case of Alexandria. In the narrative of Arrian and Plutarch, no springs occur; instead the location of the city to be exhibits fresh as well as salt water and Plutarch's account of how the birds ate the barley-meal-marking of the city-wall is instantly transformed into a positive omen for the socio-economic future of the city.[25]

The location of Alexandria is not easily categorised in simple geographic or geo-political terms. Was the founding carried out in "Egypt," at the very border of Egypt, in a border zone at the fringes of Lower Egypt, or at the Nile Delta? Again, Arrian's narrative explains the location of Alexandria as the very spot where Egypt as one entity meets another, the Mediterranean world, and thus represents a location where the best of two worlds meet, exchange and are upgraded beyond known standards. Thanks to its unique location and the divine ancestry of its founder, the seer Aristander pronounced Alexandria as a place of future prosperity, industry and vigour as well as being large, and perhaps most important: fashionable and up-to-the-minute!

The vexed question of the definition of *polis* thus presents itself. First, the three authorities on the founding presumably understood and used the phrase πόλις of the physical city, and we have to consult further evidence dealing with the Ptolemaic period in order to be able to identify additional definitions with relevance for Alexandria. As demonstrated above by Plutarch and Arrian's excurses, the city's foundation mythology is almost entirely concerned with the formation of the *asty*, the nucleus or the built-up area within the city-walls. The *chōra*, the rural part of the territory, is only vaguely alluded to by the combination of agricultural produce with the future prosperity of the city. Accordingly, the later traditions of the city's founding, as reflected by Plutarch and Arrian, unfolds without the assistance or even presence of the population that eventually constitutes the substance of the city's *asty* and *chōra*. The selection of the spot by Alexander as well as the emptiness of the location classifies the site as the virgin *space* of a border-region, on the very fringe of Egypt of the past. Thus, the foundation my-

---

hunting and how he effectuated the capture of a large snake which became an attraction of the city. Hence, Philadelphus would follow Alexander's example, and also become a tamer of snakes (Diod.Sic. 3.36.3-5; 3.37.7-8).

A somewhat reversed usage of the snake theme is to be found in Plutarch's biography of Cleomenes of Sparta, who, during the process of his execution became the object of a serpentine emergence of the kind in which the animal crept around the exhausted body of the dying king (Plut. *Cleom.* 32-3; also Polyb. 5.35-39). This observation I owe to Dr. Karen Rørby Kirstensen. See further in Shimron 1972, 64-6, and Cartledge & Spawforth 1989, 57-62, mostly on the consequences of Cleomenes' death. In this particular usage, I believe, we are faced with a virtual example of how the *Agathos Daimōn* (Alexandria) – in the guise of the snake – overwhelmed and devoured the fallen king in a symbolic expression of his downfall. Thus, the last character to enter the drama, the viper that allegedly bit Cleopatra VII, ensured that the history of the Ptolemies in Egypt began and ended with the interference and involvement of snakes. The fate of royalty is determined by the outcome of their encounter with the symbolic manifestation of the chthonic world and the divinities that belong to it.

25 Plut. *Alex.* 26.3-10; Arr. *Anab.* 3.1.5-2.2; Pseudo-Callisthenes 1.32.

thology serves as a narrative of how this particular *space* was transformed into not any *place*, but that of a Greek city founded by a divinity in his very name.

Additionally, the instigator of the event is exclusively the *oikist* Alexander and this particular aspect immediately creates or reflects the "royal" aspect and dimension of the city's founding. In fact, an archaic-classical Greek *oikist* did identify and define the potential of *place* within *space* – alternatively with the specific help from a god (Apollo) – and subsequently executed or drew up the conditions for the development of the colony as *place* sometimes by the creation of laws. Therefore, the later Ptolemaic subscription to the founding as a royal achievement agrees well with the idea that the city was a *polis* only in the way that its history and development could be brought in contact with and made part of Ptolemaic royal ideology. Thus, the tradition insists on the fact that the citizenry and its adjacent political institutions emerged at Alexander's initiative. This end was met by the fact that the first citizens of Alexandria were also soldiers in Alexander's and Ptolemy's armies – that is, persons who were either engaged in the process of conquest, or colonisation, or both. The "spear-won" land was the prize for military audacity and success, predominantly reflected by royal military potency, but also echoed in the ways that Alexandrines dealt with and processed their Greek ancestry, heritage and history. Hence, the on-going re-enactment of the classical citizen-soldier ideal in the Graeco-Macedonian context of Alexandria secured and fixed a unique "moment" that was intimately dependent upon the very history of the city's creation. The mid-third century papyri include several allusions to the *pompē* or *kōmos* of the Ptolemaeia, in which military settlers presumably from the entire *chōra* were summoned to pay allegiance to Ptolemy and, presumably, to perform their part in the dionysiac inspired *kōmos* as representatives and "heirs" of the first Alexandrine inhabitants.[26]

The narrative of the founding of Alexandria accordingly presents a coherent and intelligible example of how the birth and building of a Classical Greek *polis* was potently exploited by its focus on the transformation of *space* into *place*. Thus in a sense, in the literary "mythologies" of later Antiquity regarding the founding of Alexandria Alexander was the force that transformed Herodotus' Greek notion of Egypt as "space" into a new version of Egypt with a Greek *polis* as "place". However, the process of founding or rather colonisation commenced after Alexander's lifetime. This phase initiated by Ptolemy Soter and carried on by Ptolemy Philadelphus, included the important project of creating lasting bonds between the *oikist* and the city and the formal establishment and consolidation of Alexandria as the official residence of the royal family.

3. Alexandria as Ptolemaic *Place*

Although numerous questions have been asked (and many incomplete answers produced) concerning the history of the dominant buildings, sanctuaries, monuments and harbours of early Alexandria, it is safe to suggest that these markers of Ptolemaic achievement constitute and frame Alexandria as a Ptolemaic *place*. Undoubtedly, contemporary so-

---

26 See further below on the Ptolemaeia. *P. Cairo Zeno* 59341 (a), ll. 17-22 and *P. Freib.* 7.l.7.

ciety as well as scholars of later periods associated these numerous physical markers and exhibitions with reflections of the city's identities. It goes beyond the limitations of this paper, however, to delve further into the relationships between monumentalisation, city outline and *place*.[27] We shall therefore, concern ourselves with some examples of how and to what ends the first Ptolemies created and prepared some of Alexandria's religious institutions which would support the transformation of the city into a Ptolemaic *place*.

In concert, much energy has been invested in revealing the many facets of Ptolemaic propaganda and royal ideology, and the details of this field are better left in the hands of specialists.[28] In a number of ways, the first of the Ptolemies, Ptolemy Soter and perhaps most importantly, his son Ptolemy Philadelphus, incorporated and exploited what I shall name "the notion of Alexander" as one of the focal elements in the early versions of the Ptolemaic royal ideology. Although only scant evidence exists, it has been argued that Ptolemy Soter created and exploited the particular relationship between the founder and his city; and that this ideological anchorage acted as a point of departure for the formulation of a distinct Ptolemaic royal ideology.[29] Thus, the second focal element in the development of Ptolemaic royal ideology was obviously the history of the Ptolemies themselves and their varying though always extensive involvement in religious innovation and development. In the case of Ptolemaic Egypt, there are, however, two distinct ways of understanding and articulating the relationship between identity and ideology: the first deals with the relationship with the outer world for example the other Hellenistic kingdoms. In this type of relationship it is important to stress the connection to the Greek world and the (potential) roles of the Ptolemies as heirs to Alexander, his Empire, and his Graeco-Macedonian roots. The second way to understand the relationship between identity and ideology is an inward exercise which deals with Ptolemaic adherence to and control over Egypt. In this case, it is important to stress the mythological "fact"; the Ptolemies created a distinctly unique frame of reference, which allowed for its development to commence in its own right and on its own terms.

Presumably, the early phase of the city's history, during which the Library and the Museum were founded by Ptolemy Soter and Philadelphus, in addition to a number of sanctuaries, the general outline of the city itself marked significant steps towards the establishment of the city as a show-piece of the Ptolemaic version of Greek urban culture.[30] In one way, the transference of residence from Memphis to Alexandria in 311 BCE marked the official beginning of Alexander's city as the administrative and ideological focal point of the Ptolemaic kingdom.[31] However, Ptolemy's possession of the body of

---

27 Good points of departure in Hoepfner and Schwandner 1994, 235-56, and Empereur 1998, *passim*.

28 See the Introduction and discussions in Hazzard 2000.

29 Bingen 2007, 15-30.

30 Modern discussions on the form and content of these institutions are extensive. See further in Fraser 1972, 312-25. For a short but very accurate discussion of the "…fact of their existence at all" see Erskine 1995 and Jensen in this volume.

31 The evidence for this date is derived from the so-called Satrap Stele of 311 (Cairo, Egyptian Museum, Cat. Gén. 22181). For different opinions among modern scholars on the date of the transfer

the deceased Alexander, its transfer to Alexandria and the subsequent establishment of the cult of Alexander in his "name-city" contained a strong ideological potential, which was readily exploited by Ptolemy.[32] Recently, Bingen suggested that the establishment of the cult of Alexander undoubtedly extended Ptolemy's control and the allegiance of the army a first and most important tool for the power base he was building.[33] However, the importance of carrying out the retrieval of the "war-dead" king acted as a forceful agent for the merger of the land "won by the spear" by Alexander with Ptolemaic authority and legitimacy.[34] The return of Alexander to Alexandria also constituted a powerful ingredient in the religious and mythical basis of Alexandria as *place*.

The creation of the city as the location of Alexander's burial site confirms yet another element of the archaic formula of founding cities: that of burial of the *oikist* in his city, along with making his tomb an object of worship.[35] Ptolemy Soter understood this potential. He exploited it and made it a prime asset as an element of the arsenal of ideological constructs and elements ready for the royal house to exploit time and again until the very last of the Ptolemy's, Cleopatra VII.[36] Thus, the usage by Cleopatra of the notion "fatherland" in her royal titulature was not a deliberate attempt to anchor her self-representation in a Macedonian context – by allusion to the paternal figure of Alexander, though, could easily so be understood as an allusion to the Alexandrian context and its many "fathers," Alexander, Ptolemy Soter and Ptolemy Philadelphus.[37]

4. Cult and *Place* in the Early Ptolemaic Period

Subscribers to the *polis* religion tenets argue with great confidence that the constant redefinition and change of polytheistic religion acted as a positive complement to the construction of civic identity and ideology in the cities of mainland Greece of the classical and Hellenistic period.[38] Thus, according to this logic one would expect the Greek cults of Alexandria to reflect and develop in accordance with the ongoing socio-

---

of the capital city see Hölbl 2001, 26, with note 78. A translation of the stele is to be found in Bevan 1927, 28-32.

32 Bingen 2007, 20.

33 For an excellent discussion of the nature and relationship of Greek and Ptolemaic monarchy see Bingen 2007, 17-25. Especially, the idea of Ptolemy as a transitory type of monarch – one "in between" fourth-century Greek and later Hellenistic style monarchy – seems attractive. Distinctions are made to e.g. the Homeric monarchy and the very Greek question (Aristotle) of how a king might either prevent or further the citizens of a city in sharing freedom and liberty. The Macedonian element and its influence is, however, less explicit.

34 See Shipley 2000, 36-58, on legitimacy of power, reign and territorial dominance among the Diadochi.

35 References in note 20 above.

36 Bingen 2007, 63-79.

37 Regarding Cleopatra and Aulic titulature see further Bingen 2007, 263.

38 The tenets of the polis-religion approach have not yet been subjected to exhaustive examination, as has been the case of the Classical period.

economic and political developments of Ptolemaic society.[39] However, the nature and implications of religion in the Ptolemaic period have been exploited to communicate something quite distinct and definite about the relationship between Greeks and others in the Egyptian and Alexandrine contexts. During the nineteenth and twentieth centuries, Droysen, Rostovtzeff and Préaux among others prepared the ground for the notion of Greek dominance of Alexandrine religion.[40]

However, numerous debates on various aspects of this topic have been carried out over the years. One position claims that a rather clear order of religious spheres was established by the first Ptolemies between Memphis, devoted to traditional Egyptian religious tradition and on the other hand Alexandria dominated by the aspirations of the Greek populace, demanding Olympian Gods for worship.[41] Apart from the overall dichotomy and its ethno-geographical divide (Greeks and Barbarians), two points of view from the later decades include some geographic aspects. In 1972 Fraser observed that after the Ptolemies assumed power a rapid religious evolution took place in "the *chora* of Egypt" and that this development was different from that in Alexandria where the "racial elements" of the city remained more or less intact in the third century BCE.[42] Regarding Egyptian religion in Alexandria, Fraser noted that: "From the Old Kingdom to the Saite period and later, the deities of Pharaonic Egypt were closely linked to a specific city or locality," and further "In this framework of traditional local worship Alexandria had naturally no place, and the Ptolemies do not seem to have favoured the establishment of purely Egyptian cults in the city".[43] Although appealing, this statement is not self evident and further speculation is in order.[44] These ways of thinking about "the religious landscape" of Ptolemaic Egypt agree with the view shared by many scholars that the "ancient Pharaonic" part of Egypt represented a somewhat time-locked and static religious concept. On the other hand, the syncretised cults of Alexandria, which derived partly from an ancient Egyptian context, were calibrated to meet the religious demands of the Hellenised world. This complies with the notion of Hellenistic religion as one characterised by internationalism and an essentially Panhellenic nature. The proof of this general understanding, it is argued, is the very fact that the cults of Serapis and Isis spread to the wider Graeco-Roman world in the years after Alexander's death.[45] However, as Samuel observed, the inclusion of Isis into the Alexandrian *pantheon* by Alexander reflected the fact that Isis was known to the Greeks before the founding of Alexandria and so the goddess was, in one way or another, already known to the Greeks in their homeland.[46]

---

39 Good introductions are to be found in Zaidman & Pantel 1992 and Sourvignou-Inwood 1990.

40 Droysen 1952-53; Préaux 1939; 1947. Rostovtzeff 1941.

41 Préaux 1939. E.g. see Hölbl 2001, 90-8.

42 Fraser 1972, 189. This observation did not prevent Fraser from presenting numerous speculations concerning potential religious syncretism particularly between Greek and Egyptian divinities in the following pages.

43 Fraser 1972, 190.

44 E.g. see the excellent arguments in Clarysse 1985; 2000; Koenen 1983; 1993.

45 See, for instance, Samuel 1983, 75-6.

46 Samuel 1983, 82-3. The Athenian context provides evidence for the establishment of the Isis cult

First, if Fraser's analysis is correct, the Egyptian element of Alexandria's population must have had no choice but to pay tribute to the divinities introduced by Alexander and the Ptolemies; as Fraser himself insists, this would only pass if these non-Greeks could speak, or learned to speak Greek.[47] Moreover, it seems certain that the Egyptian segment of the population would have continued to perform religious practices which have not been recorded; one cannot imagine this segment of the population without its own religious needs and desires. However, if the former possibility was indeed the case the Greek understanding of temporal-spatial order, religion and cult and therefore also of a common perception and dependency on history and tradition must have been part of the religions of all "Alexandrines" alike.

Although very little can be said regarding the popular religious beliefs and affiliations of early Alexandria, one alternative to Fraser's perception is to see these "syncretic" cults as "contexts" or "common grounds" where different purposes and desires were pursued by supplicants in need of different aspects of the religions offered. For rulers of a newly founded city of many nationalities the opportunity to exploit the religious development to create concord and unity were great indeed. As Fraser argues, however, there remains the question of whether this was indeed what happened.[48] Thus, both Greeks and non-Greeks would find content, logic and meaning in the cult of Serapis and Isis but not necessarily out of the same reasons or desires.[49] At the very least, we can contemplate the creation of a principle in which the mixed population of Alexandria was brought together in a particular cult, which shared a common *geographic place*, though not necessarily representing a shared *place of identity.* Presumably, the erection of a statue of Serapis "in the Hellenic fashion," and Ptolemy Soter's financing of the burial of the Apis bull, signal important steps towards redefinitions of the cults as Alexandrine *places* rather than a desire to promote a strict and coherent Hellenic religious discourse.[50] Hence, by these acts, Ptolemy contributed to the creation of the cults of Serapis and of Isis, not as the creations of fundamentally new Hellenistic and internationalising religions, but as Alexandrine *places*.

5. Alexandria's Pantheon and the Ptolemies

The League of Islanders, originally founded by Antigonus Monophthalmus in 315/14 BCE and lost by Demetrius Poliorcetes, fell sometime before 280 BCE (probably 286 BCE) to the Ptolemies and became a vehicle for their imperial ambitions for the following 30 years.[51] Undoubtedly, the role of Alexandria as the focal point of Ptolemaic

---

in the Piraeus before 333/2 BCE, cf. *IG* II² 337. See further Garland 2001, esp. 126-8, 228.

47 Fraser 1972, 192.

48 Fraser 1972, 189-201. See also Swinnen 1973.

49 See also the many observations in Stambaugh 1972.

50 On the statue of Serapis from Sinop: Tac. *Hist.* 4.83-4; Plut. *De Is. et Os.* 28. On the Apis bull: Diod.Sic. 1.84.8.

51 *Syll.*³ 390, decree of the League of Islanders on the acceptance of the Ptolemaia. Fraser 1972,

imperialism was strengthened by the affiliation of the member states of the *League of Islanders* to the Alexandrine contest and games of the Ptolemaeia. Scholars generally agree that the great *pompē* of Ptolemy Philadelphus as described in Athenaeus was part of the quinquennial celebration of the Ptolemaia in 270/1 BCE or 263/2 BCE, which according to the Islanders' decree *Syll.³* 390 was designed to honour Ptolemy Soter.[52] It is, however, of some importance, to note the clearly expressed ambition of Philadelphus that of making the contests of the Ptolemaeia equal to those at the Olympic Games, a claim to be repeated several times in the Islanders' decree. Undoubtedly, the Grand Procession is a most potent example of a Ptolemaic framing of Alexandria displaying the grandeur and majesty of the royal house and Philadelphus' city of residence. The very fact that the massive numbers of animals and artefacts were successfully matched with the dimensions of the city would, at the very least, ensure the "majesty" of the city.[53]

Athenaeus' narrative of the Ptolemaeian *pompē* reveals some information regarding Alexandria's pantheon at the time.[54] It has often been assumed that the *pompē* displayed and reflected the hierarchy amongst the gods of the Alexandrian pantheon.[55] As Fraser noted, one would be on relatively safe ground in deducing that the prominent role of Dionysus in the *pompē* reflected his important role for the Ptolemies. This impression is confirmed by the additional documentation of Dionysus' primacy, compared with that of the remainder of Alexandrine deities.[56] An analogy to the Classical Greek context suggests that leading the sacrificial victims to the altar was the practical purpose of a

---

224, 231; Bagnall 1976, 136-58; Buraselis 1982, *passim* on the history of the Antagonids in the third-century Aegean. Hölbl 2001, 19, 23-4, 28, 40, 93-4. Translation in Austin 1981, no. 218. The discussion of the *space* and *place* dimensions of the Ptolemaic Empire is beyond the limits of this paper.

52 Rice 1983 argued against the identification of the Ptolemaeia with the procession described in Ath. 5.202f-203e = Callixinus of Rhodes *FGrH* 627 F 2. See, however, the exhaustive treatment in Hazzard 2000, esp. 59-79.

53 The discussion of the *space* and *place* dimensions of the Ptolemaic Empire is beyond of this paper. It is, however, of some importance to stress again the importance of exclusiveness, which is created by the exploitation of religious events as political events. See e.g. Sholten 2000, esp. 39-45, 97-102, 235-52. On religious exploitation by the Aetolian league.

54 Ath. 5.202f -203e = Callixinus of Rhodes *FGrH* 627 F 2.

55 Fraser 1972, 202. It seems, however, that the Ptolemies were particularly involved with those Olympian gods who could either support their own claims to divine status – e.g. Aphrodite – or act in ways that supported the Alexandrine economy, which would include Demeter (in the great Procession Philadelphus is aligned with Triptolemus) and Apollo-Sarapis. Documentation in Fraser 1972, 196-209. See Manning 2003 on Ptolemaic economy and land tenure.

56 Fraser 1972, 201-7, on Dionysus. Fraser even goes as far as to suggest that all the remaining Olympic gods were subjugated to Dionysus although he also ponders whether the *Agathos Daimōn* was indeed the patron god of Alexandria; and he speculates further that the importance of Zeus was reduced in the sense that he is made equal to the Ptolemies although he certainly is included in the city-oath. Fraser 1972, 194, 209 on *Agathos Daimōn*. Fraser's many speculations on the syncretic nature of Alexandrine religion, a point of view backed by the unsubstantiated insistence on the "eclectic" nature of the Alexandrine Greeks, is somewhat futile.

pompē. Clearly, we are not dealing exclusively with the initial stages of a bloody sacrifice, something else was also at work. Greeks were summoned from the *chōra*[57] and from the rest of the Greek communities from all over the Aegean region including representatives of the member states of the *League of Islanders*.[58]

The fact that Dionysos played a significant role in the Ptolemaeia invites speculation about this *pompē* in terms of Dionysian revelry in which case the Ptolemaeia would also involve elements of the *kōmos* and re-occupation of the city as *place*. In the Athenian Great Dionysia the *kōmos* served to re-take or repopulate the city. Most importantly, perhaps, is the element of "gathering," which involved invitations to join in and participate in the contest and festival. Louise Bruit Zaidman and Pauline Schmitt Pantel summarise the many functions of procession rituals:

> One was publicity: the reason for the festival was broadcast, and an invitation to join in was extended to all along the way. Other functions included renewal, a reactivation of the benefactions and virtues of the god whose statue was sometimes carried, and a reaffirmation of the sanctity of the different sites where the crowd halted, especially alters. Speaking generally, the procession served as a symbolic re-appropriation of the city's space by the community.[59]

As Fraser observed, the Ptolemaic claim of descent from Dionysus is of some relevance for an interpretation of the Ptolemaeia. In the narrative of Athenaeus, Dionysus of the Ptolemaeia returned from the "Indian Campaign" but Alexander not the god is the "true hero of the Indian section," a feature which most clearly associates and combines Soter and his heir with Dionysus and Alexander.[60] Once again, we return to the relevance of the founding of the city and its *oikist*. By this framing, the royal house and its city of residence added further weight to the claim of Alexandria as the *place* where the Ptolemaic mythology would become the experience of all the Alexandrine "actors" through the re-enactment of the homecoming of Dionysus at the Ptolemaeia. The re-populating of the city and the renewed commitment to the mythology of the royal house and its

---

57 *P. Cairo Zeno* 59341 (a), ll. 17-22; *P. Freib.* 7.l.7.

58 Fraser 1972, 218, 224, 228, 231-2, 288. The mutual support of the Athenians and Ptolemy "the younger" is made explicit in a decree honouring Callias of Sphettus (270/69 BC). Here, Ptolemy furnishes the new robe for Athena *Archēgetis* at the Panathenaea and Callias is honoured for paying the cost of sending a sacred embassy to the Ptolemaeia and generally for acting as the contact between Athens and Ptolemy. See further the *editio princeps* by Shear 1978, 2-4; and Austin 1981, no. 44. Some intriguing similarities are to be found, I believe, in comparisons with the context of the Athenian Panathenaea and its iconographic representation. See further in Hurwit 1999, 222-8 for an excellent discussion of the interpretative possibilities of the Parthenon frieze. On Samian tributes to the Ptolemaeia see *SEG* 1.366.26-35. See the exhaustive treatment in Mikalson 1998 on Hellenistic religion in Athens in which a good argument for the continuance of classical religious "ideology" and practice is deployed.

59 Zaidman & Pantel 1992, 106, 199-207 on Dionysus in general.

60 Fraser 1972, 202.

city would take place under the guidance and protection of Ptolemy.[61] Thus, the Ptolemies understood how to develop Alexandria as a positive *place*, operational for future formulations of the kingdom's mythology.

6. Ruler Cult

Time and again it has been repeated how cults, especially ruler-cults and the spectacular festivals introduced by the first Ptolemies created a religious framework for display of royal ideology. Price's important observation, that ruler cult derived from the need in Greek cities "to represent this new power [the Hellenistic kings] to themselves" also applies to the case of Alexandria, in the sense that the population of the city needed to deal with the Ptolemies and chose to do so in the traditional fashion of divine worship. The deviation from the examples discussed in Price is, however, that the ruler cult of Alexandria and Egypt was directly promoted by the Ptolemies: it was not promoted through the initiative of the Egyptian populations, it seems.[62]

The dependence of the ruler cult on *place* is obvious and in the Alexandrine example essential to understanding the special mechanics involved. Whereas the question of the relationship between "Greek" and "Egyptian" gods is extremely complex and vexed, the special history of the ruler cult in Ptolemaic Egypt seems to solve and unite more than not. Undoubtedly, the Ptolemaic version of the ruler cult originates from the desire to "manage" the heritage of Alexander in the most potent manner, that being to make Alexander the subject of a founder hero cult in his name-city. This important step, which is most dependent on a fixation in time and space, would eventually lead to the creation of the Ptolemaic version of the ruler cult.[63] Thus, in Egypt, the Ptolemies introduced a version, which involved the deification of the dead royalty by administrative measures; by the deaths of Arsinoe and Philadelphus, their cults were attached to that of Alexander and the concept of "Brother-Sister Gods" thereby created. As Chaniotis observed, "…this cult in Alexandria was transformed into an eponymous state cult; the reference to its eponymous priest in the dating formula of documents fulfilled an important symbolic function, underlining both dynastic continuity and the monarchy's divine nature".[64] The development that began as a conscious act in the race "for the spoils of Alexander" would eventually led to the founding of Alexandria as a Greek *place* and *polis* in the early days of Alexander and Ptolemy Soter; but the development into a

---

61 See further in Hazzard 2000, 59-79 on The Grand Procession and its relevance for the formation of Ptolemaic propaganda; id. 156-9 on the ambitions of Ptolemy Philadelphus, and how they developed in the broader historical perspective until the time of Cleopatra VII.

62 Price 1984, 29-30; Hazzard 2000, esp. 156-9.

63 A good introduction to the subject and the various versions of ruler cults in the Hellenistic world is provided by Chaniotis 2003, 436-7. On the relationship between Hero cult and ruler cult see the many remarks in Kearns 1989; Larson 1995; Lyons 1997. For studies of ruler cults and its Ptolemaic aspects and versions, see further in Fraser 1972, 213-46; Koenen 1993; Bingen 2007, 31-43.

64 Chaniotis 2003, 436.

sacred *place* for the entire Ptolemaic realm in the days of Philadelphus was ensured by a careful orchestration of and constant mingling with Alexandria as Ptolemaic *place*.

7. Conclusions

A search for *place* within the Egyptian context of the Ptolemaic period enhances our knowledge of how the Greek concept of the "city-state culture" and society developed in this distinct framework. In a narrower perspective, one should also be able to say something of how Hellenistic urban centres evolved as *places* dependent on Graeco-Macedonian origins as well as how they were influenced by the parallel indigenous cultures, which continued to exercise their influences after the conquests of Alexander. The sheer number of potential questions and complexes involved in the study of Alexandria as *place* demands confinement and restraint, however; in this paper, therefore, I have chosen to explore the relationship between the later traditions of Alexandria's founding and their dependence upon the classical Greek tradition of the founding of cities. Subsequently, the elements of the parallels found have been used to say something about how the first Ptolemies exploited the classical heritage to create Alexandria as *place*. The "flexibility" of the classical Greek tradition of the founding of cities presented the Ptolemies with the opportunity to create a new essentially Greek city, which was free of obligations of a political or economic kind. This observation explains how the creation of Alexandria as *place* would give the Ptolemies the freedom to anchor their realm in a tradition of their own making and creation. Thus, the heritage of Alexander was brought under control by Ptolemy Soter's possession of Alexander's body, and his subsequent burial in his "name-city".

One conclusion to be drawn from the mythology of the city's founding is that Alexander was made instigator of the double dimension of the event. First, Alexander was portrayed as founder of a Greek city and as promulgator and bringer of "achievements" well-anchored in the traditions and orders of Classical Greek polis tradition. Secondly, via the display of his role of *oikist* the Macedonian monarch introduced the religious order of the Greek city to the fringe of the ancient Egyptian context. Accordingly, I believe, the testimony of the later Roman period authorities who were familiar with the traditions of classical *historia*, that a great many features of Archaic Greek colonisation and the founding of cities, were recycled in the narratives of Alexandria's beginning.

The mental exercise of transforming *space* into *place* is necessary prerequisite for the formulation of individual as well as group identities. This particular action can have many guises and commence under different headlines, and so be named accordingly, *diaspora*, colonisation, nation-building, etc. A fundamental feature of this process, however, is that a distinct identity or set of identities emerges from this process. Furthermore, we must expect the nurturing of a given *place* to be a continuous process, constantly or momentarily involving calibrations of the minor and major details of the space-place-identity continuum. Thus, the continued introductions and calibrations of religious institutions by the first Ptolemies demonstrate a deep and profound interdependency and dialogue with Alexandria as *place*. The Ptolemies claimed their royal house to be the one focal point, which maintained Egypt as a coherent entity in the sense that Alexandria would function as the *place* where "state" and "nation" would meet in joint celebration of the royal house – as in the example of the Ptolemaia.

References

Agnew, J.A. 1987 *Place and Politics: the Geographical Mediation of State and Society* London: Allen and Unwin.

Anderson, B.R.O.G. 1991 *Imagined Communities: Reflections on the Origin and Spread of Nationalism* London-New York: Verso (second edition).

Anderson, G. 2003 *The Athenian Experiment. Building an Imagined Political Community in Ancient Attica, 508 – 490 B.C.* Ann Arbor: University of Michigan Press.

Austin, M.M. 1981 *The Hellenistic World From Alexander to the Roman Conquest. A Selection of Ancient Sources in Translation* Cambridge: Cambridge University Press.

Bagnall, R.S. 1976 *The Administration of the Ptolemaic Possessions outside Egypt* Leyden: Brill.

Bagnall, R.S. 1997 "Decolonizing Ptolemaic Egypt" in: P. Cartledge, P. Garnsey & E. Gruen. *Hellenistic Constructs: Essays in Culture, History, and Historiography* Berkeley: University of California Press, 225-41.

Bagnall, R. S. & Derow, P. S. 2004 *The Hellenistic Period: Historical Sources in Translation* Oxford: Blackwell.

Barth, F. 1969 "Introduction" in: F. Barth (ed.) *Ethnic groups and boundaries: the social organization of culture difference* London: George Allen & Unwin, 9-38.

Bernal, M. 1987-2006 *Black Athena. The Afroasiatic Roots of Western Civilization*, (3 vols.) New Bunswick, NJ: Rutgers Unievrsity Press.

Bevan, E. 1927 *A History of Egypt Under the Ptolemaic Dynasty* London: Methuen.

Bilde, P., Engberg-Pedersen, T., Hannestad, L. & Zahle, J. (eds.) 1992 *Ethnicity in Hellenistic Egypt* Aarhus: Aarhus University Press.

Bingen, J. 2007 *Hellenistic Egypt. Monarchy, Society, Economy, Culture*, (edited with an introduction by Roger S. Bagnall) Edinburgh: Edinburg University Press.

Bourdieu, P. 1977 *Outline of a Theory of Practice* Cambridge: Cambridge University Press.

Brock, R. & Hodkinson, S. (eds.) 2000 *Alternatives to Athens. Varieties of PoliticalOrganization and Community in Ancient Greece* Oxford: Oxford University Press.

Bulloch, A. W., Gruen, E. S. Long, A. & Stewart, A. (eds.) 1993 *Images and Ideologies: Self-definition in the Hellenistic World* Berkeley and Los Angeles: University of California Press.

Buraselis, K. 1982 *Das hellenistische Makedonien und die Ägäis* München: C.H. Beck.

Buxton, R. 1994 *Imaginary Greece. The Contexts of Mythology* Cambridge: Cambridge University Press.

Cartledge, P. & Spawforth, A. 1989 *Hellenistic and Roman Sparta: A Tale of two Cities* London-New York: Routledge.

Chaniotis, A. 2003 "The Divinity of Hellenistic Rulers" in: A. Erskine (eds.) *A Companion to the Hellenistic World* Oxford: Blackwell, 431-445., 431-445.

Clarysse, W. 1985 "Greeks and Egyptians in the Ptolemaic army and administration" *Aegyptus* 65, 57-66.

Clarysse, W. 1998 "Ethnic diversity and dialect among the Greeks of Hellenistic Egypt" in: A. Verhoogt & S. Vleeming (eds.) *The Two Faces of Graeco-Roman Egypt. Texts and Studies Presented to P.W. Pestman* (Papyrologica Lugduno-Batava 30) Leiden: Brill, 1-13.

Clarysse, W. 2000 "The Ptolemies visiting the Egyptian chora" in: L. Mooren (ed.) *Politics, Administration and Society in the Hellenistic and Roman World. Proceedings of the International Colloquium, Bertinoro 19-24 July 1997* (Studia Hellenistica 36) Leuven: Peeters, 29-53.Cresswell, T. 2004 *Place. A Short Introduction* Oxford: Wiley-Blackwell.

Dougherty, C. 1994 "Archaic Greek Foundation Poetry: Questions of Genre and Occasion" *The Journal of Hellenic Studies* 114, 35-46.

Droysen, J.G. 1952-53 *Geschichte des Hellenismus* (3 vols.) Tübingen (= Darmstad: Primus Verlagt 1998).

Empereur, J.-Y. 1998 *Alexandria Rediscovered*, New York: George Braziller.

Erskine, A. 1995 "Culture and Power in Ptolemaic Egypt: the Museum and Library of Alexandria" *Greece and Rome*, 42, 38-48.

Fraser, P.M. 1972 *Ptolemaic Alexandria* (3 vols.) Oxford: Clarendon Press.

Fraser, P.M. 1996 *Cities of Alexander the Great*, Oxford: Clarendon Press.

Garland, R. 2001 *Piraeus. From the fifth to the first century BC* London: Gerald Duckworth (second edition).

Goudriaan, K. 1988 *Ethnicity in Ptolemaic Egypt* Amsterdam: Gieben.

Hall, J. 1997 *Ethnic identity in Greek antiquity* Cambridge: Cambridge University Press.

Hammond, N.G.L. 1983 *Three Historians of Alexander the Great: The So-called Vulgate Authors, Diodorus, Justin and Curtius* Cambridge: Cambridge University Press.

Hazzard, R.A. 2000 *Imagination of a Monarchy: Studies in Ptolemaic Propaganda* (Phoenix Suppl. 37) Toronto: University of Toronto Press.

Hoepfner, W. & Schwandner, E.-L. 1994 *Haus und Stadt im klassischen Griechenland* (Wohnen in der klassischen Polis 1) Münch: Deutscher Kunstverlag (new edition).

Hölbl, G. 2001 *A History of the Ptolemaic Empire* London-New York (trans. from orig. *Geschichte des Ptolemäerriches*, 1994).

Hurwit, J.M. 1999 *The Athenian Acropolis. History, Mythology, and Archaeology from the Neolithic Era to the Present* Cambridge: Cambridge University Press.

Huss, W. 1995 "Memphis und Alexandreia in helle-nistischer Zeit" in: *Alessandria e il mondo ellenis-tico-romano: I centenario del Museo Greco-Romano (Alessandria, 23-27 novembre 1992). Atti del II Congresso Internationale Italo-Egiziano* Roma: L'Erma di Bretschneider, 75-82.

Kearns, E. 1989 *The Heroes of Attica* (Bulletin supplement 57) London: University of London.

Koenen, L. 1983 "Die Adaptation ägyptischer Königsideologie am Ptolemäerhof" in: E. van't Dack, P. van Dessel & W. van Gucht (eds.) *Egypt and the Hellenistic World* (Studia Hellenistica 27) Lovanii, 143-90.

Koenen, L. 1993 "The Ptolemaic king as a religious figure" in: A.W. Bulloch, E.S. Gruen, A. Long & A. Stewart (eds.) *Images and Ideologies: Self-definition in the Hellenistic World* Berkeley-Los Angeles: University of California Press, 25-115 (Response Walbank, 116-29).

Kühr, A. 2007 *Als Kadmos nach Boiotien kam. Polis und Ethnos im Spiegel thebanischer Gründungsmythen* (Hermes Einzelschriften Band 98) Stuttgart: Franz Steiner Verlag.

Larson, J. 1995 *Greek Heroine Cults* Madison, Wis.: University of Wisconsin Press.

Lyons, D. 1997 *Gender and Immortality: Heroines in Ancient Greek Myth and Cult* Princeton, NJ: Princeton University Press.

Malkin, I. 1987 *Religion and Colonization in Ancient Greece* (Studies in Greek and Roman religion 3) Leiden: Brill.

Manning, J.G. 2003 *Land and Power in Ptolemaic Egypt: The Structure of Land Tenure* Cambridge: Cambridge University Press.

Mikalson, J.D. 1998 *Religion in Hellenistic Athens* (Hellenistic culture and society 29) Berkeley-Los Angeles: University of California Press.

Mitchell, B. 2000 "Cyrene: Typical or Atypical?" in: R. Brock & S. Hodkinson, *Alternatives to Athens. Varieties of Political Organization and Community in Ancient Greece* Oxford: Oxford University Press, 82-102.

Morris, I. 1987 *Burial and Ancient Society: The Rise of the Greek City-State* Cambridge: Cambridge University Press.

Mossman, J.M. 1988 "Tragedy and Epic in Plutarch's Alexander" *The Journal of Hellenic Studies* 108, 83-93.

Ogden, D. 1997 *The Crooked Kings of Ancient Greece* London: Gerald Duckworth.

Osborne, R. 1996 *Greece in the Making 1200-479 BC* (Routledge history of the ancient world), London: Routledge.

Powell, J. E. 1939 "The Sources of Plutarch's Alexander" *Journal of Hellenic Studies* 59, 229-240.

Préaux, C. 1939 *L'Économie royale des Lagides* Bruxelles: Édition de la Fondation Égyptologique Reine Élisabeth.

Préaux, C. 1947 *Les Grecs en Égypte: d'après les ar-chives de Zénon* (Collection Lebègue, 7th series 78) Bruxelles: Office de Publicité.

Price, S.R.F. 1984 *Rituals and Power. The Roman Imperial Cult in Asia Minor* Cambridge: Cambridge University Press.

Rice, C.C., 1983 *The Grand Procession of Ptolemy Philadelphus* Oxford: Oxford University Press.

Rostovtzeff, M. 1941 *The Social and Economic History of the Hellenistic World* (3 vols.) Oxford: Oxford University Press.

Rudhardt, J. 1992 "Les attitudes des Grecs a l'égard des religions étrangères" *Revue de l'histoire des religions* 209, 219-38.

Samuel, A.E.S. 1983 *From Athens to Alexandria: Hellenism and Social Goals in Ptolemaic Egypt* (Studia Hellenistica 26) Lovanii.

Scholten, J.B. 2000 *The Politics of Plunder: Aitolians and their Koinon in the Early Hellenistic Era, 279-217 BC* Berkeley-Los Angeles: University of California Press.

Shear, T.L. 1978 *Kallias of Sphettos and the Revolt of Athens in 286 BC* (Hesperia Supplement 17) Princeton: American School of Classical Studies at Athens.

Shimron, B. 1972 *Late Sparta: The Spartan Revolution 243-146 BC* (Arethusa Monographs 3) Buffalo, NY: State University of New York.

Shipley, G. 2000 *The Greek World after Alexander 323-30 BC* (Routledge History of the Ancient World) London-New York: Routledge.

Sourvignou-Inwood, C. 1990 "What is Polis Religion?" in: O. Murray & S. Price (eds.) *The Greek City from Homer to Alexander* Oxford: Clarendon Press, 295-322.

Stambaugh, J. 1972 *Sarapis under the Early Ptolemies* (Études préliminaires aux Religions orientales dans l'Empire romain 25) Leiden: Brill.

Swinnen, W. 1973 "Sur la politique religieuse de Ptolémée Ier "in: *Les Syncrétismes dans les Religions Grecque et Romaine (Colloque de Strasbourg, 9-11 June 1971)* (Travaux du Centre d'Études Supérieures Spécialisé d'Histoire des Religions de Strasbourg) Paris: Presses Universitaires de France.

Tatum, W.J. 1996 "The Regal Image in Plutarch's Lives" *The Journal of Hellenic Studies* 116, 135-51.

Taylor, P.J. 1999 *Modernities: A Geohistorical Interpretation* Cambridge: Polity Press.

Tuan, Yi-Fu, 1974 *Topophilia: A Study of Environmental Perception, Attitudes and Values* Englewood Cliffs, NJ: Prentice Hall.

Tuan, Yi-Fu, 1977 *Space and Place. The Perspective of Experience* Minneapolis-London: University of Minnesota Press.

Vian, F. 1963 *Les origines de Thèbes: Cadmos et les Spartes* Paris: Librarie C. Klincksieck.

Whitley, A.J. 1988 "Early states and hero cults: a reappraisal" *The Journal of Hellenic Studies* 108, 173-82.

Whitley, A.J. 1994 "The monuments that stood before Marathon: tomb cult and hero cult in Archaic Attica" *American Journal of Archaeology* 98, 213-30.

Whitley, A.J. 1995 "Tomb cult and hero cult: the uses of the past in Archaic Greece" in: N. Spencer (ed.) *Time, Tradition and Society in Greek Archaeology: Bridging the "Great Divide"* London: Routledge, 43-63.

Zaidman, L.B. & Pantel, P.S. 1992 *Religion in the Ancient Greek City* (translated by Paul Cartledge) Cambridge: Cambridge University Press.

CHAPTER 2

Theatrical Fiction and Visual Bilingualism in the Monumental Tombs of Ptolemaic Alexandria

Marjorie Susan Venit

Almost from the foundation of their city, Alexandrians constructed monumental tombs as communal spaces for both burial and veneration of the dead. Born in the soil of Alexandria – or more literally, in the substratum of soft limestone that underlies the spit of land on which Alexandria was founded – these tombs are unique and, until their dissemination across the north coast of Egypt and to the eastern Mediterranean, they stand unparalleled as monuments to a complex vision of the afterlife.

Two seemingly disparate elements contribute to the singularity of Alexandrian tombs: the first is their incorporation of Egyptian elements into the fabric of an initially and fundamentally Hellenically-inspired monument; the second is their inclusion of theatre. From their inception, Alexandrian monumental tombs integrate two culturally distinct architectural traditions and, very shortly after their inception, they also intermingle two ethnically discrete visual systems as well. From their very beginning, too, Alexandrian monumental tombs construct a purposefully designed space within which, and against which, the human drama of the funerary ritual was to be played out.

The unifier for these two apparently unrelated visions for the monumental tomb is an intentional overriding conceptualisation that, from the outset, forms the basis of the tomb's design. Underlying the fabric of every Alexandrian monumental tomb that is well enough preserved to be considered are external references that point to a purposefully fabricated character as the basis for its design. Although fully functional as burial places, the singular quality of Alexandrian mortuary buildings is the metaphorical quality of their design. The incorporation of a theatrical framework to envelop the ritual performance and the insistence on a bilingual visual vocabulary both provide fictions that preclude historically derived ethnic specificity. Creating a new mortuary building type, independent of place and time and so ideational in its goals, must have served to encourage in the polyglot population of Alexandria an identity as Alexandrians as it also concretised their eschatological ideals.

During the Ptolemaic period, most Alexandrians, independent of their own or their family's country of origin, were buried in similarly conceived funerary buildings and, indeed, often in the very same monumental tomb. The general architectural framework of these monumental tombs is Greek, and the language of the inscriptions found in the tombs – with the exception of rare and unreadable (and almost certainly feigned) hieroglyphs – is also Greek. These tombs contained both inhumations and cremations[1] and even the occasional mummified body,[2] but given the rich population of non-Greek foreigners in Ptolemaic Alexandria and of Egyptians,[3] it is surprising that the tombs record little evidence that speaks specifically to their non-Greek occupants. Slight evidence indicates that Egyptians who wished to maintain a separate identity may have been buried in rock-cut surface graves[4]; some other non-Greeks may have been interred in surface graves that have found little record in the archaeological literature or, less likely, entombed in parts of the necropolises not yet explored; but on current evidence, similarly fashioned monumental tombs seemed to have served the entirety of the culturally assimilated population of Ptolemaic Alexandria. The so-called Soldiers' Tomb,[5] irregularly by Alexandrian standards explicitly built for Gauls who died in Alexandria, was nevertheless a typical Alexandrian monumental tomb. More commonly, though, inscriptions indicate that peoples of multifarious ethnic origins generally shared the same burial space.[6] Jews are a case in point: Although most of the evidence for Jewish burials stem from the period of Roman rule, these burials seem to confirm that cemeteries and

---

1   See Venit 2002, 11, and, for cremation burials in the Roman period, see, e.g., Rowe 1942, 38.
2   For evidence for mummification in Alexandria see Venit 2002, 11; for mummies in the monumental tombs at Anfoushy see Botti 1902, 14, where he mentions two mummies lying in the debris on the floor of the Tomb I, Room 4. He describes them in place as if they must have been deposited in wooden coffins set on the left and back walls of the room (see p. 36 and the plan of the hypogea in Botti 1902, at the back of the volume). See also Breccia 1921, 67, for two mummies possibly disposed in painted mummy cases found in a small room (or large *loculus*) in Anfushy Tomb VI. For "hundreds" of mummies found in *loculi* in a hypogeum at Ras el Tin dated by coins of Cleopatra and Augustus to the late-Ptolemaic period see Breccia 1913, 9. The Ras el Tin and Anfushy mummies are unquestionably found in Greco-Roman context, and may be of late Hellenistic date rather than from the earliest period of Roman rule. Whether by this date mummification indicates Egyptian ethnicity, however, is moot, since it must be remembered that according to Dio Cassius (51.15) the bodies of both Antony and Cleopatra were mummified.
3   See Venit 2002, 10.
4   Botti 1899, 44, notes undated graves with mummies found in the area of Fort Saleh in the quarter of Gabbari. The mummies were discovered in limestone mummiform coffins set in graves that had been precisely cut out to receive the coffins. A small stone monument indicated the presence of a group of two to four coffins. This mummification was not carefully done, especially in the case of children. Some mummies (or, more likely, mummy cases) were, however, very brightly coloured. Botti also reports hieroglyphic writing, traces of gilding, and small leaves of gold. Hieroglyphic writing is almost entirely absent from tombs of the Greco-Roman type, and the hieroglyphs might indicate that these were mummies of Egyptians who retained their traditional practices.
5   Brown 1957, *passim* and esp. 5-20.
6   See Enklaar 1985, 145 and map on 146 and Breccia 1911, *passim*.

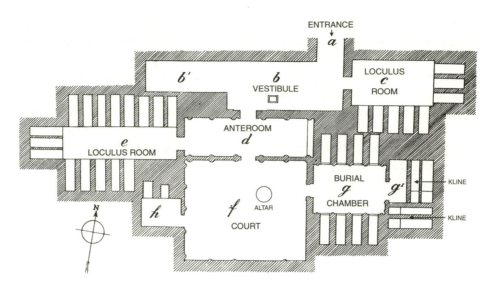

even tombs were conceived as multiethnic.[7] Later Christian burials alongside pagans in reused monumental tombs[8] are also suggestive of the inclusive character of the cemeteries.

It is certainly presumptuous to insist that each Alexandrian individual saw his or her own relation with the afterlife as interchangeable with his (or her) neighbour's. A single individual may have been a member of a number of different cults or religious guilds or a family may have privileged one cult or burial guild over another. Yet despite any individual or familial differences that might be expected, and despite the ethnically distinct divisions that current thought imposes on the population of Ptolemaic Alexandria (and that may have well existed in everyday affairs), the city's monumental tombs suggest an inclusiveness and a commonality of purpose within the rite of burial. And the tombs argue, too, that the mode of burial stressed both the tombs' performative-embracing function and its Egypto-Hellenic intellectual content.

Even one of the very earliest extant monumental tombs, Hypogeum A (**Fig. 1**) which dates to the early third century BCE,[9] incorporates both the architectural fiction inherent in the Ptolemaic Alexandrian tomb (that seems to be a precursor to its fulfilled theatricality) and the bilingualism that bridges the city's two most dominant cultural and ethnic strains. In its original phase (see Fig. 1: *a, b, d, f, g,* and *g'*), Hypogeum A already shows the elements that delineate the plan of the Alexandrian monumental tomb: an entrance

---

7   For a summary of reported Jewish burials in Alexandria see Venit 2002, 20-1. Many of those based on archaeological "evidence" cannot be substantiated; the "Jewishness" of others based on "Jewish" names can also be questioned.

8   See, for example, Empereur & Nenna 2001, *passim.*

9   See Venit 2002, 30-3 for the arguments for the date.

stair (here destroyed) leading down from the surface into the tomb, an intermediary space (here both the vestibule and the anteroom perform that function), a court open to the sky with an altar, a burial room with *loculi* for the body's final disposition, and a *klinē* room with a place to lay out the body (g').

Like the city of Alexandria built for its live inhabitants and like later Alexandrian tombs, Hypogeum A relies heavily on Greek architectural elements and a general Greek interest in illusionistic fiction as the foundation of its visual form. Today the rooms and court of Hypogeum A are filled with gravel and mud to half their height, but still visible in the burial chamber (g) are the delicate engaged Ionic columns that flank the *loculi* and, beyond the door leading into the *klinē* room (g'), two *klinē*-sarcophagi, which are cut from the living rock to replicate Greek wooden couches, are set at right angles to one another. Later *klinē* rooms, such as one in the monumental tomb Moustapha Pasha 2, will add a *trapeza* in front of the table (though no evidence disproves Hypogeum A employing a removable one) and others will, as Hypogeum A, employ two *klinai*, but Hypogeum A stands alone among recorded tombs in setting two *klinai* at right angles to one another to present an immediately recognisable extract from a Greek dining room.[10] Thus, very early in the history of its funerary monuments, Alexandrians conceived of the tomb as a performative space, in this case to re-enact the *prothesis*, which had already been performed in the house of the deceased. Yet, not only did the mourners replicate the *prothesis* within the fabric of the tomb but they elaborated upon it, making the *prothesis* not only a laying out of the body but ensuring that the action would also be read as a metaphor for the banquet of the dead.

Illusionistic fiction is the basis of theatrical design and despite (or perhaps because of) the early date of Hypogeum A, the tomb contains some of the most sophisticated examples of illusionistic fiction of any Alexandrian tomb. Although all details are now lost to time and weather, Evaristo Breccia's excavation reports preserve elements of the tomb's initial aspect that are no longer visible.[11] The long walls of the court (f) were articulated by engaged columns (which can no longer be made out), which were painted white. Between the columns, the court's walls were painted blue, simulating sky and air, and against the blue, rich swags of garlands were painted as if hung between the rock-cut columns. Most remarkably, above the garlands were painted fluttering birds, even further visually piercing the stone and rendering the walls of the court as insubstantial as its roof, open as it was to the sky above.

Yet most remarkable in Hypogeum A, and a detail found with such subtlety in no other Alexandrian tomb, are the fictive windows that penetrate the wall between the anteroom (d) and the vestibule (b) beyond. The wall, with its engaged-half-fluted columns, is treated in Greek zone-style with orthostats, a string course, and a main frieze. And, in the main frieze, and carved as half open, shutters are painted yellow against the blue of the remaining stone (**Fig. 2**). Yet Breccia's drawing is deceiving. First, the colours

---

10 See Venit 2002 for Breccia's drawing of the *loculi* (30, fig. 13) and for a photograph of the two *klinai* (31, fig. 15).

11 See, e.g., Breccia 1905; 1908; 1909; 1910; 1912.

Fig. 2   *Hypogeum A: section of the wall between the anteroom and the vestibule (after Adriani 1966, pl.
45, fig. 171)*

are not just painted on the flat surface of the stone, but the stone itself is partly pierced.
And second, the window is not precisely half open, but only partly opened, the second
"shutter" placed not at a right angle to the surface of the wall, but at an angle oblique
to the stone's surface, giving the impression that someone, who has lazily pushed it
open, has just passed through the scene – populating the uninhabited anteroom with
a human agent as other painted details had populated the empty court with birds.

Hypogeum A provides a cogent model for our understanding of later Ptolemaic
tombs. Insofar as its component parts, only a well for water, common – but not required – in later Ptolemaic-period tombs, is lacking. In its reliance on fictive architectural elements appropriated from Greek monumental civic and religious buildings, in
its use of *trompe l'oeil* painting and furnishings from Greek domestic context, and in
its architectural provisioning for the funerary rites, Hypogeum A stands at the head of
a series of Alexandrian tombs that reach into the Christian era.

Although the fictive architecture of Hypogeum A cannot be argued to carry the same
weightiness of theatricality as that of later tombs, its *trompe l'oeil* backdrop against which
the rites are played out shows a nascent impulse toward the theatre, while its banquet
klinai in the *klinē* room and its altar positioned in the open court indicate the performative aspect of the tomb that permits the playing out of burial and commemorative
rites within the bounded space of the monument. This concretising of the funerary rites
within the very fabric of the building, as well as the fiction involved in such an act, is
elaborated upon in later tombs.

In a first century BCE tomb discovered in the gardens of John Antoniadis in Alexandria in the last years of the nineteenth century,[12] for example, the *klinē* – functional in
all other Alexandrian tombs – is reduced to an elaborately carved facade. The Antoniadis
Garden Tomb's bed, therefore, could neither have supported the deceased in *prothesis*

---

12   For the tomb and previous bibliography see Venit 2002, 41-4.

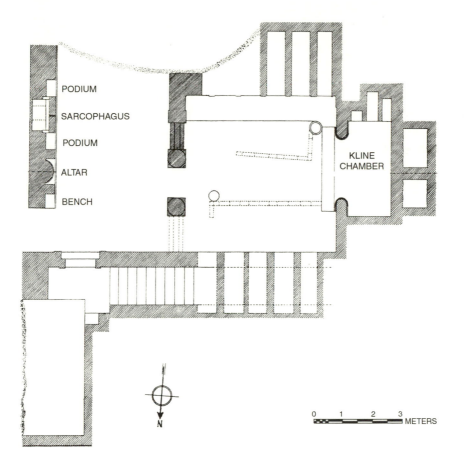

PODIUM

SARCOPHAGUS

PODIUM

ALTAR

BENCH

KLINE
CHAMBER

N

0   1   2   3
METERS

Plan of Wardian Tomb 1 (after Riad 1967, plan 1)   **Fig. 3**

nor in fictive funerary banquet nor have served as his or her coffin. In the Antoniadis
Gardens Tomb, the function of the *klinē* is quite clearly the emblematic value it incorporates. The *klinē*'s complete disdain for functional reality demonstrates the intention
inherent in Alexandrian monumental tombs to create an environment in which each
element – fictive or real – fulfils its necessary role in the ritual performance for the dead.

No tomb better illustrates the artifice that the Alexandrian monumental tomb embraces, the tomb's literal embodiment of the funerary ritual, and its incorporation of
the funerary ritual as part of the scene building than a second-century BCE tomb
from the region of Wardian in Alexandria's ancient western cemetery.[13] Wardian Tomb
1 (**Fig. 3**) is remarkable for the rock-cut features that line the east wall of the court.
These elements: a throne, an altar with a possible broken lintel (an important Egyptian
motif, which will be considered further), and a sarcophagus framed by two podiums
encompass all aspects of the funerary ritual except (as in Hypogeum A) that of water.

13   For the tomb and previous bibliography see Venit 2002, 99-100.

These three elements, calcified in rock, denote the furniture essential to the performance of the mortuary drama, signifying, as they do, the bonds of family, the sacrifices to the deceased, and his or her place of final rest. The sculpted wall of Wardian Tomb 1 stands as the quintessential calcification of the funerary ritual in an Alexandrian tomb and, with the wall's lack of any but ideational functionality, testifies to another and different use of a theatrical model in Alexandrian tombs – a stage set itself that provides a unique backdrop to the funerary drama.

Chatby's Hypogeum A, aside from its early sense of theatricality, also embraces bilingualism, though in the most restricted way of all Alexandria's monumental tombs, since all its architectural details, as well as its banqueting metaphor, are emphatically Greek. Nevertheless, the burial of its occupants – certainly a major function of the monument – in *loculi* is of Egyptian origin.[14] Thus, from their very beginning, as well, although in a limited manner, Alexandrian monumental tombs speak in two tongues The tombs, though, that can most easily serve as archetypes for Ptolemaic-period Alexandrian tombs and the earliest ones that best combine visual bilingualism and theatrical fiction stem from the eastern Alexandrian quarter of Moustapha Pasha (now called Moustapha Kamel) from which the *trapeza* in the *klinē* room of Moustapha Pasha 2 has already been mentioned. The tombs at Moustapha Pasha are slightly later than Chatby's Hypogeum A, dating approximately to the mid-third century BCE.[15]

Like Hypogum A, the Moustapha Pasha tombs are constructed around an open court, and as in Hypogeum A, the court centres on an altar. Also as in Hypogeum A, a *klinē* room is the focal point of mortuary ceremony, though – unlike Hypogeum A and as is more often the case in Alexandrian Ptolemaic-period tombs – the *klinē* rooms in Moustapha Pasha complex are reduced to a single *klinai*. As in Hypogeum A, the walls of Moustapha Pasha Tomb 1 (the walls of the other tombs are not well enough preserved to comment upon) are treated in Greek zone-style (itself a fiction, as it reproduces the outer wall of monumental civic or religious buildings on the interior of much lesser ones) but, unusually in Alexandrian tombs, this fiction is carried out not only in paint, but also in plaster, with both the string course and the orthostat blocks carved as if carrying drafted margins.

Because it is built around a court open to the sky, the Alexandrian tomb has been identified as replicating a Hellenistic house, and other of its other details – the *klinai* and the treatment of the walls – accord with those found in domestic interiors. Nevertheless I should argue that the replication of a house is not the major intent of the monument: In the tomb, each fictive element that seems to duplicate an element of a domestic building stands independently as a single sign, unrelated spatially or conceptually to the next. Although individual units may be dependent on elements of domestic architecture, their parts do not add up to a single whole. This disjunction is made abundantly clear, when a generic Hellenistic house plan is superimposed upon a tomb.[16] Only the

---

14 For a brief discussion of the origin of *loculi* and for previous bibliography see Venit 2002, 16.
15 For the tombs at Moustapha Pasha (Kamel) see Venit 2002, 44-67.
16 Grimm 1998, 41, fig. 39. A closer parallel to Alexandrian tombs now would be the Ptolemaic-period

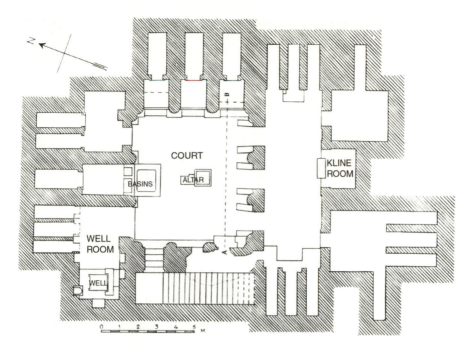

Plan of Moustapha Pasha Tomb 1 (after Adriani 1966, pl. 48, fig. 181)

Fig. 4

central court of the tomb conforms spatially to any aspect of a Hellenic-house plan, as one should expect when comparing two monuments with greatly different functions.

Rather than merely replicating domestic architecture, the monumental tombs of Alexandria are intended, as I hope I have made clear, as a stage-set within which the funerary drama is played out. And both the individual units of the tombs at Moustapha Pasha (among others) and the construction of the fictive architecture that fashions these individual units (again, at Moustapha Pasha among others) bears out this interpretation. The tomb best preserved from the complex, Moustapha Pasha 1 (**Fig. 4**), makes the point most clearly, for beyond its seemingly domestic fiction, it employs specific devices borrowed from the theatre, as Margaret Lyttleton has pointed out.[17] In the monumental south wall of the tomb, with its three doorways recalling those of scene buildings, the tomb uses a stratagem specifically adopted from contemporaneous stage design: The jambs of each doorway, instead of being cut at right angles to the facade, splay outward toward the viewer in the court, and the bottom of the lintel, instead of being parallel to the floor, rises obliquely to the ground (**Fig. 5**). This same conceit, as

pseudo-peristyle houses recently unearthed at Kom el-Dikh in Alexandria (communication by G. Majcherek, December, 2004), but the point remains that the Alexandrian tomb is a collection of domestic-like elements rather than the replication of a domestic structure.

17 Lyttelton 1974, 43.

Fig. 5
*Moustapha Pasha
1: southwest
doorway (author
photograph)*

noted by Adriani,[18] is found in Anfushy Tomb II, a first-century BCE tomb (that will be discussed at length later) from a cemetery on the island of the Pharos, indicating both the intentionality and the longevity of the device. As in the theatre buildings in which they are found, these departures from the horizontal-vertical axes are intended to heighten, and thus falsify, the sense of perspective, and the inclusion of this visual device in Alexandrian tombs – unessential as it is to any physical function of the building – argues the tombs' indebtedness to theatre.

The single facet in Moustapha Pasha Tomb 1, however, that is perhaps most instru-

18   Adriani 1952a, 67.

Outlet pipe and   **Fig. 6**
basins in the court
of Moustapha
Pasha 1 (author
photograph)

mental to argue a dramatic underpinning for the design of Alexandrian tombs is the part that water plays in the production. The very western end of a room in the northwest corner of the tomb is given over to a well (see **Fig. 4**), around which a balustrade (only one side of which is still extant) was later added. A basin, set at kitchen-counter height into the north wall of the room, faces the well and drains through a pipe set into the wall. Precisely how the pipe continued through the building cannot be determined since the wall was intact when the tomb was excavated, but its exit point is clear: It is found in a hole fitted with a pipe in the north wall of the court just above the westernmost of two basins (**Fig. 6**). These basins are carved from the bedrock (forming a double sink, as it were) and, beneath them; another basin is carved into the floor of the court. The

Fig. 7   *View of Moustapha Pasha Tomb 3 (author photograph)*

water that has its origin in the well finally gushes from the outlet in the wall of the court into the westernmost basin of the double sink, from where it flows through a hole near the bottom of the basin – which, therefore, cannot be an overflow hole but must be a more purposeful one – into the second basin, from which it streams forth toward the basin cut into the rock of the flooring of the court.

Hypogeum A aside, most Ptolemaic-period monumental tombs contain a means for water within the fabric of the building, since water is necessary for ablution in the funerary rites, but the complicated water system that Moustapha Pasha 1 offers is completely superfluous: Practical necessity is elsewhere easily served through cisterns and wells. In contrast to other Alexandrian tombs, in Moustapha Pasha 1, water becomes a palpable agent. It gushes forth, streaming from basin to basin, its source (shielded from a direct view from the court) perhaps intended as miraculous. In Moustapha Pasha 1, aside from and perhaps beyond the theatrically derived architecture, water becomes a leading actor in the production of the burial rites.

So far as any Alexandrian tomb is concerned, however, Moustapha Pasha 3 (**Fig. 7**) is the most unquestionably theatrical, though it may not be a tomb at all. Although a Hadra hydria was discovered in the excavation, which might argue for at least one cremation burial,[19] no *loculi* or any other accommodation for burial was discovered. It is therefore conceivable that Moustapha Pasha 3 may have been devoted entirely to the funerary rites, which would explain its unique design.

19   Venit 2002, 65.

Yet beyond these speculations of absolute function, there is no question that Moustapha Pasha 3 makes use of a theatre metaphor, since it not only preserves a stage, but also a scene building, and covered stairways to facilitate entrances and exits to the stage. Behind the scene building is an intermediary space with an altar and, beyond that, a *klinē* room. The space for participants in the vast court and in a smaller, covered exedra at the end opposite the stage, and the open stage and shrouded *klinē* room beyond, suggest that the building served for dramatic performances that accommodated both public ritual and more private rites. And the transformation from light to shade and back to light as the participants moved throughout the tomb, a drama repeated in all Alexandrian Ptolemaic tombs whose courts were open to the sky, calls to mind the experience of the petitioner in the great sanctuaries in the Hellenistic world like Didyma, Lindos, Kos, and others, who proceeded from light into shadow and again into light until the most sacred space was finally revealed.

Mourning in both the ancient Greek and ancient Egyptian world is a constructed performance with ritualised gestures and ritualised acts. Thus it is scarcely surprising to find in the architectural fabric of Alexandrian monumental tombs the employment of dramatic elements inherent in both Hellenistic sacrificial ritual and in the theatre itself.

A further and different use of artifice and metaphor that addresses the experience of death is also characteristic of Alexandrian Ptolemaic tombs. In 1961, in an article that has had resonance throughout later scholarship, Laszlo Castiglione defined a "dual style" characterising the funerary art in Roman-period Egypt.[20] The dual style Castiglione identifies depicts the deceased male or female in naturalistic Roman terms and dressed in Roman garb but portrays the surrounding figures, which are usually deities, represented as Egyptian in both in style and subject. Castiglione's dual style is an important contribution to the study of Roman-period funerary iconography in the *chōra* of Egypt, yet it is rare that the model he identifies is applicable to material from Alexandria during either the Roman or the Ptolemaic period.

Yet beyond the specific form of the "dual style" identified by Castiglione, or the "bilingual style" (a term coined by the authors who published a remarkable Alexandrian Roman-period tomb niche[21]), a visual bilingualism can be applied to Alexandrian Ptolemaic-period tombs. This bilingualism can be seen both in the tombs' figured decoration and in their architectural detail. We have already noted that elements from Greece and Egypt early merge in Alexandrian tombs – Egyptian *loculi* couple with Greek architectural detail and Greek domestic furniture to form the substance of the tomb – but the bilingualism I address here goes beyond this union. This bilingualism speaks to the incorporation of Egyptian cultural material into the fabric of a visibly Greek tomb and to the incorporation of Egyptian eschatological visual signs into a Greek eschatological system.

The earliest extant example of this visual bilingualism known to me is telling in

---

20 Castiglione 1961.
21 See Guimier-Sorbets & Seif el-Din 1997.

both its sophistication and its form. In front of the south facade of the court of Mou-stapha 1, sphinxes crouch on pedestals guarding the entrances to the burial chamber (see **Fig. 5**). Sphinxes are a very old Greek guardian of the tomb.[22] Though in Greece proper this function rarely outlives the sixth century BCE, it survives elsewhere in the Hellenically-influenced world,[23] so it is not surprising that is emerges in third-century pan-Hellenic Alexandria. Greek sphinxes, wherever they are found, are normally winged, female, and sit back on their haunches with their forelegs firmly planted, not unlike ungainly dogs or cats. Egyptian sphinxes, however, perform a different function, assume a different physique, and strike a different pose. They are not tomb guardians but are instead connected with royal power, and they normally lack wings, are male, and crouch like lions. Yet although the sphinxes in the Moustapha Pasha tomb are set up like Greek sphinxes to guard the tomb, they are Egyptian sphinxes in form, pose, and attribute. They are wingless like Egyptian sphinxes, crouched like Egyptian sphinxes, and wear the royal *nemes* head cloth of Egyptian sphinxes. The sphinxes guarding the entrances to the burial chamber in Moustapha Pasha 1 function as Greek sphinxes, but they incorporate all the iconographic trappings of their Egyptian counterparts. With sophisticated efficiency, these sphinxes incorporate the efficacy of Egyptian antiquity into its Greek visual synonym, and by means of this Egyptian reference, create a new and more greatly nuanced image of supernatural protection for this monumental tomb. Scholarship identifies Greek stage buildings as assuming the architectural facade of palaces, and the appropriation of the Egyptian sphinx permits the south facade of the court of Moustapha Pasha 1 to be simultaneously viewed as stage-set and as palace. This royal reference is not limited to Moustapha Pasha Tomb 1, but appears in another context and employing a very different metaphor, as shall be demonstrated shortly.

Conceptually similar to the synthetic sphinxes in Moustapha Pasha 1 is a hybrid from the second-century BCE Sāqiya Tomb, which was painted on the face of a *klinē*-sarcophagus cut into the court of the tomb (**Fig. 8**). Though recognised as an Egyptian *ba*-bird by the papyrus on which it perches and the *nemes* head cloth and the *uraeus* that it wears (neither of which, though, follows a true Egyptian model), the composite creature is so close in form to a Greek siren – which since at least the early fifth century BCE has also had funerary connotations – that the creature is much more likely to have been intended as a syncretism of the two culturally distinct concepts than one that is

---

22 Similar sphinxes once guarded the Hellenic (and theatrically-inspired) doorway to the first suite of burial rooms of Anfushy Tomb II and were also placed in front of the Egyptianised doorway between Rooms 1 and 2 of the same tomb (see discussion of the other Egyptianising elements in Anfushy Tomb II below and, for the sphinxes, Venit 2002, 80 and 82).

23 Sphinxes continue to guard tombs in Lycia, Etruria, and Cyprus, for example. Note the tomb from Xanthus in the British Museum (London B 290) dated 480, with two confronted sphinxes guarding a "false door" and the later Tomb of Merehi from Xanthus (London 1848.19-20.143), dated 390-350, which also shows confronted sphinxes in its gable. See also, for example, the Cypriot sarcophagus (New York 74.51.2453), dated to the second quarter of the fifth century, with sphinxes as corner acroteria and the Etruscan sarcophagus of Vel Urinates (London GR 1838.6-8.12), dated 325-250 with Greek sphinxes as central acroteria at either end of the roof.

Sāqiya Tomb: facade of klinē-*sarcophagus with* ba-*bird (author photograph)*

Fig. 8

either purely Egyptian or purely Greek. The form (as we see it here) and the funerary connotations of the Greek siren may well have originally been imported from Egypt,[24] but the Sāqiya Tomb soul-bird has acquired aspects from its earlier sojourn in Greece, lacking the arms and hands that are often included in the later-period Egyptian *ba*-birds. The integration of the Greek siren with the Egyptian soul-bird in the Sāqiya Tomb accords with the treatment of the sphinxes in Moustapha Pasha Tomb 1 and argues for an intentional conflation of the heretofore ethnically specific eschatological signs.

In a very different way, monumental tombs on Alexandria's Island of the Pharos, first cut in the second-century BCE, also demonstrate Alexandrian bilingualism and the conceptual and visual richness that results. Accessed by a covered stair and built around an open court provided with wells or cisterns, the tombs at Anfushy and Ras el-Tin follow the same plan as earlier Alexandrian tombs. Extending from the open court are two suites of rooms, in each of which a long anteroom precedes a smaller burial chamber. Rock-cut *klinai* have been found in only two of the Pharos Island tombs unearthed, and it is probable that in the others wooden *klinai* served in their stead.

Obviating any possibility of these tombs being those of Egyptians native to Pharos Island as argued by Adriani,[25] Anfushy tombs retain their Graeco-Roman underpin-

---

24 Proposed as certain by Vermeule 1979, 75, despite the female-headed bird already having been known in the Aegean Bronze Age (*ibid*. 231, note 69).

25 Adriani 1952a, 128.

ning well into the first century CE. Room 3 of Anfushy Tomb I,[26] the only tomb that is reconfigured architecturally, is refashioned with three brick-built sarcophagi forming a metaphorical *triclinium*, using as its architectural basis the *triclinium* dining room favoured by the Romans. This model is one that Roman-period Alexandrian tombs often adopt as they transform the earlier Greek banqueting metaphor of the *klinē* to a form paradigmatic of the Roman period, as seen, for example, in the actual *triclinium* and in the *triclinium*-shaped Main Burial Chamber in the Great Catacomb at Kom el-Shoqafa.[27] Whereas Anfushy Tomb I shows a Roman-lineage reconfiguration to its original plan, the original decoration of the other tombs at Anfushy demonstrate their Hellenic heritage. Their walls are decorated in Greek zone-style, seen earliest in extant Alexandrian monumental tombs in Hypogeum A, with a socle, a course of orthostats treated, as is normal in Alexandria, as if made of alabaster, a string course, and a main frieze painted to simulate isodomic blocks. Ceilings of the rooms are most often painted to simulate coffered blocks, also a Hellenic reference. Yet, despite the Hellenic skeleton that underlies the plan and the Greek zone-style division of the walls in the tombs at Anfushy, Egyptian decorative elements are also included, either added to the originally Hellenically based tomb or incorporated into the original decorative scheme.

Anfushy Tomb II,[28] for example, shows a restoration which includes the main frieze of the wall of one anteroom, Room 1, redecorated with a checker pattern intended to replicate faience tiles and a new Egyptianising doorway between the anteroom and its burial chamber (**Fig. 9**). The doorway, whose Egyptian vari-coloured columns support a segmental pediment with a central disk, and which shows a frieze of *uraeae* above the doorway and a broken lintel framing it (which, on Egyptian temples, Diana Wolfe Larkin[29] has seen as heralding and marking the epiphany of a deity), is clearly intended to denote Egypt as is the checker-patterned main frieze, which is intended to replicate faience tiles.

Faience tiles appear in Egypt as early as Dynasty I, but they are most frequently attested in the New Kingdom where they are found in palace context creating opulent wall coverings. Perhaps because of their prevalence in New Kingdom palaces and the cultural value thus accrued, actual faience tiles are also found in Alexandria: Sixty faience squares were excavated in the Ptolemaic Royal Quarter, their findspot arguing for their having decorated some part of the palace complex.[30] Their discovery in the Royal Quarter also argues that the faience tile retained into the Ptolemaic period the Egyptian-palatial connotation that it carried in the Pharaonic period, and argues, too, that in a tomb complex, such as the one at Anfushy, that normally shuns figurative content and relies on illusionistic architecture to make its iconographical statement, the faience tiles must stand (as they undoubtedly do in the Ptolemaic palace) as a referent

26 Venit 2002, 74-7.
27 See plan, for example, in Venit 2002, 126, fig. 104.
28 For the tomb and previous bibliography see Venit 2002, 77-85.
29 Larkin 1994, 122-6.
30 For evidence for faience tiles in Egypt and for the sources of the evidence see Venit 2002, 73.

Anfushy Tomb II, Room 1 (author photograph)

Fig. 9

to Egypt. Like the crouched sphinxes that guard the entranceways to the burial rooms at Moustapha Pasha Tomb I, the faience tiles in the tombs on Pharos Island articulate the intention to entomb the dead within a complex with palatial implications.

The burial room beyond the anteroom in Anfushy Tomb II shows an even greater embrace of the two major cultures of Alexandria: On the one hand, its focus is an Egyptian-style *naiskos* and its walls are entirely devoted to a simulacrum of faience tiles; on the other, its painted ceiling shows a complex pattern of interlaced elements that form a trellis supporting a fictive tapestry into which are woven paintings of Greek mythological figures, unfortunately no longer visible even with infra-red photography, but preserved in drawings made upon their discovery. These figures, drawn in a style that is clearly classical, have been seen as having Dionysiac connotations,[31] which – given the cult of Dionysus in Alexandria and his Mysteries[32] – is a fitting subject for a burial room. In this room, as in the anteroom, the ceiling with its Greek associations is retained, even though a ceiling could have been contrived using the motif of faience tiles that can be seen in other Anfushy tombs. Yet, in the refurbishing of Tomb II, despite the simulacra of the faience squares that replaced both the string course and the main frieze of the wall (and despite the inclusion of the Egyptianising doorframe),

31 Adriani 1952a, 72-6.
32 See Fraser 1972, 201-6.

the orthostats and the decoration of the ceiling remain in their original Hellenic style, providing a bilingual message – on the one hand Egypt, on the other Greece.

Probably at the same time in the first century BCE that the doorway embrasure was added and the tomb was redecorated with the faience-tile pattern, three Egyptianising paintings were added to the walls of the staircase. The one on the first landing shows the dead person led by Horus and welcomed by two other figures – presumably Egyptian deities – who are presented in a reasonably accurate, although generalised, Egyptian form. This mode of representation, in which deities lack attributes or in which attributes are awarded cavalierly without respect to tradition, is an aspect that grows more prevalent during the centuries of Roman rule. But in both the Ptolemaic and the Roman period this inconclusive iconographic treatment indicates the efficacy that the Egyptianised image itself carried, independent of the veracity of its form or the specificity of its narrative.

Thus Anfushy II, originally conceived as a purely Greek tomb becomes bilingual in the first century BCE by the retention of the Greek zone-style system (and a number of its decorative components) coupled with the addition of the Egyptian-referenced treatment of its main frieze, the new Egyptian doorframe, the Egyptian *naos*, and the Egyptian paintings on the entry stair. Anfushy Tomb II, which begins as a tomb based fully on Hellenic components, evolves into one that is bilingual.

In contrast to this apparent evolution, other tombs from the Island of the Pharos and elsewhere in Alexandria show concurrence in their incorporation of Egyptian and Greek elements.

On the Island of the Pharos, this intent to preserve the coexistence of two culturally distinct styles is rendered clearest by another tomb, Anfushy V.[33] In contrast to Anfushy II, Anfushy V was planned from its inception to simultaneously incorporate both Greek and Egyptian systems of wall decoration. The doorway to one of its anterooms (Room 1) is Doric, and the walls flanking the entrance and the room's two long walls are conceived in Greek zone style, yet the wall facing the entryway is Egyptianising, with rows of checkers alternating with bands of fictive alabaster. In addition, an alabaster band, similar to the end wall's dividing bands, runs around the entire room at the top of the wall linking the two modes of decoration, and the Egyptian treatment of the ceiling – alabaster strips alternating with checkered tiles – counterbalances the seeming ethnic inequality of the walls. The middle strip of fictive alabaster reads as a ridgepole, and the other bands can be read as beams intended to support a light ceiling of faience tiles, a conceit that at once simplifies and Egyptianises the fictive trellis in the burial chamber of Anfushy II, while adding to the palatial associations of the burial chamber.

Room 4 in Anfushy Tomb V shows the same bilingual style as the last, juxtaposing Greek with Egyptian elements. Unlike the Doric doorway to the first suite of rooms, however, the one to Room 4 displays an Egyptianising embrasure. Similar to the first anteroom, this room too presents Greek zone-style decoration on its long walls and Egyptian polychrome faience tiles on its back wall. And in contrast to the Egyptian

---

33   For the tomb and previous bibliography see Venit 2002, 85-90.

doorframe leading into the suite of rooms, the entrance door between the anteroom and the burial chamber (Room 5) receives a Greek embrasure with white painted uprights crowned by a moulding of Lesbian leaf. Among the remarkable features of Room 4 is a huge *loculus* characterised by a richly articulated *loculus*-closing slab set into an equally extraordinarily rich plaster framework, which occupies the entire height of the wall and even extends up onto the ceiling (**Fig. 10**).[34]

The *loculus* slab and its plaster embrasure are astonishingly complex and embody components of a true Egyptian *naos* of which the interior elements (now to a large extent destroyed) are indicated in several planes. This fictive *naos*, which occupies the liminal space between the room and the entombed deceased, acts like the broken lintel on the door frame to the burial room in Anfushy Tomb II and is another testament both to the vigorous penetration of Egyptian motifs and beliefs into a once Hellenic milieu and to the genuine understanding of these beliefs and motifs as they are concretised in the city's tombs.

A further expression of the bilingualism that informs Alexandrian tombs comes from the *klinē* niche of Tomb 8 (**Fig. 11**)[35] in the necropolis beneath the palace grounds at Ras el Tin (now lost to view) that originally must have been part of the same necropolis now

34 For a reconstruction drawing of the closing slab and its embrasure see Venit 2002, 89, fig. 74, after Adriani 1940a, 92, fig. 54.
35 For the tomb and previous bibliography see Venit 2002, 72-3.

Fig. 11   Klinē *niche in Ras el-Tin, Tomb 8 (after Adriani 1952b, pl. 32, fig. 2)*

called Anfushy.[36] The niche encloses a Greek *klinē* laid with a thin mattress and furnished with cushions at its head and a bier cloth, which is decorated with birds (the type of *klinē* that the soul-bird from the Sāqiya Tomb presumably would have inhabited). But this fully Greek *klinē* is set behind a facade that recognises Egypt, composed, as it is, of Egyptianising columns – striped red and white, capped with composite capitals and the high impost block that characterises Egyptian post-and-lintel architecture – that support an Egyptian segmental pediment. The wall behind the *klinē* is itself bilingual with painted checkers replicating Egyptianising faience squares and painted columns creating the illusion of spatial recession – a classicising conceit found, for example, in a third-century BCE Alexandrian tomb at Sidi Gabr.[37]

Beyond the Island of the Pharos, Alexandria's western cemetery also yields tombs fashioned as bilingual, and the Sāqiya Tomb,[38] the most unusual of all tombs from the western necropolis and seemingly the most Hellenised, nevertheless, stands as an exemplar of the tradition (**Fig. 12**). The tomb takes its name from the water-lifting device that constitutes an element in the largest remaining painting in the tomb, which shows a piping boy walking around the *sāqiya*, accompanying the oxen that turn the wheel.

---

36   For an image see Adriani 1952b, pl. 32, fig. 2; Venit 2002, 72, fig. 55 (after Adriani).
37   See Venit 2002, 38-41.
38   For the tomb and previous bibliography see Venit 2002, 101-18.

Sāqiya Tomb painted slabs (author photograph)

Fig. 12

Painted on the short wall perpendicular to the *sāqiya* scene, is a bearded herm of Pan set in a woodland enclosure. On the wall perpendicular to that one and on what must have been the jamb leading into a second room, a shepherd overlooks his flock, painted below, and protects it from the lurking jackal at the bottom of the picture. He holds an animal across his shoulders and stands in an easy chiastic pose. The scene finds a close visual parallel in Tomb 3 from Ras el-Tin,[39] which also shows a decorated door jamb that is also divided horizontally into two halves. On the lower part of the Ras el-Tin slab, a hoopoe perches on a plant and, above, Heracles dominates the jamb – as does the shepherd – although the Ras el-Tin Heracles stands in a much less convincing pose. The style of all the scenes in the Sāqiya Tomb is Greek and its images, with the exception of the waterwheel itself, which is a Hellenistic invention, are found in the Greek visual repertoire as early as the sixth century BCE.

In concert with walls of the courts of the Sāqiya Tomb that retain figures painted in a Hellenic style, the burial chamber adds facing *klinai* each set into an *arcosolium*. *Arcosolia* characterise Roman-period and early Christian tombs throughout the Mediterranean world, and the Sāqiya Tomb's *arcosolia* are among the earliest. Painted on the back wall of the niche formed by the *klinai* are birds (reminiscent of the treatment in the court of Hypogeum A) and fictive columns creating the impression of a third dimension, at

39 See Venit 2002, 71, fig. 54.

in Ras el-Tin Tomb 8 (see **Fig. 11**), and on the back wall of the *klinē* chamber, itself, a male reclines under a fruited arbour.

Two other elements in the Sāqiya Tomb, however, conspire to add this tomb to the inventory of Alexandrian bilingual monuments. First is the *klinē*-sarcophagus, which has already been noted, with its painted facade slab bearing the *ba*-bird or siren (see **Fig. 8**), which must have come from the wall of the court facing the *sāqiya* scene. Despite the pseudo-Egyptian style of the image, however, details such as the fine, black, pen-like calligraphic lines, which are repeated in the other paintings from the court, suggest that the *ba*-bird (or siren) is by the same hand that painted the other images in the tomb and thus coeval with the remainder of the painted program.

The second Egyptianising element is found in the room adjacent to the court, which is entered through the doorway with the shepherd and his flock on its jamb. Similar to the repainted walls in Anfushy Tomb II on the Island of the Pharos, this wall shows a plinth, orthostat blocks in mock alabaster, and – in the main frieze – a black and white checker pattern, though in the Sāqiya Tomb, the "faience squares" are above a double string course (see **Fig. 12**). This string course is a vestigial element, since it is eliminated in the repainting of Anfushy II and in other tombs from Anfushy, and its retention suggests that the Sāqiya Tomb predates those of Pharos Island, probably dating to the late-second century BCE. Though the images in the Sāqiya Tomb are painted in a style that evokes the Hellenic world, the zone-style wall, as in the tombs on the Island of the Pharos, incorporates Egypt.

The bilingual Sāqiya Tomb, then, introduces into a basically architectural Hellenic tomb – marked by its *klinai*, the *klinē*-sarcophagus, and the zone-style wall – an Egyptian faience-tile main frieze, and it commingles with its Hellenic illusionism of birds flitting among fictive columns and its Greek landscapes, the Egyptianised *ba*-bird of the *klinē*-sarcophagus. It also localises the imagery, combining a specifically Alexandrian landscape – that of the *sāqiya*, a device that was almost certainly invented in Alexandria – with the landscapes that are generically Greek.

In addition, the Sāqiya Tomb is bilingual in yet another way, since the landscapes also can be read to embrace both Hellenic and Egyptian eschatological viewpoints. I have argued[40] that the Sāqiya Tomb's landscapes perfectly parallel those evoked in the shepherd's song in the *First Idyll* of Theocritus – the poet-in-residence in the Ptolemaic court in the 270s – as articulated by Charles Segal,[41] and I have also argued, that these landscapes in the Sāqiya Tomb (as those in Theocritus' poem) can be interpreted metaphorically to address the range of human experience, the first two landscapes – those of the *sāqiya* and the herm – expressing the polarities of the human psyche: Civilisation, and the triumph of culture, is epitomised in the land that is brought under human control by the invention of the *sāqiya*, while the untamed aspect of the human condition is delineated in the rustic sanctuary of the rustic Pan. Between these two extremes stands the third image: the shepherd guarding his flock. The pastoral land he exemplifies

---

40 Venit 2002, 116-8.
41 Segal 1981.

mediates between the cultivated and the undomesticated, for it is at once beneficial to mankind, since it supports his flocks, and yet it is unaltered by human intervention. Thus, the three paintings of the court embrace the complexity of nature in its relationship to humankind. And, in doing so, they also speak to Egypt. S.C. Humphreys[42] has proposed that the thrice-yearly harvest in the Egyptian Isles of the Blest indicates not only perpetual abundance but also an unchanging state that echoes the timelessness of the existence of the dead, and the paintings in the Sāqiya Tomb may be intended to evoke a similar metaphor, as they too denote a fully rounded vision of the completeness and the permanence of nature and, by extension, the immutable eternal life of the deceased buried within the monument. Thus, though at times in ways very different from one another, both the second-century BCE Sāqiya Tomb and the slightly later tombs from the Island of the Pharos, continue, amplify, and further nuance the bilingual quality of earlier Alexandrian tombs.

It is somewhat more difficult to argue that either the Sāqiya Tomb or the tombs from the Island of the Pharos carry the same degree of "theatricality" as the earlier tombs. Yet even in this later Ptolemaic period the theatrical metaphor is not absent from Alexandrian tombs. One aspect of the theatrical character of Tomb II at Anfushy has already been mentioned: The outward splaying of the jambs of the door embrasure that leads to its first suite of burial rooms employs the same device to create a heightened perspective as do the doorways of Moustapha Pasha Tomb 1. In fact, in the much more tightly contained court of the Anfushy tomb, the resulting effect would have appeared even more dramatic than in Moustapha Pasha Two other elements, both of which are unique in the form they take at Anfushy, are also best explained by citing the theatre, though unlike the architectural treatment of Anfushy II's door embrasures, no definitive theatrical parallels can be adduced for either. The first is found on the north wall of the court of Anfushy II (**Fig. 13**). It takes the form of a very large shallow niche, decorated in Greek zone style and framed to either side with engaged piers, about four meters high and occupying almost the entire length of the wall.[43] This niche has no structural function in the tomb and, positioned at right angle to the tomb's entrance, as it is, it does not act as the focal point for a visitor entering the court either. It can best (and perhaps, only) be explained in concert with the well cut into the contiguous northern corner of the court's west wall – and, with the water system in Tomb 1 at Moustapha Pasha in mind – as a framing device to contain the part of the funerary drama concerned with water.

The original plan of Tomb I at Anfushy – the tomb mentioned earlier that contained a room reconfigured as a mortuary *triclinium* – also incorporates a device that might be viewed as theatrical. The funnel-shaped opening cut above the doorways that mediate between the court and the anterooms (including the reconfigured one), and that terminates about a meter into the room, can also be added to the catalogue of theatricality in Alexandrian tombs. These oblique openings fashion a vehicle for a dramatic focusing of

---

42 Humphreys 1981, 275-8.
43 For a drawing of the niche see Venit 2002, 80, fig. 62, after Adriani 1952a, 65, fig. 35.

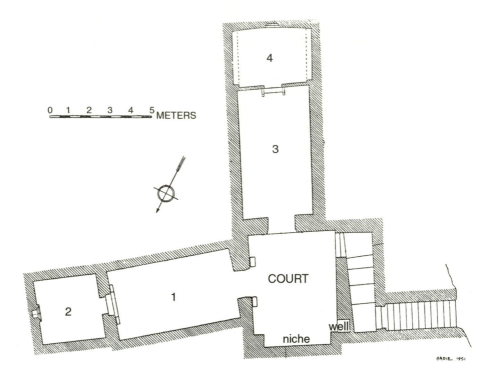

Fig. 13 *Plan of Anfushy Tomb II indicating the niche and the well in the court (after Adriani 1952a, 62, fig. 32)*

light. They are intended to concentrate the light from the court and direct it into the interior of the long narrow room, illuminating with natural daylight and, depending on the position of the sun, perhaps spotlighting the memorial rites that must have been performed in the anterooms of the tomb.

In addition to the seemingly theatrical devices in the Anfushy tombs, one might propose that the paintings of the *ba*-bird from the *klinē*-sarcophagus and the landscapes from the court in the Sāqiya Tomb add another kind of theatricality to the Alexandrian mortuary monument – that of "theatrical" fiction. That is to say, the images of the court and the others in the tomb create an extended metaphor that emerges as a dramatic narrative that forms the basis of theatrical performance.

Both visions – bilingualism and theatricality – incorporate into their fabric the fiction that is the underlying basis of Ptolemaic-period Alexandrian tombs, and both fictive situations, apart and in concert, establish the mortuary buildings of Ptolemaic Alexandria as bi-cultural monuments that can only have had their genesis in the peculiar construct that was ancient Alexandria. It is this bi-ocular modality that separates Alexandrian tombs from other tomb types in the ancient world, as they employ formal characteristics to express the singular eschatological vision that marks the monumental tombs of ancient Alexandria.

References

Adriani, A. 1952a "Nécropoles de l'île de Pharos. B) Section d'Anfouchy" *Annuaire du Musée Gréco-Romain* 4 (1940-1950) Alexandria: Société de publications égyptiennes, 55-128.

Adriani, A. 1952b "Nécropoles de l'île de Pharos. I. Section de Ras el Tine" *Annuaire du Musée Gréco-Romain* 4 (1940-1950) Alexandria: Société de publications égyptiennes 4 (1940-1950) Alexandria: Société de Publications Égyptiennes, 48-54.

Adriani, A. 1966 *Repertorio d'arte dell'Egitto Greco-Romano* (series C) Rome: L'Erma di Bretschneider.

Botti, G. 1899 "Études topographiques dans la nécropole de Gabbari" *Bulletin de la société (royale) archéologique d'Alexandrie* 2, 37-56.

Botti, G. 1902 "Première visite à nécropole d'Anfouchy à Alexandrie" *Bulletin de la société (royale) archéologique d'Alexandrie* 4, 13-15.

Breccia, E. 1905. "La necropoli di Sciatbi" *Bulletin de la société (royale) archéologique d'Alexandrie* 8, 55-100.

Breccia, E. 1908 "Fouilles et trouvailles. La Nécropole de Chatby" *Rapport sur la marche du Service du Musée pendant l'Année 1907* Alexandria, 3-4.

Breccia, E. 1909 "Fouilles et trouvailles. La Nécropole de Chatby" *Rapport sur la marche du Service du Musée pendant l'Année 1908* Alexandria, 3-4.

Breccia, E. 1910 "Fouilles et Trouvailles. La Nécropole de Chatby" *Rapport sur la marche du Service du Musée pendant l'Année 1909* Alexandria, 7.

Breccia, E. 1911 *Iscrizioni greche e latine. Catalogues général des antiquités égyptiennes du Musée d'Alexandrie, nos 1-568* Le Caire: Imprimerie de l'Institut français d'archéologie orientale (reprint Osnabrück: Otto Zeller 1976).

Breccia, E. 1912 *La Necropoli di Sciatbi* Cairo: Imprimerie de l'Institut français d'archéologie.

Breccia, E. 1913 "Fouilles 1. – Fouilles d'Abou Girgeh" *Rapport sur la marche du Service du Musée en 1912* Alexandria: Société de Publications Égyptiennes, 3-14.

Breccia, E. 1921 "Fouilles. II.– Nécropole d'Anfouchy" *Rapport sur la marche du Service du Musée Gréco-Romain pendant l'exercice 1919-1920* Alexandria: Société de Publications Égyptiennes, 55-69.

Brown, B.R. 1957 *Ptolemaic Paintings and Mosaics and the Alexandrian Style* Cambridge, MA: Archaeological Institute of America.

Castiglione, L. 1961 "Dualité du style dans l'art sépulcral égyptien à l'époque romaine," *Acta Antiqua* 9: 209-30.

Empereur, J.-Y. & Nenna, M.-D. (eds.) 2001 *Nécropolis 1.(Études alexandrines* 5) Cairo: Institut français d'archéologie orientale.

Enklaar, A. 1985 "Chronologie et peintures des hydries de Hadra" *Bulletin van de Vereeniging tot Bevordering der Kennis van de Antike Beschaving* 60, 106-51.

Fraser, P.M. 1972 *Ptolemaic Alexandria* Oxford: Clarendon Press.

Grimm, G. 1998 *Alexandria. Die erste Königsstadt der hellenistischen Welt. Bilder aus Nilmetropole von Alexander dem Großen bis Kleopatra VII* Mainz am Rhein: Philipp von Zabern

Guimier-Sorbet, A.M. & Seif el-Din, M. 1997 "Les deux tombes de Perséphone dans la nécropole de Kom el-Chougafa à Alexandrie" *Bulletin de correspondance hellénique* 121, 355-410.

Humphreys, S.C. 1981 "Death and Time" in: S.C. Humphreys and H. King (eds.) *Mortality and Immortality: the anthropology and archaeology of death* London: Academic Press, 261-83.

Larkin, D.W. 1994 *The Broken-Lintel Doorway of Ancient Egypt and its Decoration*, (dissertation) New York: New York University, Institute of Fine Arts

Lyttelton, M. 1974 *Baroque Architecture in Classical Antiquity* Ithaca, NY: Cornell University Press.

Riad, H. 1967. "Quatre tombeaux de la nécropole ouest d'Alexandrie" *Bulletin de la société (royale) archéologique d'Alexandrie* 42, 89-96.

Rowe, A. "New Excavations at Kôm el-Shukafa" *Bulletin de la société (royale) archéologique d'Alexandrie* 35, 5-45.

Segal, C. 1981 "'Since Daphnis Dies': the meaning of Theocritus' First Idyll" in: C. Segal, *Poetry and Myth in Ancient Pastoral. Essays on Theocritus and Virgil* Princeton, NJ: Princeton University Press: 25-46.

Venit. M.S. 2002 *Monumental Tombs of Ancient Alexandria. The Theater of the Dead* Cambridge: Cambridge University Press.

Vermeule, E. 1979 *Death in Early Greek Art and Poetry* Berkeley: University of California Press.

CHAPTER 3

Language and Race: Theocritus and the Koine Identity of Ptolemaic Egypt

George Hinge

1. Race

Admittedly, the word "race" is rather discomforting. Since I have nevertheless chosen to include it into the title of this article, I suspect I have to clarify my motives and my position first. It is radical to claim that any application of the concept of race must be, at the same time, racist. Yet, even if I shall not deny that man differs in physical appearance, the division into definite races presupposes that the accidental difference in phenotype has social implications as well. Therefore, any use of the word outside physical anthropology must be considered suspicious and perilous. In German and Danish, the corresponding words "Rasse" and "race" are in fact used only of physical differences. In English, on the other hand, the word covers at least three different meanings. Besides the continental denotation, it is also used synonymously with "species," when one speaks about, say, "the human race" or even "extraterrestrial races," to my mind a dangerous extension of the word. Furthermore it designates a cultural unit sharing a common history, language, culture and origin. One may speak about "the Greek race" for instance. Even though I consider the last-mentioned extension of the word no less dangerous than the first one, it is ethnicity and not physical race to which the title of my article alludes. The juxtaposition of the two words "language" and "race" was simply too catchy to resist.

It need not be said that the theory combining cultural and physical races experienced a well-deserved setback after the monstrous excesses of the Holocaust. Because the grotesque and so to speak gothic construction of the Aryan race was based partially on linguistic arguments, historical linguistics as such has been considered suspicious by post-war scholars, even though hardly any serious Indo-Europeanists would ever claim the existence of Indo-European genes (and only few of them did in fact subscribe to the Aryan hypothesis before the War).[1] Ironically enough, the marginalisation af classical

---

[1]   For an exhaustive discussion of the evidence regarding the phenotype of Early Indo-Europeans and its significance for reconstructing the prehistory of Indo-European see Day 2001.

historical linguistics has, at the same time, opened the way for a new genetic approach to the dispersion of language and culture.[2] This is, however, another story. So, the present article does not claim that language is correlated to physical race in any way. It will, however, be argued that language played a major role in the ancient concept of ethnicity; and linguistic differences and similarities were, to a certain extent, shaped by the ethnic divisions and groupings.

2. Linguistic identity in Classical Greece

A celebrated passage of Herodotus' *Histories* sums up Greek ethnicity with the following words put into the mouths of the Athenians to a Laconian delegation as an argument of their alliance in the war against the Persians (8.144.2):

> There are many reasons why we should not do this, even if we wanted to: First and foremost, they have burnt and destroyed the statues and temples of our gods, and we are obliged to revenge them as far as possible rather than conclude a treaty with the offenders. <u>Furthermore, there is the Hellenicity, consisting in the same blood and the same language, the common shrines of gods and cult and the same way of life</u>, which the Athenians should not betray.

> Πολλά τε γὰρ καὶ μεγάλα ἐστὶ τὰ διακωλύοντα ταῦτα μὴ ποιέειν, μηδ᾽ ἢν ἐθέλωμεν, πρῶτα μὲν καὶ μέγιστα τῶν θεῶν τὰ ἀγάλματα καὶ τὰ οἰκήματα ἐμπεπρησμένα τε καὶ συγκεχωσμένα, τοῖσι ἡμέας ἀναγκαίως ἔχει τιμωρέειν ἐς τὰ μέγιστα μᾶλλον ἤ περ ὁμολογέειν τοῖσι ταῦτα ἐργασαμένοισι· <u>αὖτις δὲ τὸ Ἑλληνικόν ἐὸν ὅμαιμόν τε καὶ ὁμόγλωσσον καὶ θεῶν ἱδρύματά τε κοινὰ καὶ θυσίαι ἤθεά τε ὁμότροπα</u>, τῶν προδότας γενέσθαι Ἀθηναίους οὐκ ἂν εὖ ἔχοι.

Accordingly, ethnicity can be defined in terms of four components: origin, language, cult, and culture. The last three of these components are in fact the main criteria for ethnicity in the ethnographical parts of Herodotus' *Histories*. Thus, in the Scythian logos, different tribes are dissociated from the Scythians on the basis of their language, cult, and culture (cf. 4.23.2, 4.106, 4.108.2, 4.109, 4.117), and it is evident that Scythian language was to Herodotus an important prerequisite of Scythian ethnicity.[3] In the first book, Herodotus offers a short excursus on the origin of the Greek tribes (1.56-8). We are told that the Hellenic tribe (τὸ Ἑλληνικὸν ἔθνος) originally lived in Central and

---

2   Cavalli-Sforza 2000, 133-72, points to a correspondence between genetic cladistics and linguistic cladistics. Undeniably, people who speak similar languages are often similar genetically as well; yet, at closer inspection there are many important exceptions (besides the well-known modern ones), for instance the Ethiopians who speak a language related to Arabic and Hebrew in spite of the large "racial" difference. Genetically, Iranians are closely related to the other people of the Middle East, but they speak an Indo-European language. The examples are *legio*.

3   Hinge 2005.

Northern Greece but later invaded the Peloponnese and was by then called Doric. The Athenian tribe (τὸ Ἀττικὸν ἔθνος), on the other hand, was autochthonous and originally Pelasgic. Herodotus concludes that, since the contemporary Pelasgians, i.e. those living in the northern Aegean, speak a non-Greek language (βάρβαρον γλῶσσαν), the Athenians were originally Barbarians, but after they went over to the Greeks (ἅμα τῇ μεταβολῇ τῇ ἐς Ἕλληνας), they learnt the Greek language as well. The historicity of this reconstruction is questionable.[4] What matters here is the line of argumentation. It supports once again that language is quintessential to Herodotus' concept of ethnicity.

This fact may seem uncontroversial, and it has been so for some centuries. However, Jonathan Hall, who has written two significant books[5] about the construction of Greek ethnicity, claims that language played only a minor role. Instead the Greeks formulated their ethnicity in terms of fictitious genetic relations, mythical genealogies. Significantly enough, Hall considers Herodotus a possible exception to this rule, but he nevertheless underscores the role of language here too. Thus he says:[6]

> … it is clear that the "Hellenic tongue" (*Hellas glossa*) is not based on any empirically-derived observations referring to the isoglosses that separate the myriad of local Greek dialects from the non-Greek languages. It is rather an abstract reification that assumes the prior existence of an "imagined community" defined according to other criteria.

Since no language can be separated from closely related languages 100 % empirically, one must say that Hall makes an unfair demand on Herodotus and the Greeks. Yet, even if it is impossible to draw an unambiguous line between language and dialect, there can be no doubt that Classical Greece encompassed a linguistic community which included a range of mutually intelligible dialects. There may have existed border cases. The Macedonian dialect is probably a good example of that and an example invoked by Hall. Both the ancients and the modern scholars disagree as to the ethnic affiliation of the Macedonians. The birth of the Slavic Republic af Macedonia in the 1990s has made the Hellenicity of the ancient Macedonians a matter of high political and scholarly priority. Thus, many scolars now conclude that the ancient Macedonians were in fact some kind of Dorians.[7] However, the glosses of the ancient lexicographers give the impression of a language that was closely related to Greek, but different in some fundamental aspects,[8]

---

4   The alleged autochthony of the Athenians implies that Hellenicity is not something constant and natural. Cf. also Hinge 2005, 107-15.

5   Hall 1997; 2002.

6   Hall 2002, 191-2.

7   E.g. Brixhe 1999; Kapetanopoulos 1999; O'Neil 2006; Panayotou 2007. Their main evidence is two inscriptions in the Doric dialect found in Macedonia, but they prove only that Greek was gaining ground in Macedonia in the Classical age already (later, under Philip II, the inscriptions were written in pure Attic Greek).

8   The Macedonian personal names and the glosses of Hesychius exhibit IE *b^h > β instead of Gk. φ, e.g. Βερενίκη = Φερενίκη. Here, Brixhe (1999, 51-62) assumes a retrograde development *b^h > Gk.

and the Macedonian dialect seems to have been unintelligible to the Greeks (cf. Curt. 6.11.4). To my mind the linguistic ambiguity of the Macedonian dialect is not only parallel, but also correlated to the ethnic ambiguity of the Macedonian people. At any rate, the Classical Greeks probably had an intuitive approach to the dialect division. They may not have known exactly where to put the finger, but they were certainly able to tell the provenience of a fellow-Greek by his accent alone.

Even if the concept of isoglosses (characteristic features dividing dialects of a language) is a complex issue, of which the ancients were perfectly unaware – as are most modern people –, they did play a role in the linguistic and social reality of the Greek world. Isoglosses may be described as fossils of both previous and present ethnic differences. If modern linguists detect a bundle of isoglosses between two areas, it is a clear sign that the two areas differ, or once differed, in their ethnic identities. Conversely, if the isoglosses are blurred through new common developments, it indicates that the areas in question have started to construct convergent identities. In the homeland it mattered what sort of Greek you were – a Spartan, an Argive, an Athenian etc. However, the great waves of colonisation in the eighth and seventh centuries BCE contributed to the construction of a Greek identity in opposition to the non-Greek natives in Cyprus, Egypt, Libya, Sicily, Italy or Scythia. The otherness of those "Barbarians" and the complete unintelligibility of their languages, which were frequently compared to the chirping of birds, made the existence of a specific Hellenic identity obvious. For instance, Sophocles contrasts Greece with the languageless people (*Trach.* 1060 οὔθ᾽ Ἑλλάς, οὔτ᾽ ἄγλωσσος).

3. Koine and Panhellenisation

It cannot, however, be stressed often enough that this identity is not natural *per se*, but a cultural construction. The linguistic, cultural and religious similarity of the future Greeks, which already existed as a consequence of the cultural convergence in the Mycenaean Age,[9] was an impetus to this construction. At the same time, the invention of a Hellenic identity that emphasised these parallels would naturally minimise the differences and maximise the similarities. The process that eventually led to the creation of a Koine is a clear evidence of the importance of language in Greek ethnicity. It will therefore not be superfluous to look closer at this process, and as we shall see, this path will in the end lead us to Alexandria.

The Finnish scholar Jaakko Frösén has suggested that Koine originated through a creolisation of a pidgin that was used as a means of communication between heterogeneous Greek dialects in the fifth century BCE.[10] There is, however, a fundamental difference between pidgin and koine. A pidgin bridges a language barrier between people

---

φ > Mac. β. However, it is to my mind more economical to relate this feature to the unanimous *b* of the neighbouring Indo-European dialects of Central and Eastern Europe (Phrygian, Thracian, Illyrian, Celtic, Balto-Slavic, Iranian etc.).

9   Finkelberg 2005, 109-39.
10 Frösén 1974.

speaking completely different languages. The grammar and the phonology are reduced to an absolute minimum. If the pidgin becomes a permanent language, it will eventually develop a complete grammar and phonology, a process known as creolisation.[11] The Greek dialects were, however, anything but mutually unintelligible in the Archaic and Classical Ages. The grammar and the vocabulary were largely identical, and nothing indicates that a Greek from one city would not readily understand a Greek from another city – on the contrary.

The Koineisation is therefore better described as a gradual convergence of related linguistic norms towards an imagined superregional standard ("dialect levelling").[12] In the Archaic Age, the dialects spoken in the southern Balkan and in the western Asia Minor started to orientate themselves towards each other. The concept of a Hellenic ethnicity was introduced, and one of its main pillars was the realisation that the Hellenes shared a common language, i.e. they were able to understand each other even if their various idioms were different. We are dealing with the concept of Panhellenisation. Local deities were integrated into one and the same Olympian pantheon, and the hymns of the local cults were formulated in a new common linguistic and poetic form. As I have pointed out in my study of the language of Alcman[13], poetry composed in the Archaic Age was basically formulated in the same language (deep structure), even if the actual poems were performed with different accents (surface structure). Panhellenisation was relevant not only to the literary language, but also to the local dialects, which were now conceived not as independent entities, but as epichoric units of a Panhellenic whole. The Laconian, Boeotian and Athenian dialects were no longer autonomous systems, but parts of a linguistic collective. The dialects, which had been drifting apart in the Dark Ages, now started to converge. Since the Archaic Koineisation or Panhellenisation was primarily poetic and oral, it tended to ignore the phonetic differences of the dialects and worked in the phonological deep structure of the language. In the Classical Age, with the emergence of a written prose culture, people started to be more aware about the dialectal peculiarities of the surface (pronunciation and orthography), and the Koineisation took another direction, as it is evident from the fact that Ionic and Attic prose was written by men speaking other dialects.

The Hellenistic Age led to an intensification of the Koineisation. Greeks coming from different regions of the Greek world were integrated into new societies together with non-Greeks. An important example is the city of Alexandria. Let us therefore move our focus to the capital of Ptolemaic Egypt. The life of the city is nowhere put so vividly into scene as in Theocritus, writing at the court of Ptolemy II Philadelphus ca. 275 BCE. The most interesting piece in our context is the *Fifteenth Idyll*, where a linguistic and ethnic consciousness is formulated dissociating itself from the Doric ethnicity of Syracuse on the one hand and from the Egyptian ethnicity on the other.

---

11 Thomason 2001, 157-95; Mufwene 2008 downplays the difference between creoles and "natural languages".

12 Cf., for the Hellenistic and Roman periods, Bubeník 1989; 1993.

13 Hinge 2006; cf. also Hinge 2009.

The main characters of Theocritus' *Fifteenth Idyll* are the ordinary housewives Praxinoa and Gorgo, who decide to go up to the palace of Ptolemy to see a festival of Adonis. As soon as they step out on the street, they meet the mob of Alexandria. The street is one chaos, and as they approach the palace, the situation gets even worse. They have to fight themselves through to the gate. People are jostling and trampling on each other's feet. Finally they succeed in entering the palace and gaze at the extraordinary tapestries. All the way the two women have been chatting, and at last a man interrupts them and asks them to shut up; he is fed up with their broad accent (v. 88). He uses the uncommon verb πλατειάσδοισαι, i.e. "broadening." In his work *On the genres*, Hermogenes comments that Theocritus refers to the Doric habit of pronouncing an alpha all the time; the same interpretation is given in the scholia as well.[14] There can be no doubt that the retention of the long ᾱ, where Attic-Ionic and Koine had a long η, was considered one of the most remarkable linguistic features in the speech of a Dorian.

Commenting on this very passage, Jonathan Hall[15] objects that the preservation of the long ᾱ was by no way restricted to Doric, which is certainly true since all dialects outside the Attic-Ionic branch shared this archaism. He concludes that the Greeks were not able to distinguish the single dialects sufficiently because they could not survey the complicated web of isoglosses which made up the Greek dialectological landscape; they simply described a dialect as Doric because it belonged to a city whose population was Doric according to a traditional mythological reconstruction and not on the basis of a linguistic analysis of the dialect in question. His criticism is, however, totally unfair. It reminds me of Socrates, who claims that a horse dealer knows nothing about horses just because he cannot define a horse scientifically. Just as one can have a practical approach to horses, there can, in my eyes, be no doubt that an average Greek was able to tell if a person came from, say, Sparta or Boeotia from his accent alone. There was a whole range of diagnostic features that made the identification obvious to a native Greek, even if he was not able to draw a dialectological map of these isoglosses or even verbalise his intuitive judgment. Similarly, every Dane can tell if a person comes from the islands of Bornholm or Funen, even if he is perfectly unaware of concepts like palatalisation or glottal stop.

4. The dialect of Theocritus' idylls

Theocritus' idylls are for the most part written in some kind of Doric themselves, even though it has remained a matter of debate which kind of Doric it is. Since Theocritus originally comes from Syracuse, it has been suggested that the Syracusan dialect was his primary model. However, the Doric idylls present some peculiarities which are not compatible with what we know about the Syracusan dialect, the primary sources

---

14 Hermog., *Id.* 1.6: ὁ γὰρ Θεόκριτος ἀχθόμενόν τινα πεποίηκε δωριζούσαις γυναιξὶ διὰ τὸ πλατύνειν τῷ α τὰ πλεῖστα χρωμέναις τὴν φωνήν; Sch. Theocr. 15.87-88 τὸ γὰρ "πλατυάσδοισαι" τοιοῦτόν ἐστιν, ὅτι πλατυστομοῦσιν οἱ Δωριεῖς τὸ α πλεονάζοντες.

15 Hall 1997, 176.

of which are the fragmentary comedies of Epicharmus and Sophron. Therefore, the Dutch linguist Cornelis Ruijgh has conjectured that Theocritus attempted to imitate the dialect of the common Alexandrian population.[16] It is true that no extant epigraphic or papyrological sources support that Doric was ever spoken in Alexandria. However, since a large part of the population may have come from the neighbouring colony of Cyrene, as we know at least in the prominent case of Callimachus, Ruijgh considered it highly probable that the Cyrenaean Doric dialect was prevalent in Alexandria in the early Ptolemaic era.

Thus, Theocritus has in the feminine of the participle the ending -οισα instead of -ουσα, which is known in the Doric dialects only in Cyrenaean. In Theocritus' Doric idylls, a regular ζ of Koine is regularly replaced by σδ. Ruijgh speculates that this pronunciation was retained in the Cyrenaean dialect. The inscriptions write ζ, but it cannot be ruled out that it was in fact pronounced [zd]. Ruijgh assumes that in the *Fifteenth Idyll*, σδ is written when the speaker uses the Alexandrian Cyrenaean dialect, whereas the text has ζ when the ladies switch back to their Syracusan dialect. Yet, considering the unstable transmission of the Theocritus corpus, it is extremely difficult to draw conclusions about the presence of a specific pronunciation in a specific word; the papyri and the manuscripts are very often at variance. In the oldest papyrus containing examples of this phoneme, P.Oxy. 2064, from the second century CE, ζ is written in nine instances, and we find no examples of σδ. The papyrus may have been anomalous, but the Theocritean corpus shows a tendency towards an increasingly Doric surface in the *paradosis*.

Both features are known from the transmitted fragments of the Archaic poet Alcman as well.[17] Ruijgh explains this agreement with reference to the theory of Ernst Risch[18] according to which the Alexandrian scholars have altered the text of Alcman to fit the model of the neighbouring Cyrenaean dialect, which was in their eyes the ideal form of Doric. However, this assumption is not only improbable *a priori* since the Alexandrian philologists would definitely have distinguished Old Laconian and contemporary Cyrenaean. It is also invalidated by the fact that the participle in -οισα is common not only in Alcman, but in practically all lyric poetry of the Archaic and Classical Ages. The manuscripts and papyri of Pindar usually have -οισα, and it is also relatively frequent in Archaic and Classical inscriptions, which were certainly free from Alexandrine alterations.[19] Since the puzzling digraph σδ is not attested in any epigraphic sources before the Roman Age, its presence in Alcman, Sappho, Alcaeus and Theocritus must be explained by a convention of the Alexandrian philologists. I am convinced that it is not what it looks like, i.e. a testimony for the hypothetical pronunciation [zd], but I shall not lay forth my arguments here.

---

16 Ruijgh 1984.
17 Hinge 2006, 43-6, 91-9.
18 Risch 1954.
19 *CEG* 352 ε]ὐμένοισα (Corinth, seventh cent. BCE), *CEG* 114]οισα (Boeotia, 479 BCE?); Page 1962, nos. 938(e) Μοῖσα (*c.* 480 BCE), 938(c) ἄγοισα (*c.* 450 BCE), Wachter 2001, nos. COR 36 Μοῖσαι (Corinth, sixth cent. BC), COR 96 Πνατομέδοισα (Corinth, sixth cent. BCE).

The vocalism of Theocritus' Doric idylls is particularly complicated: As a rule one can say that the secondary long *ē* (originating from compensatory lengthening or contraction) is written ει in Theocritus as it is in Attic-Ionic and Koine, whereas the secondary long *ō*, which Attic-Ionic and Koine represents with ου, normally appears as ω in Theocritus. The Syracusan dialect has ει and ου, whereas the Cyrenaean dialect has η and ω. In other words, Theocritus' dialect cannot be reconciled with either Syracusan or Cyrenaean without further ado. Ruijgh assumes a partial influence from Koine, which is rather unsatisfying. Another Dutch scholar, Jelle Abbenes, has suggested that Theocritus' choice of vocalism is influenced by the text of Alcman.[20] His examples from the Alcman corpus are, however, incomplete, and his conclusions therefore inaccurate.[21]

Teresa Molinos Tejada, who has written a thorough dissertation on the language of Theocritus, assumes that the *Fifteenth Idyll* was originally composed in Syracusan.[22] She bases her conclusion on the fact that the cases of irregular ου accumulate exactly in this idyll. The word "acumulación" is, I must say, an exaggeration. The primary sources of the secondary long *ō* are found in the endings of the genitive singular and the accusative plural of the 2nd declension. The most complete papyrus fragment of the *Fifteenth Idyll*, the Antinoë Papyrus from ca. 500 CE, has twenty examples of the genitive singular and three examples of the accusative plural; respectively three and one of these are written with ου:

	-ω	-ου	-ως	-ους
PHamb. 201 (1st cent. CE)	1	1	1	-
POxy. 1618 (5th cent. CE)	-	-	1	-
PParVind. (5th cent. CE)	3	-	-	-
PAnt. (ca. 500 CE)	17	3	2	1

In other words, the idea that certain poems or parts of poems imitate the habits of particular Doric dialects cannot be supported by the evidence. The *Fifteenth Idyll* is written neither in Syracusan nor in some hypothetical Ptolemaic Cyrenaean, but in an artificial colloquial Doric which combines linguistic features from different traditions. It may of course seem ironic that the man, who criticises the chatting Syracusan women, speaks the same Doric dialect as they do: He uses the "flat" Doric ᾱ (δύστανοι, ἀνάνυτοι) and the feminine of the participle in -οισα (κωτίλλοισαι, πλατειάσδοισαι). On the other hand, the dialect serves not as a parody of the persons, but lends a certain ethos to the scene as such. The linguistic and metric form marks the text as a hybrid of mime, lyric and epos.[23]

---

20 Abbenes 1996.

21 Abbenes claims that Alcman has no examples of η before original *rw*; there are however, two possible cases: 3 fr. 11 πήρα[(= πέρας, πεῖραρ) and 7 fr. 1.14 ἀπήρ[ι]τον (= ἀπείριτος). Cf. Hinge 2006, 25-30.

22 Molinos Tejada 1990, 73, 377-8.

23 Hunter 1996. He supposes that Theocritus does in fact imitate Alcman in the *Eighteenth Idyll*, but

5. Linguistic prejudices in Ptolemaic and Roman Egypt

Even if we cannot use the *Fifteenth Idyll* as a testimony to the spoken language of the streets of Ptolemaic Alexandria, it is an important document of the *attitudes* towards language. The city is indeed pictured as a cultural melting-pot. The streets are crowded to the bursting point with both native Egyptians and Greeks from diverse parts of the world. In her book on the so-called "urban" mimes of Theocritus, Joan Burton argues that the *Second, Fourteenth* and *Fifteenth Idylls* describe the new cosmopolitan identity of Alexandria and at the same time contribute to the construction of that identity.[24]

In the *Fifteenth Idyll*, the journey of the two Syracusan ladies from their homes through the crowded streets to the royal palace symbolises the integration of the citizens into a new urban identity under the auspices of Ptolemy. The climax of the poem, and the goal of their journey, is a religious festival sponsored by Queen Arsinoë. It is tempting to analyse the development of the poem in terms of a rite of passage:

1) Rite of separation: the domestic scene (vv. 1-43).
2) Rite of liminality: the crowded streets, the urban jungle (vv. 44-77)
3) Rite of aggregation: the entrance into the palace and Queen Arsinoë's Adonis chorus (vv. 78-149).

Through this rite of passage, the women change their identity, from Sicilian immigrants to Alexandrine citizens, from bumpkins to cosmopolites. As soon as they enter the palace, a stranger reproaches them with their broad Doric accent. In other words, the new identity as an Alexandrian cosmopolitan required the abandonment of the old epichoric dialects and the adoption of Koine since in the multiethnic milieu of Alexandria, the old local affinities have lost their meaning. Praxinoa argues that they are Syracusan women and therefore Corinthians. Consequently, they speak Peloponnesian, and she adds, "*Dorians are in my opinion allowed to speak Doric*" (vv. 92-93 Πελοποννασιστὶ λαλεῦμες, Δωρίσδειν δ᾿ ἔξεστι, δοκῶ, τοῖς Δωριέεσσι). She is not ready to give up the old linguistic discourse just like that. The anachronism of Praxinoa's Doric identity is, however, emphasised by her invocation of the mythical figure Bellerophon (vv. 91-92 ὡς εἰδῆς καὶ τοῦτο, Κορίνθιαι εἰμὲς ἄνωθεν, ὡς καὶ ὁ Βελλεροφῶν). Furthermore, Praxinoa is pictured, though with great empathy, as a ridiculous narrow-minded housewife. She is unreasonable to her slave girl Eunoa and negligent of her infant boy Zopyrion. Her perseverance in the Doric dialect is yet another example of her stubbornness.

In modern western societies, underclass and middleclass women generally speak a variant which is closer to the standard than the variant spoken by their male peers, whereas Praxinoa and Gorgo allegedly spoke a more regional variant.[25] The difference

---

it is a generic *mimesis* (pp. 153-5).

24 Burton 1995.

25 Willi 2003, 157-97, surveys the concept of "female speech" in Classical Athens. For a critical discussion of language and gender see Eckert & McConnell-Ginet 2003, 266-304.

may be explained by different gender roles in modern times and in antiquity: When modern working class women speak a middleclass dialect, it is an indication of their higher social and linguistic ambitions. In Ptolemaic Alexandria, women were apparently less ambitious, or that is at least the impression that Theocritus wants to give us.

Praxinoa is also a racist. When on the street, she cries out (vv. 44-50, transl. Gow 1950):

> Heavens, what a crowd! How and when are we to get through this plague? They're like ants – there's no numbering or counting them. You've done us many a good turn, Ptolemy, since your father was in heaven. Nowadays no ruffian slips up to you in the street Egyptian-fashion and does you a mischief – the trick those packets of rascality used to play, one as bad as another with their nasty tricks, a cursed lot.

Andrew Gow elucidates in his commentary, with a somewhat racist malice, "*the Egyptians had by long tradition a bad reputation in such matters.*"[26] Praxinoa's unjust prejudice may in fact have been shared by many Greeks in Alexandria. As pointed out earlier in this article, Greek ethnicity was after all to a great extent formed in direct opposition to the non-Greeks in the colonies.

The question is, however, how one qualified to be a Greek. Fluency in Greek was without doubt a prerequisite. Not being able to speak Greek was equivalent to being a barbarian. Herodotus states that the Egyptians made a similar distinction; they labelled all that did not speak their language as "barbarians" (2.158.5 βαρβάρους δὲ πάντας οἱ Αἰγύπτιοι καλέουσι τοὺς μὴ σφίσι ὁμογλώσσους). On the other hand, it need not be an unchangeable status. We have already seen that Herodotus derived the Athenians from the Pelasgians, who spoke a non-Greek language; so, a barbarian might become a Hellene under certain circumstances. Dorothy Thompson has demonstrated that a targeted language policy was exacted in Ptolemaic and Roman Egypt.[27] Thus, not only were Greeks and Persians excepted from the obol tax, but teachers of Greek were also exempted for the heavier salt tax. She concludes that in Egypt those were Hellenes who had learnt Greek language at the gymnasium; from these Hellenes the corpse of bureaucrats and officers was recruited. This conclusion is of course extremely attractive, not only because it would support the importance of language in Greek ethnicity, but also because it would exonerate Ptolemaic Egypt of the charge of being an apartheid society. The assumption is, however, anything but certain. Herbert Youtie has argued that literacy was not demanded of a person holding a higher administrative post.[28] On the other hand, fluency in Greek is not the same as being able to read and write it fluently. At any rate, the considerable amount of documents in Greek speaks for itself. Even though the majority of the population in Upper Egypt remained Egyptian-speaking,

---

26 Gow 1950.
27 Thompson 1992; 1994.
28 Youtie 1971.

the Greek language gained more and more importance throughout antiquity, whereas Demotic suffered a gradual loss of domain.

A widespread bilingualism would show in two ways: Egyptian interference in Greek and Greek interference in Egyptian. The Greek interference in Egyptian is minimal in the Demotic documents, but in the Coptic language it is rather impressive. Not only is the alphabet Greek (with some additions), but there is also a considerable amount of Greek loan words. That these loans are not learned, but parts of the colloquial language can be demonstrated by two examples: 1) Greek θάλασσα was borrowed into Coptic as *thalassa*, but subsequently, the aspirate was conceived as the definite article, *t* + an initial *h*; accordingly, the indefinite form is written *halassa*.[29] Such false word divisions are commonplace in the history of language, but it is at the same time a clear proof of the fact that the Greek loanwords did not belong to the learned and literate layer of the language. *thalassa* must have become an integrated part of the spoken language before it was analysed as *halassa*. 2) It is quite astonishing that Coptic has borrowed a large amount of common Greek conjunctions and particles such as *alla, gar, de, kan, oute, hina, hos* and many more. What is more, in the Coptic translations of the New Testament, these conjunctions are used not only where they are found in the Greek original. They are also used as translations of other Greek conjunctions. *alla* translates not only ἀλλά, but also δέ and καί; *gar* corresponds not only to γάρ, but occasionally also to ὅτι, etc. In other words, the Greek particles were not only leftovers from the translation, but part of the Coptic language as well.

The Egyptian interference in Greek is harder to detect. The documentary papyri of Egypt show several orthographical aberrancies from the norm of Koine. Frequently the voiceless stops π, τ, κ are written instead of the voiced stops β, δ, γ and *vice versa*. Francis Gignac attributes this fluctuation to a Coptic substratum.[30] In Coptic the distinction between voiced and voiceless stops is phonologically irrelevant (like in modern Danish, where the opposition *p, t, k ~ b, d, g* is a matter of aspiration, not voice). On the other hand, as Sven-Tage Teodorsson points out, most of the orthographic aberrancies are in accordance with the general development of the Greek language; the insecurity in the representation of the voiced and voiceless stops may just as well be a consequence of the reorganisation of the Greek phonological system, according to which the voiced stops were developing into fricatives, i.e. [β], [ð], [γ].[31] The substratum theory was introduced in the 19th century by the Italian scholar Graziadio Isaia Ascoli[32], who attributed the particularities of the different Romance dialects to the influence of pre-Latin, primarily Celtic, languages. Accordingly, the French [y] for Latin *ū* was allegedly caused by a pronunciation habit of the ancient Gauls.[33] Even though it is incontestable that one

---

29 Rahlfs 1900.

30 Gignac 1970.

31 Teodorsson 1977; Bubeník 1989, 221-5, insists on "bilingual interference from the Coptic substrate".

32 Ascoli 1881.

33 Ascoli argues that [y] for Latin *ū* occurs in French, Occitan and North Italian, i.e. in the areas inhabited by Celts in Antiquity. However, there is no proof that the kind of Celtic spoken in Gaul

can never learn to speak a foreign language without an accent, it is questionable if such lack of competence would be hereditary as a matter of course. We have still not left the matter of the present article, the interdependence of language and race: The substratum theory assumes, overtly or tacitly, that language is a consequence of race; for some reason, the Celtic or the Egyptian "race" cannot pronounce a close back vowel or a voiced stop properly, and this defect remains even after they have become fluent in their new languages.

On the other hand, one shall not disregard the importance of language as a marker of identity. When speaking a second language, one of course makes errors; the inaccuracies of my own English pronunciation are not a deliberate choice, but an inescapable condition. However, to become standard in a language community, such deviations must have become markers of a desirable identity.[34] There can be no doubt that the persons that wrote the Greek papyri aimed at a correct Koine. As a matter of fact, the spelling errors are an indication of a high competence in Greek rather than the opposite: They demonstrate that the writers have not learnt fixed formulas by heart, but mastered the language orally; they have not learnt Greek for writing purposes only, but must have practiced it in their everyday life. I therefore tend to agree with Teodorsson, who attributes the orthographical deviations to an inner-Greek development, originating in Classical Attic; the Egyptians that identified with the Greek Koine took over the substantial speech habits of the ethnic Greeks as well.

6. Conclusion

Language and race are both cultural constructions. They are expressions of man's attempt to organise the world around him in a meaningful way. Thus, if we establish that a Laconian and an Argive speak Doric, it is equivalent to saying that they have orientated themselves in the same direction through the history of the dialects. They have shared an identity at least periodically. When the local dialects are replaced by Koine, it is not just a practical way of bridging a language barrier, but the symptom of a new identity, and not only a symptom, but also a most powerful contribution to that identity. In the Classical Age, inner-Greek ethnic affiliation was formulated mythologically in terms of genealogy and expressed linguistically through different manners of speech, regional dialects. In the Hellenistic Age, Greek identity was first of all a matter of *paideia*, to which the Museum and the Gymnasium of Alexandria were invaluable contributions. The timeless and superregional Koine was the natural vehicle of this common Hellenic

---

had the pronunciation habit. On the contrary, Gaulish $\bar{u}$ is rendered with ου in Greek sources, even though Classical Greek did have the vowel $\bar{y}$ (e.g. Λούγδουνον = *Lyon*). Welsh has [i:] for Celtic *$\bar{u}$, presumably by the way of *$\bar{y}$. However, in the Latin words borrowed into Welsh, $\bar{u}$ is usually retained (e.g. *mūrus* > *mwr*); in other words, the substratum influence did not work in the only dialect in which we have positive evidence for $\bar{u}$ = [y:].

34 Mufwene 2008 describes contact changes and creoles with reference to the societal ("ecological") function of the varieties in question.

identity. It is significant that the disappearance of the spoken epichoric dialects coincides with a growing interest in the literature transmitted in those dialects (Alcman, Sappho, Alcaeus) and the construction of a new literary pseudo-colloquial Doric dialect. It is no coincidence that this antiquarian interest in the old dialects is centred exactly in Ptolemaic Alexandria, where the cosmopolitan milieu deprived the classical linguistic identities of their meaning. Theocritus' *Fifteenth Idyll* bears testimony to that development both in its linguistic form and its discourse.

References

Abbenes, J.G.J. 1996 "The Doric of Theocritus: a literary language" in: A. Harder, R.F. Regtuit & G.C. Wakker (eds.) *Theocritus* Groningen: Egbert Forsten, 1-17.

Ascoli, G.I. 1881 "Una lettera glottologica" *Rivista di filologia classica* 10, 1-79 (German excerpt in R. Kontzi (ed.) *Substrate und Superstrate in den romanischen Sprachen* (Wege der Forschung 165) Darmstadt: Wissenschaftliche Buchgesellschaft 1982, 29-54).

Brixhe, C. 1999 "Un "nouveau" champ de la dialectologie grecque: le macédonien" in: A.C. Cassio (ed.) *Katà diálekton* Napoli: Istituto Universitario Orientale di Napoli, 41-71.

Bubeník, V. 1989 *Hellenistic and Roman Greece as a Sociolinguistic Area* Amsterdam-Philadelphia: John Benjamins.

Bubeník, V. 1993 "Dialect contact and koineization: the case of Hellenistic Greek" *International Journal of the Sociology of Language* 99, 9-23.

Burton, J.B. 1995 *Theocritus' Urban Mimes: mobility, gender, and patronage* Berkeley London: University of California Press.

Cavalli-Sforza, L.L. 2000 *Genes, Peoples and Languages* New York: North Point Press.

Day, J.V. 2001 *Indo-European Origins: The Anthropological Evidence* Washington, DC: The Institute for the Study of Man.

Eckert, P & McConnell-Ginett, S. 2003 *Language and Gender* Cambridge: Cambridge University Press.

Finkelberg, M. 2005 *Greeks and Pre-Greeks* Cambridge: Cambridge University Press.

Frösén, J. 1974 *Prolegomena to a study of the Greek language in the first centuries A.D.* Helsinki.

Gignac, F.T. 1970 "The pronunciation of Greek stops in the papyri" *Transactions and Proceedings of the American Philological Association* 101, 185-202.

Gow, A.S.F. 1950 *Theocritus* Cambridge: Cambridge University Press.

Hall, J.M. 1997 *Ethnic Identity in Greek Antiquity* Cambridge: Cambridge University Press.

Hall, J.M. 2002 *Hellenicity. Between Ethnicity and Culture* Chicago / London: The University of Chicago Press.

Hinge, G. 2005 "Herodot zur skythischen Sprache" *Glotta* 81, 86-115.

Hinge, G. 2006 *Die Sprache Alkmans: Textgeschichte und Sprachgeschichte* (Serta Graeca 24) Wiesbaden: Dr. Ludwig Reichert Verlag.

Hinge, G. 2009 "Cultic Persona and the Transmission of the Partheneions" in: J. Jensen, G. Hinge, P. Schultz & B. Wickkiser, *Aspects of Ancient Greek Cult* (Aarhus Studies in Mediterranean Antiquity 8) Aarhus: Aarhus University Press, 213-34.

Hunter, R.L. 1996 *Theocritus and the Archaeology of Greek Poetry* Cambridge: Cambridge University Press.

Kapetanopoulos, E. 1999 "Alexander's *patrius sermo* in the Philotas affair" *The ancient world* 30, 117-28.

Molinos Tejada, T. 1990 *Los dorismos del Corpus bucolicorum* Amsterdam: Adolf M. Hakkert.

Mufwene, S.S. 2008 *Language Evolution: Contact, Competition and Change* London-New York: Continuum.

O'Neil, J.L. 2006 "Doric forms in Macedonian inscriptions" *Glotta* 82, 192-209.

Page, D.L. 1962 *Poetae melici Graeci* Oxford: The Clarendon Press.

Panayotou, A. 2007 "The position of the Macedonian dialect" in: A.-F. Christidis (ed.): *A History of Ancient Greek: From the Beginnings to Late Antiquity* Cambridge: Cambridge University Press, 433-44.

Rahlfs, A. 1900 "θαλασσα im Koptischen" *Zeitschrift für ägyptische Sprache und Altertumskunde* 38, 152-3.

Risch, E. 1954 "Die Sprache Alkmans" *Museum Helveticum* 11, 20-37.

Ruijgh, C.J. 1984 "Le dorien de Théocrite: dialecte cyrénien d'Alexandrie et d'Égypte" *Mnemosyne* 37, 56-88.

Teodorsson, S.-T. 1977 *The phonology of Ptolemaic Koine* Göteborg: Acta Universitatis Gothoburgensis.

Thomason, S.G. 2001 *Language Contact. An Introduction* Edinburgh: Edinburgh University Press.

Thompson, D.J. 1992 "Language and literacy and early Hellenistic Egypt" in: P. Bilde, T. Engberg-Pedersen, L. Hannestad & J. Zahle (eds.) *Ethnicity in Hellenistic Egypt* Aarhus: Aarhus university Press, 39-52.

Thompson, D.J. 1994 "Literacy and power in Ptolemaic Egypt" in: A.K. Bowman & G. Woolf (eds.), *Literacy and Power in the Ancient World* Cambridge: Cambridge University Press, 67-83.

Wachter, R. 2001 *Non-Attic Greek Vase Inscriptions* Oxford: Oxford University Press.

Willi, A. 2003 *The Languages of Aristophanes* Oxford: Oxford University Press

Youtie, H.C. 1971 "Ἀγράμματος: an aspect of Greek society in Egypt" *Harvard Studies in Classical Philology* 75, 161-76.

CHAPTER 4

Homeric Scholarship in Alexandria

Minna Skafte Jensen

1. The Library

The present paper has a twofold aim: first to describe the great Alexandrian Museum and the research conducted there, especially the Homeric studies (the object of lively discussion in recent years), and next to discuss its role in the multicultural project that is the common theme of this volume.

The Library of Alexandria was established by Ptolemy Soter at the beginning of the third century BCE and soon became justly famous.[1] It was given abundant funding and seems to have had as its ambition to collect the entire written literature of the Greeks. Anecdotes tell how all ships that called at the harbour of Alexandria were searched for books, and how the Athenian state exemplar of the three great tragedians ended up in the Library.[2] Estimates of its size vary from 200,000 volumes to 700,000.[3] The variation may be explained as representing different phases of the Library's history, or perhaps rather as indicating that its precise size remained unknown, but that it was considered to be huge.

The Athenian scholar Demetrius of Phalerum was responsible for its initial arrangement. He was a pupil of Aristotle's, and among various literary activities he is said to have had the Aesopic fables recorded in writing. He was also an active statesman who had governed the Athenian state for the Macedonians in 317-7 BCE. In Egypt he seems to have taken Aristotle's library at the Lyceum as his model when designing the new book collection, and also to have planned to outdo it. Libraries were still at this time a fairly recent phenomenon in the Greek world, Aristotle's being the first Greek library to deserve the name, in the sense of including more than what its owner would conveniently need for his own entertainment and study. But the world had, of course, seen great libraries before, such as that belonging to the Assyrian king Assurbanipal

---

[1]   Pfeiffer 1968, 87-233, 252-79 is the basic modern discussion of Alexandrian scholarship. For more readable descriptions see Reynolds & Wilson 1991, 5-16, and Pöhlmann 2003, 26-40.

[2]   Gal. 17.1.606-7.

[3]   200,000 according to Aristeas *Ad Philocratem epistula* (*c.* 150 BCE according to Honigman 2003, 11). Seneca, *Tranq.* 9.5, says, referring to Livy, that it contained 400,000 volumes at the time of Caesar's fire. Tzetzes 1975, 32, says 490,000 volumes + 42,000 in the Serapeum. Gellius 7.17.3 and Ammianus Marcellinus 22.16.13 say 700,000 before the fire.

four centuries earlier. In this as in so many other respects Greek culture was provincial as compared to that of the great Mesopotamian centres.

Plato's Academy and Aristotle's Lyceum had been sited at a dignified distance outside Athens. The Ptolemies, however, placed their Museum conspicuously in the middle of the city, immediately adjacent to the palace.[4]

They invested not only in books, but also in brains. The best Greek scholars in both the humanities and the sciences – to use modern terminology – were invited to the Museum, where they had free board and lodging and access to the books, and during the Hellenistic period this "centre for advanced study" achieved brilliant results in the full spectrum of research fields known to the ancient world. Euclid established his system of geometry, which became the model of scientific and scholarly method right up to early modern times, Eratosthenes developed ways in which to measure the circumference of the globe, and Heron invented the steam-engine, to mention only a few of the most remarkable achievements.

For literary studies, the work carried out by the poet Callimachus (*c.* 305-240 BCE) was of paramount importance. His *Pinakes* (= tablets) in 120 volumes was compiled as a catalogue of the Library, but were at the same time a registration and first systematisation of Greek literature, and as such it is best understood as part of the general peripatetic attempt at registering the phenomena of the world.[5] Through his and his colleagues' work, a system of literary genres was established, and a canon of the best authors defined. The Alexandrians performed the first, fundamental studies of Homer, Hesiod, Pindar and other early poets as well as of Athenian drama, and they worked at orthographic and prosodic problems. For instance, they uncovered the system of response in choral songs and arranged the texts accordingly. Also prose writers such as Herodotus and Thucydides, Plato and Demosthenes were subjected to their editorial scrutiny. The first century and a half constituted not only the founding period but also the heyday of the Library. A first crisis occurred when in 145 BCE Ptolemy VIII came into power by having his predecessor killed, and expelled the leading philologists for having supported Ptolemy VII. Another catastrophe occurred with a fire in 48 BCE in connection with Caesar's Alexandrian war. According to some ancient sources, the Library was destroyed.[6] Modern scholars have considered this exaggerated and have pointed to the exact wording in Dio Cassius, suggesting that only a magazine was burned.[7] However, the independent information that Mark Antony presented Cleopatra with 200,000 books from the Pergamene library and that Augustus dedicated a new Alexandrian library to Caesar in 12 BCE corroborates the tradition that the Library

---

4   Ancient sources do not distinguish clearly between "museum" and "library". I use "museum" for the institution, "library" for the book collection.

5   For the *Pinakes* see Pfeiffer 1968, 126-34. However, Pfeiffer argues against the opinion that the library was peripatetically inspired (Pfeiffer 1968, 95). For the opposite view see Fraser 1972, I, 313-16.

6   Sen. *Tranq.* 9.5; Gell. 7.17.3; Amm. Marc. 22.16.13.

7   Dio Cass. 42.38, cf. Fraser 1972, 334-5, and Pöhlmann 2003, 39.

actually suffered severely in the fire.[8] Whatever the case, Alexandria continued to be an important centre of intellectual activity during the following centuries, even though Rome gradually took the lead. For instance, the learned Didymus was still able to perform Homeric studies in Alexandria during the second half of the first century BCE.

2. The sources

Research into the Homeric poems constitutes the most celebrated and also best-known part of the Alexandrian philologists' literary studies. Most modern scholars agree that the *Iliad* and the *Odyssey* as we know them today found their final form at the Museum,[9] and the names of the leading Homeric scholars are well known: Zenodotus of Ephesus (b. *c.* 325), Aristophanes of Byzantium (*c.* 257-180) and Aristarchus of Samothrace (*c.* 217-145). But exactly what their critical activities were and what part each of them had in creating the remarkably uniform text transmitted in medieval manuscripts (usually called the Vulgate) is a matter of dispute. It might even be claimed that besides the well-known Homeric Question of how the two epics were originally composed, there exists an Alexandrian Homeric Question of similar complexity. That this is so is due to the nature of the sources.

The scholars' own works have not survived, but are known to us through quotations in the so-called *scholia*, commentaries that accompany the epics in some of the medieval manuscripts. The richest source is *Venetus Marcianus Graecus 454* (tenth century CE), a huge copy of the *Iliad* written in a careful bookhand, surrounded by a compact frame of comments to form an elegant overall design (see Fig. 1). Other manuscripts, such as the similar, but less sumptuous *Codex Townleyanus* of the *Iliad* (dated 1059), share some of their material with *Venetus 454*, but also supply much of their own. The scholia to the *Odyssey* are much briefer and their documentation later; the oldest manuscripts containing comments on the *Odyssey* are from the thirteenth century CE. Whereas these compilations are anonymous, we have a full commentary on both epics composed by Bishop Eustathius of Thessalonica (twelfth century CE). The bulk of his comments are of the same kind as the scholia, but he also drew on other sources, some of them lost to us. Furthermore, Byzantine lexica now and then contain fragments of Alexandrian learning. To these medieval sources may be added papyrus fragments of ancient commentaries as well as mentions of Alexandrian scholarship made by other ancient authors, most notably by Athenaeus in his *Deipnosophistae* (second century CE).[10]

The scholia contain material compiled over many centuries, normally without any indication of source, and it is up to modern scholars to distinguish among its different layers. But at the end of each book of the *Iliad*, *Venetus 454* says: "The following works

---

8 Mark Antony: Plut. *Ant.* 58; Augustus: Philo *Legatio ad Gaium* 151. Finkelberg 2006, 240, accepts the stories of the fire and Marc Antony's gift without discussion.
9 Margalit Finkelberg has recently questioned this opinion, see Finkelberg 2006.
10 Ath. 1.22; 4.184b-c; 5.203e. – Matthaios 1999, 7, gives a survey of the sources for Aristarchus' research in grammar.

Iliad 18.580-604 *as represented in the manuscript* Venetus Marcianus Graecus 454 *(tenth century* **Fig. 1**
CE). Size of the original: 39.3 x 27.8 cm.

are used: Aristonicus" *Signs* and Didymus' *About Aristarchus' Revision*, and also something from Herodian's *The Prosody of the Iliad* and from Nicanor's *About Punctuation*." None of these works has survived, but their authors are known individuals. Aristonicus and Didymus were late followers of Aristarchus attached to the Museum towards the end of the first century BCE, whereas Herodian and Nicanor conducted their Greek scholarship in the second century CE. Since Karl Lehrs it has been the general opinion that in Late Antiquity these works were excerpted and transformed into the so-called *Viermännerkommentar*, and that this was in turn the main source of the scholia.[11] Thus, the studies that were begun by Zenodotus and continued by his colleagues passed through many hands during more than a millennium before they found the form in which they meet us in the medieval manuscripts.

It has cost generations of modern scholars huge efforts to sift through all this material and extract from it as much information as possible about the kind of scholarship pursued at the Museum. The discussion has intensified over the last decades, first in connection with the new editions of scholia to the *Iliad* by Erbse and of Eustathius by van der Valk, then with the new editions of the poems themselves, by van Thiel and West.

3. The scholarship

It is at all events clear that the main questions handled in Alexandria were concerned with the interpretation of difficult words and passages and with evaluation of critical problems. Such discussions had begun long before the Museum; they turn up already towards the end of the 5th century BCE, and when the *Iliad* and the *Odyssey* were studied at school, much energy was invested in intralingual translation, in which the archaic poems were paraphrased in standard prose as a way to ensure proper understanding of the text.

a) Textual criticism
The activity for which the Alexandrians are best known is their systematic criticism of the Homeric text. It is in itself interesting that the scholars did not take for granted that the two epics from beginning to end were composed by Homer, but that verses might have been added and passages changed. Such verses were athetised, i.e. marked as being spurious. A puzzling fact is that most of the verses condemned by the Alexandrians are actually transmitted in the medieval manuscripts. We still read Book 10 of the *Iliad*, even though the Alexandrians considered it a Pisistratean addition, and the *Odyssey* does not end at book 23.296, as Aristophanes and Aristarchus wanted it to.[12]

---

11 Lehrs 1832, 1-32.

12 The scholiast says that they considered this to be the *telos* or *peras* of the poem. Some scholars have explained this to mean not the end, but the climax of the poem, e.g. Gallavotti 1969. But the words, especially *peras*, are more naturally understood to mean "end," and considering how much the Homeric scholars in Alexandria were concerned with athetising it is simpler to interpret the

A central topic in modern discussions has been the meaning of the terms *ekdosis* and *diorthōsis* which are used now and again in connection with Alexandrian criticism.[13] *Ekdosis* is of course the same word as Latin *editio*, but in what sense did the scholars edit the text? To us the process of editing is closely linked to the printing press or electronic media, that is to the act of multiplying the text and thus giving the public access to it. But in these earliest occurrences of the word as a technical term, what may we imagine that it means? Nothing is known of book production related to the Museum, but as we shall see, it is perhaps necessary to assume something of the kind in order to explain other facts. Anyway, a solution proposed by Franco Montanari seems to me attractive: that *ekdosis* in this case means that a scholar gave other scholars of the Library access to the exemplar he had been annotating, so that the giving out was internal in the institution, from one scholar to his colleagues.[14] *Diorthōsis* (correction, revision), on the other hand, seems to refer to the activity of marking spurious passages, and thus the two terms become almost synonymous. But *diorthōsis* may also mean the result of the process, an exemplar of the poems, as would appear from a passage in Strabo in which he speaks of the Homeric text that Alexander used to carry with him.[15]

The signs that Aristonicus wrote of must be those still found in the margins of *Venetus 454* and also encountered in some of the ancient papyri. They indicate that there is a discussion of the verse to which it is attached. An *obelos* means that a verse is spurious, a *stigmē* that it is under suspicion of being spurious, an *asteriskos* that the verse has been fetched from somewhere else in Homer, an *antisigma* that the verse is in a wrong place, a *diplē* that there is another kind of comment on the verse in question, and a *diplē periestigmenē* that Aristarchus disagreed with Zenodotus over this verse.[16]

The scholia refer to a small range of different versions of the text, most often to an *Iliad* from Marseille, but also to versions from Sinope, Chios, Argos and elsewhere, as well as to some named after persons, presumably their owners. Sometimes they refer more sweepingly to the "good" ones, the "bad" ones, or the "common" ones. Modern scholars used to imagine that the Alexandrians proceeded as they did themselves, carefully comparing all these manuscripts so as to establish in each case which reading was to be preferred. But today most scholars think instead that they worked on a single more or less carefully chosen manuscript, to which they added their notes, and refer to

---

note as referring to a discussion of genuineness than to one of narrative aesthetics, cf. Pfeiffer 1968, 175-7. Allen 1931, 199-202 presents statistics on how the Alexandrians' readings are represented in the manuscripts.

13 Pfeiffer 1968, 215-18.
14 Montanari 1998, 6-9.
15 Strabo 13.1.26-7: "*diorthōsis tēs Homērou poiēseōs, hē ek tou narthēkos legomenē*," discussed by Sauge 2000, 498-505. Irigoin 1994, 87 suggests that *diorthōsis* and *ekdosis* should be understood as the process, *hypomnēmata* as the result.
16 Schmidt 2002 gives an exceptionally clear and understandable survey of the various kinds of comment the scholia offer.

how Italian humanists set about their editorial work when preparing the first printed editions.[17]

Recently Martin West has argued for the opinion that the first Alexandrian Homerist, Zenodotus, had carried with him an exemplar from his native Ephesus, characterised by more Ionic forms than the Vulgate. West then claims that Zenodotus' *diorthōsis* consisted in marking with *obeloi* in this manuscript the verses that he athetised.[18] The signs we find in *Venetus 454* presumably transmit the system as developed by Aristarchus – like Zenodotus he provided an already existing manuscript with critical marks, but his sophisticated series of signs referred to *hypomnēmata*, comments written in a separate volume. This system must have worked smoothly: already from the sign chosen the reader received a first idea of what kind of note he would find in the commentary. Aristarchus seems to have written two such commentaries, both referring to the same Homeric text.[19] It has usually been thought that the Alexandrians' *diorthōsis* consisted in both comparing readings from various manuscripts and arguing for their own conjectures,[20] and Antonios Rengakos, who has studied Homeric allusions in Alexandrian poetry for information about the text of Homer, maintains that Callimachus and Apollonius Rhodius were familiar with more than one established text.[21] According to West, however, systematic comparison of readings was not introduced before Didymus.[22] This opinion has been vigorously contested by Gregory Nagy, who defends Aristarchus as the first scholar to have made a serious study of manuscripts.[23]

In 1963, B.A. van Groningen pointed to the strange fact that among the manuscripts called after cities no Athenian Homer occurs. This is astonishing considering both the dominant place Athens occupied in early Greek book production in general, and the various internal and external sources that assign to Athens an important role in the history of the two epics. His explanation was that the manuscript the Alexandrians took as their point of departure was the Athenian one, and that when it is not mentioned it is because it is taken for granted.[24] This ingenious hypothesis also makes it understandable why in so many cases the scholars' emendations have not been introduced into the transmitted text: if this were the exemplar they were correcting it must have been considered too authoritative to be easily changed. van Groningen's suggestion has won wide appreciation, and I find it unproblematic to unite it with West's Zenodotus and his Ephesian book. If Zenodotus had already filled one manuscript with his annotations,

---

17 Montanari 1998, 6.
18 West 2002.
19 Montanari 1998, 10-9.
20 E.g. Montanari 1998, 1.
21 Rengakos 1993; 2002.
22 West 2004.
23 Nagy 2004, 87-109.
24 Van Groningen 1963, 36-7. Irigoin 1994, 42, and Pöhlmann 2003, 36-7, also consider the basic text Athenian, but on the basis of other arguments.

Aristophanes or, rather, Aristarchus followed his method, but took another exemplar as his working copy, this time more carefully selected.

As the *Iliad* and the *Odyssey* have come down to us, they are each divided into 24 books designated after the letters of the alphabet. This too used to be ascribed to the regulating work of the Alexandrians,[25] especially concerning the arrangement of the long poems in suitable volumes. But this opinion has not remained undisputed. Already in 1967 Stephanie West pointed to details in the earliest Homeric papyri indicating that the poems were divided into books, and more recently Michael Haslam has argued from his familiarity with literary papyri in general that the Homeric books are awkward from a material point of view, being too varied in length and generally too short for a normal volume. The use of the letters of the alphabet he considers symbolical with reference to how Jesus says of himself that he is the alpha and the omega: each of the two poems contains a whole world.[26] Others, such as Keith Stanley, Bruce Heiden and the present writer, have argued from aesthetic-literary considerations that the division goes back to the original composition of the poems.[27]

Papyri that contain fragments of the *Iliad* or the *Odyssey* are known from a period of 900 years, beginning towards the end of the third century BCE and continuing until the seventh century CE. Thus they almost bridge the gap between antiquity and the oldest medieval manuscripts.

Their number has grown considerably during recent decades, and in his new edition of the *Iliad* West is able to list 704 items, adding that another *c.* 800 exemplars lie unedited in Oxford.[28]

A careful study of the earliest papyrus fragments of the *Iliad* and the *Odyssey* demonstrates that a change took place around 150 BCE. Most of these early papyri are tiny fragments, but large enough to show whether a given passage consists of the same amount of verses as it does in the Vulgate, and it is characteristic of the earliest specimens that they differ from the Vulgate, most often in containing plus-verses. Only from about 150 BCE do the papyri offer the same number of verses as the Vulgate.[29] It has of course been discussed, most recently by Nagy,[30] whether this is a sign that the poems were still being transmitted orally when the Alexandrians started their critical work, but the variations seem far too small and unimportant to be explained in that way.

It is generally thought that when plus-verses seem to disappear around 150 BCE, this must have been a result of Aristarchus' Homeric studies. By what means his *diorthōsis* of the poems reached the general reader, and how it was able to supplant other versions, is unknown. But I agree with those who imagine that the Museum offered some kind of booktrade, for instance in the sense that you could send your scribe and have

---

25 E.g. Pasquali 1934, 217-8; Pfeiffer 1968, 115-6.
26 West 1967, 18-24; Haslam 1997, 58.
27 Stanley 1993; Heiden 1996, 1998, 2000a, 2000b; Jensen 1999.
28 West 1998, LIV.
29 West 1967, 7-8 and 283-7.
30 Nagy 2004, *passim*.

him copy an authorised version.[31] In an important recent paper, however, Margalit Finkelberg has argued that when prestigious texts, such as Homer or the Bible, are standardised, this is invariably the result of the intervention of a central political power. Her hypothesis is that the standardisation was decided and carried out by Ptolemy VIII and should be understood in connection with the above-mentioned expulsion of the scholars.[32] For various reasons I remain unconvinced, but cannot discuss the question in detail here.

Another unsolved problem is how this Alexandrian text spread over the whole Greek-speaking world. Almost all known papyri are from Egypt, whereas the medieval centres of Greek manuscript production were Byzantium and Southern Italy. To judge from Homeric quotations in authors from other parts of the empire, Aristarchus' text had not yet reached them in the times of Galen or Plutarch. But when after a millennium minuscule manuscripts begin to appear, they are a direct continuation of the text known from Egyptian papyri.

b) Interpretation

We should have liked to know what criteria the scholars followed when athetising in order to understand their overall concept of the Homeric poems. But in most cases the fact that a verse or passage was considered spurious is just stated and the reasons not given. Nevertheless some patterns appear:

Verses were athetised if they differ syntactically from what is usually found in Homer or contain words or forms that are later than the main Homeric dialect. It is especially Attic forms that the Alexandrians considered suspect. It appears, then, that they had a more or less precise idea of a linguistic form they considered truly Homeric, and that this was not only viewed as more elevated and poetic than prosaic Greek of their own day, but was competently analysed as an older stage of the language.

The Alexandrians were also alert to passages they regarded as interpolated for political reasons, and here it was again Athens that was under suspicion. Their most famous political criticism concerned the entries of Athens and Salamis in the *Iliadic* Catalogue of Ships (*Iliad* 2.546-58).

Next, they were ready to expel iterated verses. In such cases they tried to decide which occurrence was the original one and athetise the rest. Considering how carefully they tried to understand Homeric usage it may seem surprising that they were not more sensitive to what in a modern reader's eyes is a dominant aspect of Homeric style. On the other hand, in the Greek intellectual circles of Alexandria poets were so intent on being new and refined that presumably also the scholars felt that the repetitiveness of Homer offended their aesthetic feelings and could not be authentic.

They also wanted to mend inconsistencies in the narrative by means of athetising. For instance, when in Iliad 13.658-9 a certain Pylaemenes participates in the lament for his dead son although he has himself been killed earlier in the poem, Venetus A marks

---

31   West 1967, 16; Reynolds & Wilson 1991, 8.
32   Finkelberg 2006.

the verses with *oboloi*, and the scholiast states that they are athetised. He also suggests, however, that there might have been two warriors of the same name.

Finally, the Alexandrian scholars wanted to expurge passages that seemed blasphemous. Already in the second half of the sixth century BCE Xenophanes of Colophon had reacted against the way in which the Homeric gods behave, and Plato had expelled them from his ideal city. In order to cope with this problem some interpreters had developed an allegorical method of reading. Such solutions occur now and then in the scholia, but generally speaking the Alexandrians seem to have been more sober than their immediate predecessors when they preferred to mend the problem of *aprepeia*, indecent behaviour, by means of athetising. After all, they were late followers of Aristotle, and they had as their colleagues poets such as Callimachus and Apollonius Rhodius.

In their literary criticism, the Alexandrians adopted the general principle of interpreting Homer from Homer, *Homēron ex Homērou saphēnizein*.[33] They seem to have accepted the *Iliad* and the *Odyssey* as a fictional universe in its own right, and their overall model for solving problems was to compare with similar passages in the poems. Both in this and in their careful "close reading" of the poems they might be considered ancient forerunners of 20th-century New Criticism.

An interesting example of the early reception of their work is to be found in some tales about the philosopher-poet Timon of Phlius (*c.* 320-230 BCE). When the poet Aratus asked him how he could get hold of a reliable (*asphalēs*) text of Homer, he answered: "Find some of the old copies and not those that are being corrected these days (*ēdē diorthōmena*)."[34] And in one of his poems he described the scholars as follows: "Many bookish cage-birds are being fed in multiethnic Egypt, infinitely fighting in the Muses' wicker cage."[35]

4. The Alexandrian melting-pot

To conclude, I shall consider the Homeric scholars of Alexandria within the overall framework of this book, and I regret to say that the impression we get in the sources does not confirm the picture of the Library as an important participant in the great interaction of cultures and religions. On the contrary, the philologists of the Library appear to have been concerned with Greek literature and nothing else. Of course, this impression may be due to the fact that these commentaries are strictly concerned with explaining a Greek author. We may even speculate that originally transcultural Alexandrian notes may have disappeared from the corpus of scholia over the centuries because later readers were not interested in such themes; but the many preserved titles of the Alexandrian scholars' works do not support such an idea. Their books all seem to have been concerned with Greek topics.

Egypt under Ptolemaic rule had Greek-Macedonian administrators in all important

---

33 Porph. *Quaestiones homericae* 1.56, cf. Pfeiffer 1968, 226-7.
34 Diog. Laert. 9.113.
35 Ath. 1.22.

posts, and Greek as its official language.[36] That Alexandria nevertheless developed a mixed Greek-Egyptian culture is clear from other fields, such as the tombs discussed by Marjorie Susan Venit in the present volume, and it is of course likely that many of its inhabitants knew both Greek and local languages. Since the city had an important harbour, it is also probable that quite a few languages from other parts of the world were spoken in its streets. For bilingualism in Hellenistic Egypt as such one might refer to Manetho's *Aigyptiaka*. This history of Egypt composed in Greek is reported to have been dedicated to Ptolemy II Philadelphus (308-246 BCE). Such a work indicates an eagerness on the part of the conquered to arouse the ruler's interest in local affairs rather than a ruler's respect for local literature. As a social phenomenon Manetho's work has a parallel in Berossus' description of Babylon (*c.* 290 BCE) dedicated to Antiochus I. Also the famous Rosetta Stone (196 BCE) with its bilingual inscription in three different scripts, dedicated by the priests of Memphis to Ptolemy V Epiphanes, bears witness to translation competence in Hellenistic Egypt.

On this background it certainly might have been expected that studies at the Library included translation activity, and that Egyptian and oriental literature was bought for the collection. As a matter of fact, that is how things are presented by the latest and most detailed source for the Library, the Byzantine scholar Johannes Tzetzes (twelfth century CE). He asserts that Ptolemy II Philadelphus collected both all Greek books and also many foreign books, especially those of the Jews, and that he had the foreign books translated into Greek by specialists. Tzetzes then proceeds to describe the *Septuagint*.[37] Sadly, he was separated from his subject by almost one and a half millennia, and it is worth noticing anyway that his only example of this translation activity is the Old Testament. If there had really been a vigorous production of translated books at the Library, would we not have come across these books here and there in Greek literature, directly or indirectly?

The so-called *Letter of Aristeas* (*c.* 150 BCE) which relates in some detail how Demetrius of Phalerum proposed to Ptolemy Philadelphus that the ruler should arrange for the Hebrew Lawbook to be translated into Greek, has been recently subjected to a subtle analysis by Sylvie Honigman. Of special interest in the present context is her demonstration of how the scholarly work at the Library is the background against which the author draws his picture of the process. Both the fact that Demetrius is made the instigator, and also the concern with which it is secured that the original text to be translated is of the highest possible authenticity reflect central aspects of the scholarly activity conducted at the Library. And when Demetrius argues that Ptolemy ought to have these books in an emended form (*diēkribōmena*), the very wording recalls the

---

36 Dunand & Zivie-Coche 2004, 197. Cf. Baines 2004, who shows how the Egyptian elite adapted itself to Hellenistic norms.

37 Tzetzes 1975, 32-3. – When MacLeod 2000, 6 states that the majority of the staff at the Library were translators, his reference is to the *charakitai* (cage-birds) in Timon's poem quoted above; but there is no reason to assume that they were specifically engaged in translating.

discourse of Homeric scholarship.[38] So even though the letter is not a reliable source as to how the Septuagint was created, it does bear witness to a link between the Library and the translation. However, this connection consists first and foremost in a general respect for philological expertise and can hardly be considered evidence that the Library actually had any hand in the translation.

Here I can only underline that non-Greek matters are conspicuously absent from the Homeric scholia. In Erbse's index one looks in vain for names of Egyptian gods, for instance. There is no Ammon, Anubis, Isis or Thoth. The name Osiris, however, is in fact mentioned twice in the scholia. The first occurrence is a note to *Iliad* 9.383 (sch. c), in which the Egyptian city of Thebes is mentioned. Here the commentary mentions that the king who built the walls was called Osiris. The other case is a discussion of the trumpet that is blown in *Iliad* 18.219 (sch. b1). The scholiast first points out that normally there are no trumpets in the epic. The poet knew this instrument, he says, but did not consider it known by the heroes. Then follows a learned list of trumpets in various cultures, among them Egypt, where the inventor of the instrument is called Osiris. That is all. The scholia offer nothing to compare with the classical Greek historian Herodotus (*c.* 484-20 BCE) and his open-mindedness in "translating" between Greek and Egyptian gods.

In modern times, Homeric scholars have been very aware of the close connections between oriental and Greek traditions. In particular, this has been a central theme in Walter Burkert's huge scholarly work, and also Martin West has done much to open classical minds to the fact that archaic Greece was deeply influenced by the dominant Near-Eastern centres.[39] But in the scholia there is nothing to suggest that the Alexandrian scholars were aware of this. There is no mention, for instance, of Gilgamesh, even though his epic was still being read in Mesopotamia in Hellenistic times.

Judging from the material I have presented here, what the Macedonian rulers did was to establish a centre of Greek learning, for which Greek books were bought and Greek scholars invited to study them. Collecting and copying Egyptian literature remained in the hands of priests in the "houses of life" associated with the temples.[40] Even though the country they had conquered was the home of one of the world's oldest and most sophisticated cultures, the Ptolemies seem to have turned their backs on it and invested only in matters Greek. The Greek poets active in Ptolemaic Alexandria such as Callimachus, Apollonius and Posidippus exhibit a similar lack of interest in Egyptian culture.[41] Actually, the Ptolemies look like Greek snobs in their provocatory lack of interest in non-Greek themes. Perhaps they were all the more snobs for being Macedonian and thus under the suspicion of being barbarian. This does not, of course, prevent me from respecting the far-sighted scholarly policies of the first Ptolemies.

Looked at in retrospect, the Ptolemaic rulers of Egypt achieved nothing more im-

---

38 Honigman 2003, 44, quoting Aristeas 31.
39 Cf. e.g. West 1997 and Burkert 1999.
40 Dunand & Zivie-Coche 2004, 233.
41 For the recently found Posidippus volume see Stephens 2004.

portant than the superb intellectual milieu established at the Museum. Whatever their intentions, the results of their generous support of learning are remarkable. To them we owe infinite gratitude for the fact that ancient Greek texts have reached us in such quantity and quality. Scientific and scholarly method was developed to a previously unknown level. Poetry flourished. And just as Alexandrian poets became the stimulating ideal for Roman poets from Ennius onwards, the Ptolemies offered themselves as worthy models for the patronage of the artists practised in Augustan Rome.[42]

References

Allen, T.W. (ed.) 1931 *Homeri Ilias*, vol. 1: *Prolegomena* Oxford: Clarendon Press.

Baines, J. 2004 "Egyptian elite self-presentation in the context of Ptolemaic rule" in: Harris, Ruffini 2004, 33-61.

Burkert, W. 1999 *Da Omero ai Magi: La tradizione orientale nella cultura greca* Venezia: Marsilio. – German translation: *Die Griechen und der Orient. Von Homer bis zu den Magiern* München: C.H. Beck 2003.

Dunand, F. & Zivie-Coche, C. 2004 *Gods and Men in Egypt 3000 BCE to 395 CE* (translated by David Lorton) Ithaca: Cornell University Press.

Erbse, H. (ed.) 1969-88 *Scholia Graeca in Homeri Iliadem (Scholia vetera)* Berlin: Walter de Gruyter.

Eustathius 1971-87 *Eustathii archiepiscopi thessalonicensis Commentarii ad Homeri Iliadem pertinentes* (ed. M. van der Valk) Leiden: Brill.

Finkelberg, M. 2006 "Regional texts and the circulation of books: the case of Homer" *Greek, Roman, and Byzantine Studies* 46, 231-48.

Fraser, P.M. 1972 *Ptolemaic Alexandria* Oxford: Clarendon Press.

Gallavotti, C. 1969 "Tracce della Poetica di Aristotele negli scolii omerici" *Maia* 21, 203-14.

Harris, W.V. & Ruffini, G. (eds.) 2004 *Ancient Alexandria between Egypt and Greece* Leiden: Brill.

Haslam, M.W. 1997 "Homeric papyri and transmission of the text" in: I. Morris & B. Powell *A New Companion to Homer* Leiden-New York-Köln: Brill, 55-100.

Heiden, B. 1996 "The three movements of the *Iliad*" *Greek, Roman and Byzantine Studies* 37, 5-22.

Heiden, B. 1998 "The placement of 'book divisions' in the *Iliad*" *Journal of Hellenic Studies* 118, 68-81.

Heiden, B. 2000a "The placement of "book divisions' in the *Odyssey*" *Classical Philology* 95, 247-259.

Heiden, B. 2000b "Narrative discontinuity and segment marking at *Iliad* 3/4, 7/8, and 10/11, and *Odyssey* 4/5, 17/18, and 23/24" *Classica & Mediaevalia* 51, 5-16.

Honigman, S. 2003 *The Septuagint and Homeric Scholarship in Alexandria: A Study in the Narrative of the Letter of Aristeas* London-New York: Routledge.

Irigoin, J. 1994 "Les éditions de textes" in: Montanari 1994, 39-93.

Jensen, M.S. 1999 "Dividing Homer: When and how were the *Iliad* and the *Odyssey* divided into songs?" *Symbolae Osloenses* 74, 5-35 and 73-91.

Lehrs, K. 1832 *De Aristarchi studiis Homericis* Leipzig: S. Hirzel (third edition).

MacLeod, R. (ed.) 2000 *The Library of Alexandria: Centre of Learning in the Ancient World* London, New York: I.B. Tauris.

Matthaios, S. 1999 *Untersuchungen zur Grammatik Aristarchs: Texte und Interpretation zur Wortartenlehre* Göttingen: Vandenhoeck & Ruprecht.

Montanari, F. (ed.) 1994 *La philologie grecque à l'époque hellénistique et romaine* Genève: Fondation Hardt.

Montanari, F. 1998 "Zenodotus, Aristarchus and the *ekdosis* of Homer" in: G.W. Most *Editing Texts: Texte edieren* Göttingen: Vandenhoeck & Ruprecht, 1-21.

Montanari, F. (ed.) 2002 *Omero tremila anni dopo: Atti del congresso di Genova, 6-8 Iuglio 2000* Roma: Edizioni di Storia e Letteratura.

Morris, I. & Powell, B. 1997 *A New Companion to Homer* Leiden-New York-Köln: Brill.

---

42 I am grateful to John D. Kendal for revising my English.

Most, G.W. (ed.) 1998 *Editing Texts: Texte edieren* Göttingen: Vandenhoeck & Ruprecht.

Nagy, G. 2004 *Homer's Text and Language* Champaign, IL: University of Illinois.

Pasquali, G. 1934 *Storia della tradizione e critica del testo* Firenze: Felice le Monnier.

Pfeiffer, R. 1968 *History of Classical Scholarship from the Beginnings to the End of the Hellenistic Age* Oxford: Clarendon Press.

Pöhlmann, E. 2003 *Einführung in die Überlieferungsgeschichte und die Textkritik der antiken Literatur* 1 Darmstadt: Wissenschaftliche Buchgesellschaft (second edition).

Rengakos, A. 1993 *Der Homertext und die hellenistischen Dichter* Stuttgart: Steiner

Rengakos, A. 2002: "The Hellenistic poets as Homeric critics" in: Montanari 2002, 143-57.

Reynolds, L.D. & Wilson, N.G. 1991 *Scribes and Scholars: A Guide to the Transmission of Greek and Latin Literature* Oxford: Oxford University (third edition).

Sauge, A. 2000 *"L'Iliade", poème athénien de l'époque de Solon* Bern-Berlin-Bruxelles-Frankfurt a.M.-New York-Wien: Peter Lang.

Schmidt, M. 2002 "The Homer of the Scholia: what is explained to the reader?" in: Montanari 2002, 159-83.

Tzetzes, I. 1975 "Prolegomena de Comoedia" in: W.J.W. Koster 1975 *Scholia in Aristophanem* (vol. 1A) Groningen: Bouma, 22-38 (text 11).

Stanley, K. 1993 *The Shield of Homer: Narrative Structure in the Iliad* Princeton, NJ: Princeton University Press.

Stephens, S. 2004 "Posidippus' poetry book: Where Macedon meets Egypt" in: Harris, Ruffini 2004, 63-86.

van Groningen, B.A. 1963 *Traité d'histoire et de critique des textes grecs* Amsterdam: N.V. Noordhollandsche Uitgevers Maatschappij.

van Thiel, Helmut (ed.) 1991 *Homeri Odyssea* Hildesheim-Zürich-New York: Olms.

van Thiel, Helmut (ed.) 1996 *Homeri Ilias* Hildesheim_Zürich-New York: Olms.

West, M.L. 1997 *The East Face of Helicon: West Asiatic Elements in Greek Poetry and Myth* Oxford: Clarendon Press.

West, M.L. (ed.) 1998-2000 *Homeri Ilias* Stuttgart-München, Leipzig: Teubner & Saur.

West, M.L. 2001 *Studies in the Text and Transmission of the Iliad* München-Leipzig: Saur.

West, M.L. 2002 "Zenodotus' text" in: Montanari 2002, 137-42. – Revised as chap. 2 in West 2001.

West, M.L. 2004 "Reply to Rengakos (BMCR 2002.11.15)" *Bryn Mawr Classical Review* 2004.04.17.

West, S. (ed.) 1967 *The Ptolemaic Papyri of Homer* Köln-Opladen: Westdeutscher Verlag.

PART II

ROME, JUDAISM
AND CHRISTIANITY

CHAPTER 5

Philo as a Polemist and a Political Apologist
An Investigation of his Two Historical Treatises *Against Flaccus* and *The Embassy to Gaius*[1]

Per Bilde

1. Introduction

Philo was a prominent Jewish citizen and writer in Alexandria in the first half of the first century CE.[2] We do not know the years of his birth and death, but as Philo in *The Embassy to Gaius* (*De Legatione ad Gaium*, henceforth *Leg.*) refers to his advanced age (*Leg.* 182), these years are often estimated to *c.* 20 BCE – *c.* 45 CE (cf. references in footnote 2), because this treatise may almost certainly be dated to 41-42 CE (cf. section 5 below).

Philo is usually not known as a politician, a polemist or a political apologist, but first of all as the author of a considerable number of exegetic, theological and philosophical writings.[3] However, it is indicated by the two texts to be investigated here as well as by

---

1   This essay is based on a lecture in Danish held on 29 October 1993 at a seminar on Philo organised by the Danish Research Council's project on *Hellenism* (1989-1995). A revised version was presented on 22 February 2005 at a seminar on Jewish apologetics at Klitgaarden in Skagen (Denmark) organised by the Faculty of Theology (University of Aarhus)'s research project on *Jews, Christians and Pagans in Antiquity – Critique and Apologetics*. This Danish version has been published as Bilde 2007.

2   Cf. Goodenough 1940; Elmgren 1939, 51-60; Sandmel 1979; Morris 1987, 809-819; Borgen 1997, 14-45.

3   Cf. Goodenough 1940 30-51; Elmgren 1939, 61-68; Morris 1987, 819-870. However, especially Goodenough has argued strongly that Philo's political activities in Alexandria were more wide ranging than estimated by earlier scholars, cf. Goodenough 1938; Goodenough 1940, 52-74. Dyck 2002 points in the same direction. Furthermore, it is pointed out, quite rightly, by Friedländer 1903, 192-328, especially 209; Krüger 1906, 1.12; Collins 1983, 112, that Philo's writings are also generally more marked by apologetic tendencies than assumed by most scholars. To this should be

Josephus (cf. *The History of the Jews* (*Antiquitates Judaicae*, henceforth *AJ*) 18.257-260) that Philo, who belonged to the most influential Jewish family in Alexandria,[4] seems to have played a significant political role in the years 38-41, a period of great importance in the history of the Jewish people in the ancient world (cf. section 2 below). Following the events of these years, probably during the year of 41-42, Philo wrote the two small books that will be discussed in this essay.

It is the aim of this investigation to present and analyse these two treatises as evidence indicating that Philo also worked as a polemist and as a political apologist. The essay is structured as follows: First, an attempt will be made at a historical reconstruction of the course of events in Alexandria in the year 38. Even though the two writings to be examined are in fact the most important historical sources of these events, we need to reconstruct and visualise what happened in order to establish some sort of yardstick to measure the interpretative accounts expressed in the two writings. On the basis of these and further sources as well as other scholars' interpretations, I will therefore try to reconstruct an outline of these events of great importance for the Jews which took place in Alexandria and Palestine in the years 38-41, i.e. during the reign of the Roman Emperor Gaius Caligula (37-41) and at the beginning of that of his successor Claudius (41-54). Second, on this background, I will turn to the main purpose of this investigation: a close analysis and interpretation of the two historical treatises *Against Flaccus* (henceforth *In Flacc.*) and *The Embassy to Gaius* (*Leg.*). Third, this analysis will be continued in an investigation of the literary genre and the aim, dating and intended readers of the two writings as well as a discussion of the question whether these writings of Philo could be perceived as a threat to Rome.

---

added that, according to Eusebius, Philo is also the author of a proper apologetic work: *Apology for the Jews* (*Apologia hyper Ioudaiōn*, *Praep. evang.* 8.11), which may be identical with the two other writings mentioned by Eusebius: *On the Jews* (*Peri Ioudaiōn*, *Hist. eccl.* 2.18.6) and *Hypothetika* (*Praep. evang.* 8.6-7).

4   In *AJ* 18.259 Josephus writes: "... Philo, who stood at the head of the delegation of the Jews, a man held in the highest honour, brother of Alexander the alabarch and no novice in philosophy, was prepared to proceed with the defence (*ep' apologiai*) against these accusations" (which the head of the non-Jewish delegation from Alexandria, Apion, had brought to the Emperor Caligula against the Jews, quoted from Feldman 1965, 155). Josephus refers several times to Philo's brother Alexander as an extremely wealthy and influential person in Alexandria, who was directly related to the imperial family in Rome as well as to the Herodian royal family in Jewish Palestine (cf. *AJ* 18.159-60; 19.276-7; 20.100). The title "alabarch" refers to a position in the Jewish society in Alexandria recognised by Rome which, according to some scholars, was responsible for the collection of certain custom duties; cf. Kasher 1985, 86.

2. The situation of the Jews in Alexandria (and Palestine) during the crisis years 38-41[5]

It cannot be claimed that the living conditions of the Jewish people were generally bad in the Roman Empire in the years from Caesar (died 44 BCE) and Augustus (31 BCE – 14 CE) until the summer of 38.[6] During that period, the Jews in Palestine and in the Diaspora were permitted by Rome unobstructed to "live according to the customs of their fathers," as it is often stated in the sources.[7] From the beginning, i.e. during the rule of Caesar and Augustus, the Jews in Alexandria and Egypt seem to have supported the Roman conquerors, whereas especially the Greeks and the Egyptians continued for a long time to consider the Romans as hostile conquerors and foreign rulers.[8]

According to Philo, this favourable situation for the Jewish population in Alexandria continued well over the first year of Caligula's rule (37-38). However, during the summer of 38, a decisive change seems to have occurred. Philo tells us that during the years 32-38, Aulus Avilius Flaccus, who had been a close friend of the Emperor Tiberius (14-37), held the post as the Roman prefect in Alexandria (and Egypt). During the months from August to September 38, Flaccus, for reasons that are not evident, seems to have cancelled the Jewish population's established right to live in Alexandria according to the customs of their fathers and under some kind of internal self-government, an institution, which in several other texts are described with the Greek expression *politeuma* ("community of citizens" or "civic association"), whereas, in Philo's two historical treatises, this right is referred to with the less exact term *politeia* ("government" or "constitution," cf. *In Flacc.* 53; *Leg.* 349.363).[9] In any case, it seems to be a right, a privilege, which was considered to be valuable and which could be acquired or lost. (cf. *In Flacc.* 172). In August 38, the newly proclaimed King Agrippa I (37/41-44) came to Alexandria on his journey from Rome to

---

5 This situation has been described by a number of scholars, especially Bludau 1906; Bell 1924, 10-21; 1926; Box 1939, XXXVIII-XLVIII; Schürer, 1973-87, vol. I, 389-394; Smallwood 1976, 235-42; Kasher 1985, 20-24; Feldman 1993, 113-7; Mélèze-Modrzejewski 1995, 165-73; Barclay 1996, 48-55. Unfortunately, I have not been able to get hold of Gambetti 2003.

6 Cf., e.g., Tcherikover 1959, 296-332; Smallwood 1976, 120-255; Schürer 1973-87, vol., III.1, 107-37; Feldman 1993, 92-102.

7 Cf., e.g., *In Flacc.* 43, 47, 52; *Leg.* 327. For an account of the general conditions of the Jews in Alexandria see Tcherikover & Fuks 1957-64, vol. 1, 93; Smallwood 1976, 224-35; Schürer, 1973-87, vol. III.1, 87-108; Collins 2005, 9-29, especially 9-14.

8 These different attitudes towards Rome was probably an important, if not the decisive, factor for the development of the tensions between the Jewish and the non-Jewish populations in Alexandria, cf., e. g., Bludau 1906, 59; Fuchs 1924, 17-8; Box 1939, XIII-XVIII; Smallwood 1976, 223-4; Kasher 1985, 12-8; Barclay 1996, 48-51.

9 There is general agreement in recent scholarship that the Jews in Alexandria did not possess full citizenship rights in the city, which might include participation in non-Jewish cults, but rather some kind of internal self-government, as indicated above, cf., e.g., Fuchs 1924, 79-105; Bell 1924, 14-6; Wolfson 1944, 165-6; Smallwood 1976, 230; Kasher 1985, 261, 356-7, 359-64; Barclay 1996, 50, 60-71. Against this understanding, Mélèze-Modrzejewski argues that the Jews in Alexandria during the Roman era did not have any kind of internal self-government, cf. 1995, 163-8 – a point of view which, however, is not very convincing to the reader.

Palestine (*In Flacc.* 25-28, cf. *AJ* 18.238). In Rome, Agrippa had recently from Emperor Caligula received the tetrarchy that had belonged to his uncle Philip, who had died in 34 CE. At the same time, Agrippa had been proclaimed king (cf. *AJ* 18.237).[10] According to Philo, Agrippa's visit to Alexandria triggered off anti-Jewish riots in the city, during which Agrippa was subjected to public ridicule (the so-called Carabas episode mentioned in *In Flacc.* 36-39), and subsequently attempts by groups among the non-Jewish population forcibly to set up images of the emperor in the Jewish synagogues ("prayer houses," cf. *In Flacc.* 41-3, 47-9, 53 and elsewhere).

Contrary to expectation, the Roman prefect did not intervene in the riots (*In Flacc.* 51). Instead, Flaccus joined forces with the "Greeks" and issued a decree (*programma, In Flacc.* 54), denouncing the Jews as "foreigners and newcomers" (*xenous kai epēludas*) in Alexandria.[11] Consequently, the Jewish population in Alexandria had no legal rights and, according to Philo, they were then exposed to direct persecution: They were driven away from four out of the five quarters of the city (*In Flacc.* 55). Some of their houses were looted and burnt (*In Flacc.* 54-7). Add to this corporeal assaults (*In Flacc.* 58-65) and confinement of the city's Jews in a very limited area, which, among other things, resulted in famine (*In Flacc.* 62). In some cases, these acts of spitefulness resulted in killing (*In Flacc.* 65) and, as a special humiliation, members of the Jewish Council (*boulē*) were publicly whipped in the theatre (*In Flacc.* 58-85), whereas some Jewish women were forced to eat pork (*In Flacc.* 96). Finally, the Roman prefect Flaccus made a systematic search for weapons in Jewish homes (*In Flacc.* 86-94).

This violent persecution of Jews seems to be something new in Antiquity. There are of course accounts in the *Book of Esther* and the books of the Maccabees, especially the *3 Maccabees*, about similar extensive persecutions of Jews in Persia, Judaea and Ptolemaic Egypt. In these books, however, it is more difficult to unravel the historical circumstances. In Alexandria in the year 38, however, a systematic persecution really seems to have taken place, an event, which several scholars describe as the first "pogrom" in history,[12] whereas other scholars refers to it as expressions of "Anti-Semitism,'[13] and some use the term "ghetto" about the quarter in which the Jews were detained.[14]

In my judgement, it is beyond doubt that the Jews in Alexandria were subjected to widespread cruel and violent persecutions in the summer of 38, even though the ac-

10   Cf. Schwartz 1990, 74-7.
11   Cf. *In Flacc.* 172 and Josephus, *Against Apion* (*Contra Apionem,* henceforth *AP*) 2.71, where the Jews in Alexandria are referred to as *peregrinos* ("foreigners").
12   Thus, e.g., Bell 1924, 16; 1926, 20; 1941, 7; Jones 1926, 23; Box 1939, XIX. XXXVIII; XLVII; Goodenough 1938, 1; Goodenough 1940, 60; Elmgren 1939, 28-30; Daniélou 1958, 29; Grant 1973, 123; Schwartz 1990, 75; Mélèze-Modrzejewski 1995, 169, 172; Barclay 1996, 48-60, 179; Horst 2005; Collins 2005, 14, 28.
13   Cf., e.g., Bludau 1906, 78; Bell 1924, 9; Bell 1941; Box 1939, XIX; Elmgren 1939, 31, 57 and elsewhere; Sandmel 1979, 12; Smallwood 1976, 233-4; Schürer 1973-87, vol. III.1, 1986, 594, 601, 607-8 and elsewhere; Schwartz 1990, 96-9; Collins 2005, 25-9.
14   Cf., e.g., Bludau 1906, 74; Fuchs 1924, 104; Bell 1926, 19; Jones 1926, 23; Box 1939, XLV; Grant 1973, 123; Smallwood 1976, 240.

tual historical circumstances cannot be established directly on the basis of Philo's very committed descriptions. We should refrain, however, when reconstructing historical circumstances in Antiquity, from using terms related to the European persecutions of Jews in the Middle Ages and in recent times. In Alexandria, the issue was most of all about ethnical, cultural and political conflicts, which, incidentally, continued and culminated in the year 66 (cf. *The Jewish War* (*Bellum Judaicum*, henceforth *BJ*) 2.487-98) and in the second great Jewish revolt against Rome which, in 115-117, took place in Cyprus, Mesopotamia, Cyrenaica (Libya) and Egypt (cf. Smallwood 1976, 389-427).

Back to Alexandria: At the accession to the throne of the Emperor Caligula in March 37, the Alexandrian Jews – like all other groups – had agreed upon a decree of congratulation, which they had asked Flaccus to send to the Emperor. Flaccus had promised to do so, but omitted it in order to discredit the Jews, as Philo formulates it (*In Flacc.* 97-101). The Alexandrian Jews then (August 38?) poured out their troubles to King Agrippa and asked him on their behalf to intervene with the Emperor, with whom he was on good terms.[15]

However, the Emperor himself seems to have anticipated this. For unknown reasons – maybe because of Agrippa's complaints (cf. Bell 1926, 22) – Caligula actually decided to remove and punish Flaccus (*In Flacc.* 104-7). The Emperor sent a police force to Alexandria, which – "during the Feast of Tabernacle," i.e. in September-October 38 – arrested Flaccus and took him to Rome, where Caligula condemned him to exile on a Greek island and later had him executed there (*In Flacc.* 109-88).

It looks as if Flaccus on that occasion was replaced as Roman prefect in Alexandria and Egypt by a certain Pollio,[16] who presumably restored order in Alexandria and thus may have given their traditional rights back to the city's Jewish population. Pollio also seems to have permitted – or maybe even ordered – each of the two contesting parties in Alexandria to appoint and send a delegation to Rome to account for their responsibility for the conflict in the summer of 38 and thus to defend themselves in front of the Emperor.[17] This may have occurred either during the winter of 38-39[18] or during the winter of 39-40.[19] However, as Philo records, both delegations seem to

---

15 Cf. *In Flacc.*103; *AJ* 18.167-8, 237-8, 289-301 and Schwartz 1990, 67-89. According to Josephus, the Herodian client-kings at the time between Herod the Great and Agrippa II several times acted as intermediaries and advocates of (part of) the Jewish people, cf. Bilde 1983, 139-41; Schwartz 1990, 76-7.

16 C. Vitrasius Pollio, cf. Bludau 1906, 80, according to whom the change of prefect occurred immediately, cf. also Bell 1924, 24.

17 This, too, was general practice in the Roman provinces. According to Josephus, *AJ* 20.179-84, for example, Jews as well as non-Jews in Caesarea after a similar conflict sent delegations to Emperor Nero, who settled the matter in favour of the non-Jews. Another example is found in *AJ* 20.193-5, where Josephus tells us that the Roman prefect in Judea, Festus, permits the leading Jewish citizens in Jerusalem to send a delegation to Rome to ask Nero to set aside an order issued by the prefect to destroy a recently built wall on top of the temple area's western colonnade.

18 Thus, e.g., Bludau 1906, 8; Fuchs 1924, 21; Bell 1924, 19; Bell 1926, 13.

19 Thus, e.g., Grant 1973, 129; Smallwood 1976, 243; Bilde 1983, 115-7.

have stayed in Rome and Puteoli (at the Bay of Naples) for a very long period of time before they were given an audience with the Emperor (cf. *Leg.* 178-83. 349-67).[20]

Shortly after the dramatic events in Alexandria, i.e., during the spring of 40 (cf. Bilde 1983, 115-121), according to both Philo and Josephus, a very dangerous conflict developed in Palestine. Philo records (*Leg.* 200-1) that the non-Jewish population had put up an altar in honour of Gaius Caligula in the city of Jamnia, which was inhabited by a mixed population. This, however, was probably considered by the Jewish population to be a desecration of the "Holy Land'. In any case, Philo tells us that the Jews destroyed the altar (*Leg.* 202). The Roman procurator of the area, Herennius Capito, reported this to the Emperor, who became enraged by this insult and decided to implement the infamous plan to have a statue of him-self erected in no other place than the very Temple of Jerusalem.[21] Caligula transferred the project to the Roman legate and proconsul of the province of Syria, Publius Petronius, and both Philo and Josephus describe in detail the riots occasioned by this project among the Jews in Palestine and elsewhere (cf. references in footnote 21).

King Agrippa I, however, also intervened in this conflict, during which the King was (again?) in Rome, and he managed to persuade the Emperor to withdraw this disastrous decision. Our sources in Philo and Josephus are characterised by some uncertainty as to what really happened at the end of the year 40: Did the Emperor's order of withdrawal reach Petronius in time, or did the news about the murder of Caligula on 24 January 41 by the praetorian tribune Cassius Chaerea reach him first and thus resolved the highly tense situation in Palestine (cf. *AJ* 18.300-308; 19.1-113)?

In Alexandria, the news about the death of Caligula seems to have resulted in a wave of Jewish revenge attacks on the city's "Greek" population.[22] Pollio seems once more to have restored order, and it is likely that he again sent two delegations to Rome to account for the latest disturbances to the new Roman Emperor, Claudius, whose way to the throne to some degree seems to have been paved by Agrippa I (cf. *AJ* 19.236-73). Furthermore, a fortunate discovery was made in 1912 of a papyrus copy of a letter of 10 November 41 from the Emperor Claudius to the two population groups in Alexandria, enjoining them to reach agreement and to restore order in the city.[23] The situation from before July 38 should thus have been re-established,[24] and this is

---

20 Scholars have discussed whether the Jewish delegation lead by Philo merely wished to re-establish the situation before the conflict/persecution, or whether it would attempt to go one step further and ask the Emperor to give full citizenship to all Alexandrian Jews, possibly to only some of them, cf. Box 1939, XXXVIII-XXXIX.

21 Cf. *Leg.* 184-348; *BJ* 2.184-203; *AJ* 18.261-309 and, further, Bilde: 1983, 62-121.

22 Cf. *AJ* 19.278-9 and further Bell 1924, 17-8.

23 Cf. *P.Lond.* 1912, which was published and translated into English in Bell 1924, 23-9; Tcherikover & Fuks, 1957-64, vol. 2, 36-55. See also *AJ* 19.280-5.

24 This meant that the non-Jewish citizens of Alexandria should now let their Jewish fellow citizens live in peace and not disturb their worship. The Jews, on the other hand, did not achieve further rights, e.g., full citizenship of the city. Instead, they had their previous rights confirmed, which probably meant their internal self-government in the form of an autonomous "citizen community"

probably the context in which Philo wrote the two historical treatises, which we will now turn to.[25]

3. *Against Flaccus*[26]

Philo introduces this writing by connecting Flaccus' "anti-Jewish" policy with a similar campaign run by Lucius Aelius Sejanus, who under the Emperor Tiberius was commander of the Praetorian Guard. In that period, the years 26-31, when Tiberius left Rome and withdrew to the isle of Capri in the Bay of Naples, Sejanus possessed the actual power in Rome and, among other things, implemented a policy against the Jews in Rome and elsewhere in the Roman Empire: "The policy of attacking the Jews begun by Sejanus was taken over by Flaccus Avillius" (*In Flacc.* 1, cf. 191; *Leg.* 159-160).[27] Then Philo describes the period when Flaccus was the emperor's prefect (*epitropos*, *In Flacc.* 2; *hē epikrateia*, *In Flacc.* 8) in Alexandria (and Egypt), from his appointment in the year 32 to his removal in the autumn of 38.

Flaccus' first six years are described in bright colours (*In Flacc.* 2-8). Then Philo mentions the reasons for the turn in Flaccus' performance of his office. Philo considers the most important reason to be Flaccus' personal relations to Tiberius, with whom he was closely connected, and to his successor, Gaius Caligula, towards whom he had felt animosity. Flaccus had preferred Tiberius' grandson, Tiberius Gemellus, to succeed Tiberius (*In Flacc.* 9). So, when Caligula after his illness, i.e. during the summer of 38, started a regular cleansing in Rome of Tiberius' relatives and "friends," Flaccus became worried that the turn would come to him, too (*In Flacc.* 10-5). According to Philo, this threatening danger from Caligula was the reason why Flaccus entered into an alliance with the heads of Alexandria's Greek population: Dionysius, Lampon and Isidorus. This alliance meant that Flaccus, in return for the city of Alexandria's support and intercession on his behalf with Emperor Caligula, should "sacrifice" the Alexandrian Jews, whom "the Greek" hated cordially (*In Flacc.* 20-4).[28]

(*politeuma*), cf. Bell 1976, 20-1.

25 Josephus wrote his two accounts later, one in *The Jewish War* in the mid-70s and one in *The Jewish Antiquities* in the mid-90s, cf. Bilde 1988, 65-79 (*BJ*), and 80-104 (*AJ*).

26 The text is from the Loeb-edition by Colson 1941, 293-403. The most important other editions are published by Box 1939; Pelletier 1967; van der Horst 2003, all with detailed introductions, commentaries and references.

27 The translation is borrowed from Colson 1941, 303. To the interpretation of the contents of the text quoted, see also the end of section 3 and section 5 below. Eusebius writes in his church history, *Hist. eccl.* 2.5.1, that "he (Philo) describes in five books the (disasters) that befell the Jews under Gaius (Caligula)." On the basis of this information, it is often assumed that Philo had also written a book on Sejanus' persecutions of the Jews in Rome, and that the two books handed down, *Against Flaccus* and *The Embassy to Gaius*, are fragments of such a large work consisting of five books, cf., among others, Box 1939, XXXIII-XXXVIII; Colson 1941, 295; Smallwood 1961, 37-43; Morris 1987, 859-63.

28 According to most scholars, the reason for this hatred was the alliance made between the Alexan-

This section is followed by a long and detailed description of the disasters brought by Flaccus upon the Alexandrian Jews (*In Flacc.* 25-101, cf. section 2 above).

In *In Flacc.* 102, Philo eventually comes to the "change" (*metabolē*, cf. *In Flacc.* 154, 159)[29] in his description in this treatise of the situation for the Jews, which Philo interprets as a just intervention of the Jewish divinity (*In Flacc.* 102, 107) through, among others, King Agrippa I. This "tremendous change" (*In Flacc.* 159) was launched by the arrest of Flaccus ordered by the Emperor (*In Flacc.* 108-15), and followed by the joy of the Alexandrian Jews at this just divine intervention (*In Flacc.* 121-4).

As mentioned in section 2 above, Flaccus was captured and taken to Rome (*In Flacc.* 125ff.), where he was sentenced by Emperor Caligula to abandon his property (*In Flacc.* 148) and to be sent into exile on the Greek island of Gyara, which was later changed to the more pleasant island of Andros (*In Flacc.* 151). The rest of this treatise (*In Flacc.* 152-90) is devoted to Philo's triumphant description of the punishment of Flaccus, of his humiliation of being an exiled prisoner, of his sufferings and ultimate bloody death when, at the Emperor's command, he was killed by sword (*In Flacc.*185-90), given as many wounds as the number of Alexandrian Jews that he had had executed (*In Flacc.* 189).[30]

Philo "piously" finishes his writing with these words: "Such was the fate of Flaccus *also*, who thereby became an indubitable proof that the help which God can give was not withdrawn from the nation of the Jews" (*In Flacc.* 191).[31] If this translation is correct, the ending of the book shows in this way, that Philo, prior to this book, had written about a "first" persecutor of the Jews, probably Sejanus, who persecuted the Jews in Rome (cf. *In Flacc.* 1; *Leg.* 159-60 and footnote 27 above).

Slightly before the end of this treatise, Philo lets Flaccus himself express the same idea about his cruel fate, being the Jewish divinity's just retribution for Flaccus' persecution of the Jews in Alexandria. Philo tells us that one night Flaccus became "possessed" (*enthous*), stepped out of his cottage and lifted his eyes to heaven saying:

---

drian Jews and leading Romans like Caesar and Octavian during the Roman conquest of Ptolemaic Egypt and Octavian's confrontation with his rival Marcus Antonius, who had formed a liaison with Cleopatra VII of Egypt (cf. section 2 above with the references in footnote 8). Alexandria's Greek-speaking citizens therefore considered their Jewish fellow-citizens as traitors to Ptolemaic Egypt. To this should probably be added the local struggles of the Jews about the right for full citizenship in Alexandria, about the degree of the internal Jewish self-government (*politeuma*) and about other issues (cf. section 2 above).

29   The same term is used by Philo elsewhere about decisive changes, e.g., about the definite eschatological change of the conditions of the Jewish people, cf. Elmgren 1939, 101.

30   Some scholars have resented this Philonic "glee," cf. Colson 1941, 301: "He (Philo) gloats over the misery of Flaccus in his fall, exile, and death, with a vindictiveness which I feel to be repulsive." To the contrary, among others, Nikiprowetzky 1968, 7-19, emphasises that Philo and the Alexandrian Jews are less pleased with the misery of their enemies than with the justice manifested through the divine providence.

31   Thus Colson 1941, 403. Similar translations are made by Box 1939, 67: "Such were the sufferings of Flaccus too …"; Pelletier 1967, 155: "Voilà, ce qu'endura Flaccus lui aussi …," and van der Horst 2003, 244-5: "Such were the sufferings of Flaccus too …"

King of gods and men – he cried – so then Thou dost not disregard the nation of the Jews, nor do they misreport Thy Providence (*pronoia*), but all who say that they (the Jews) do not find in Thee a Champion and Defender, go astray from the true creed ("sound teaching"). I am a clear proof of this, for all the acts which I madly committed against the Jews I have suffered myself (*In Flacc.* 170, cf. 174; the translation is from Colson 1941, 395).

4. The Embassy to Gaius[32]

After a very Philonic introduction (*Leg.* 1-7) about body and soul, nature and coincidence, reason and emotion, knowledge and ignorance, culminating in a confession of belief that God in his Providence (*pronoia*) looks after all people, and especially the Jewish people, who – as the only people (?) – is able to "see God" (*Leg.* 3-4), Philo goes on describing the situation when Gaius Caligula became Emperor.

Just like in *Against Flaccus*, Philo starts in a cheerful tone, describing the happiness, peace and joy that prevailed in the Roman Empire in the beginning of Gaius Caligula's reign (*Leg.* 8-13). This period lasted for about seven months, i.e. from March to October 37, when Gaius fell ill, according to Philo because of his unhealthy luxurious living (*Leg.* 14).

When the Emperor had recovered, however, according to Philo, he was completely transformed. His personality had changed from that of a "saviour" and "benefactor" to that of a cruel amok runner (*Leg.* 22). Caligula began this destructive stage of his life by murdering Tiberius' grandson, Tiberius Gemellus, who was his main rival to the office as Emperor (*Leg.* 23-31).[33] Then follows a long account of Gaius' execution of the commander of the Praetorian Guard, Macro, who had even assisted Gaius to become Emperor, of Macro's family (*Leg.* 32-74), and of other distinguished Romans (*Leg.* 66-74).

According to Philo, this massacre made Caligula believe that he was divine, and Philo provides a number of examples of how this manifested itself (*Leg.* 75-114). Only at this point, about one third into the writing, does Philo arrive at his principal issue, the Jewish people: Gaius now turned against the Jews since they were the only ones among the empire's population who, because of their religion, refused to honour him as a god (*Leg.* 115-118). "So then," Philo tells us, "a vast and truceless war was prepared

---

32   The text is published in the Loeb-series by Colson 1962. Other editions are published by Smallwood 1961; Pelletier 1972.

33   Cf. *In Flacc.* 9. The two treatises overlap in their descriptions of Caligula's cleansing of the relatives and "friends" of Tiberius in Rome and of the disasters that befell the Jewish population in Alexandria (*In Flacc.* 8-101 and *Leg.* 22-74, 120-37). There are many similarities between the two accounts, but there are also differences, which are probably due to the different aims of the two books. Whereas, in the first writing, the prefect Flaccus was charged with the responsibility for the persecution of the Jews, the second writing places the main responsibility with the Emperor Caligula.

against the nation" (*Leg.* 119, Colson 1962, 59). And the remainder of the treatise is about this war.

First, there is an account of the events in Alexandria, which here (*Leg.* 120-137) – as opposed to the account in *Against Flaccus* (25-101) – are claimed to be started by the Emperor himself and his Anti-Jewish advisers, in particular the "Egyptian" Helicon.[34] Philo maintains that in Alexandria, Gaius had an easy job, as the non-Jewish population, who had an implacable hatred of the Jews (cf. section 2-3 above), assumed that the emperor had now left the fate of the Jews to their whim (*Leg.* 120-121).

In the following section (*Leg.* 138-161), Philo contrasts this anarchy caused by Gaius and Flaccus with the traditional Roman – and earlier Ptolemaic – policy of protecting the Jews and allowing them to live according to their own laws (the Law of Moses) in Alexandria (as well as in other cities, cf. section 2 above). This policy had previously only been broken by Sejanus (*Leg.* 159-60, cf. *In Flacc.* 191 above), a fact, which, however, Philo passes lightly over here.

After this "digression" (*Leg.* 138-161), Philo, in *Leg.* 162, reverts to Caligula's "war" against the Jews, which in Alexandria was supported by the city's "Greek" population. Philo has now finally reached the "embassy," which is the main topic of this treatise. From and including *Leg.* 178 – probably in the summer of 40 (cf. section 2 above) – we are suddenly in Rome with the Jewish delegation, which, according to *Leg.* 370, consisted of five members and which, according to Josephus (*AJ* 18.259), was led by Philo. Philo now tells us that, through the mediation of King Agrippa I, the Jews had already in advance sent a long petition to the Emperor, and Philo adds that the delegation, during its stay in Rome, formulated an abbreviated version of the same petition, which they attempted to pass on to the Emperor. It was very difficult for the delegation to get to see the Emperor because access to him had to go through the Egyptian "Jew-hater" Helicon (*Leg.* 178-179). When, according to Philo, the delegation was eventually called for an audience, Caligula received them quite kindly (*Leg.* 180-181). But by virtue of his age and education, Philo was able to comprehend this kindness as hypocrisy (*Leg.* 182), and he envisaged that the Emperor in reality had hostile intentions towards the Jews (*Leg.* 183).

Then follows a new, long digression, namely a detailed account of Caligula's statue project in Palestine (*Leg.* 184-348). This digression is interlaced with a smaller digression: a new description of the traditionally positive Roman policy towards the Jewish population (*Leg.* 291-320, cf. 138-161).

In *Leg.* 349, finally, Philo returns to the principal issue of the treaty, the account of the Alexandrian-Jewish delegation's stay in Italy to plead for the Jews with the Emperor. We are now told that the delegation, this time in Puteoli, together with the "Greek" delegation, was called for a second audience with the Emperor "to take part in the

---

34 Cf. *Leg.* 166-78 (and *In Flacc.* 29). In *Leg.* 166, Philo points out that most of Caligula's servants and assistants were "Egyptians," a stereotyped feature reflecting both the traditional hostility between Jews and Egyptians and a general contempt for Egyptians in the Roman Empire, cf. Mendelsohn 1988, 116-22.

contention about our citizenship" (... *agōnisasthai ton peri tēs politeias agōna*, (cf. section 2 above)). Philo gives a vivid description of this audience. The conversation was dominated by Gaius' wish to be treated as a god (cf. also Josephus in *AJ* 18.257-258), and the Emperor again concluded with relatively gentle words to the Jewish delegation (*Leg.* 351-367). Still, Philo ends his writing in a pessimistic tone (*Leg.* 368-372) and concludes in *Leg.* 373 with the following cryptic sentence: "So now I have told in a summary way the cause of the enmity which Gaius had for the whole nation of the Jews, but I must also describe the palinode (*tēn palinōidian*)."

5. Literary genre, aim, intended readers and dating of the two treatises

The key to the correct understanding of these two writings is probably to be found exactly in *Leg.* 373, compared with the conclusion of *Against Flaccus*. In *Leg.* 373, the main problem is the interpretation of word *palinōidia*, constructed by *palin* and *aidein*, i.e. "sing again," but what does this expression mean?

In the translation of the Loeb-edition, used above, Colson omits to translate *tēn palinōidian*, or rather, he uses the English transcription "palinode,"[35] but the meaning of this is not clear either. In a note, Colson proposes to translate "palinode" to "counter-story" or "reversal."[36] At the end of the note, however, Colson proposes to change the text from *palinōidia* to *palinodia* (constructed by *palin* and *hodos*), which he interprets to mean "the opposite way" (1962, 186-7). In any case, Colson presumes that the "palinode" refers to a lost work.[37]

Pelletier, who in 1972 published *The Embassy to Gaius* in the large French edition of the complete works of Philo, *Les oeuvres de Philon d'Alexandrie*, proposes the following translation: " ... Il faudrait dire aussi le juste retour des choses."[38]

The large Greek-English dictionary (Liddell, Scott & Jones 1940, 1293), suggests to translate the word *palinōidia* into "recantation," in the sense that an author, for example, in a new poem recants previous poems, but, in my opinion, this interpretation is of little help here.[39]

---

35 Thus also Smallwood 1961, 146: "... I must now proceed to the palinode." In her commentary, Smallwood refers to the scholarly discussion about this problem and concludes as follows: "... and it therefore seems better to suppose that Philo is using the word in the unparalleled (?) sense of 'an account of a reversal of fortune.'"

36 Colson writes that such a "counter-story" probably "... gave an account of Gaius's death and probably also the change of policy adopted by Claudius, as shown in the two edicts recorded by Josephus, *Ant.* XIX. 5. If, that is, it was never written, for it is curious that Eusebius in his brief notice of the *Legatio*, see Introd. pp. XVII, shows no knowledge of it" (1962, 186-7). Colson thus interprets the word *palinōidia* in the same way as Smallwood.

37 Cf. 1962, XXIV, and references in footnote 27 above.

38 Pelletier 1972, 321. According to Pelletier, however, this work was never written but only suggested in the writing, cf. especially *Leg.* 206 (on the divine retribution towards Caligula's Anti-Jewish freedmen Apelles and Helicon) and 348 (which indicates a similar retribution towards Caligula).

39 Colson 1962, 187, note a, however, agrees to this translation of *palinōidia*, which Philo also uses

I am inclined to think that the meaning of the word should be based on an analysis and interpretation of the treatise as a whole (combined with an interpretation of *Against Flaccus*). The term *palinōidia* might in the context refer to the withdrawal by Caligula of his order to have a statue of him-self erected in the Temple of Jerusalem, which, according to both Josephus (*AJ* 18.297-301) and Philo (*Leg.* 261-329), was due to the intervention of Agrippa I. However, the last sentence of *Leg.* undoubtedly refers to a positive contrast to its first sentence, which seems to be an ultra-short summary of the entire treatise. In the context of the writing, the "cause of the enmity which Gaius had for the whole nation of the Jews" therefore most probably refers to the Jews' refusal to honour him as a god. And the "contrast" to this can hardly be anything else than the whole complex of events which are not described in Philo, but in Josephus, and which include the murder of Caligula (21 January 41), Claudius' way to the imperial throne, assisted by King Agrippa I, and Claudius' re-establishment of Rome's traditional relation to the Jewish people, including recognition of their right to live in Alexandria according to "the customs of their fathers" (cf. section 2 above with footnote 7), i.e. the Law of Moses, which again means a re-establishment of the traditional rights of the Jews in Alexandria as well as Palestine.[40]

In the light of this, I think that the "palinode" must be interpreted as an account of the Jewish divinity's just punishment of Gaius Caligula in return for his actions against the Jewish people.[41] Philo presumably refers to an account of Caligula's death on 21 January 41, Claudius' accession to the throne (cf. Josephus' detailed description in *AJ* 19.1-273) and the rescue of the Jews that was closely related to these two events (cf. section 2 above).

This "palinode" may be implicit, lost or never have been written, but it is certainly present as an idea in *The Embassy to Gaius*. And when it thus is included in the treatise, *The Embassy to Gaius* has the same dual fundamental structure as *Against Flaccus*, where both parts of this basic structure have been described in detail.[42]

This fundamental structure, however, is well-known in contemporary and earlier Jewish literature. Obvious examples are the *Book of Esther* (on the disaster for the Jewish people in Persia planned by Haman, the salvation of the Jews, and Haman's punishment), the *1 Maccabees* (on Antiochus IV Epiphanes' violent attack against the Jews in Judea,

---

in *De posteritate Caini* 179 and *De somniis* 2.232; and Colson continues: "The only sense in which the story of these events would be a recantation would be that it would force the doubters of providence to recant." This view is shared by Frick 1999, 188, who mentions that Philo in the introduction to the writing also refers to and emphasises the divine providence (*Leg.* 3).

40 Cf. Josephus in *AJ* 19.1-291 and Claudius' letter to the two opposing ethnic groups in Alexandria (cf. the end of section 2 above).

41 This interpretation is widely accepted. In addition to Colson, Smallwood and Pelletier, it is shared by, e.g., Leisegang 1938, 402; Smallwood 1976, 43-4; Morris 1987, 861; Barclay 1996, 179, note 129; Borgen 1999, 293, 302-3, 309.

42 It is easy to imagine that Philo also planned and maybe even wrote a similar account about Sejanus with the same fundamental structure, Cf. *In Flacc.* 1; *Leg.* 159-60; footnote 27 above and Bilde 1983, 62-4.

on the Hasmonean revolt against and victory over the king and thus on the Jews and the salvation of the Jews), the *2 Maccabees* (with the same content and, especially, the narrative in chapter 2 about Heliodorus' attack on the Temple in Jerusalem, Yahweh's intervention and punishment of Heliodorus and the rescue of the Temple) and the *3 Maccabees* (on the Ptolemaic King Ptolemy Philopator's threats towards the Temple in Jerusalem and towards the Jews in Egypt, and the salvation through intervention of Yahweh and his punishment of the king and the Egyptians).[43]

This type of literature, however, also includes other books in the Hebrew Bible than the *Book of Esther*, especially *Exodus* (with the description of the sufferings of the Israelites in Egypt, Moses' plea to the Pharaoh to let his people go, Pharaoh's refusal to do so and his persecution of the Israelites as well as their salvation through intervention of Yahweh and his destruction of Pharaoh and the Egyptian army).[44]

Josephus as well is writing according to this "recipe," as, for example, in his description of the fates of Antiochus IV Epiphanes, Herod the Great, Archelaus, Pilate, Herod Antipas and, of course, the Emperor Caligula.[45] In all these circumstances, Josephus explains the violent death or the tragic misfortune of the ruler concerned as a result of divine justice caused by the injustice that the ruler in question committed against the Jewish people.

Later, the Church Father Lactantius put this fundamental structure on a formula, namely through the title of his writing on the persecution of the Christians under Diocletian and his successors: *De mortibus persecutorum* (*On the death of the persecutors*).[46]

It follows that the two treatises by Philo examined in this essay seem to have been cast in a fixed, traditional and effective Jewish literary form or genre, religious apologetics, which was later taken over by and continued in Christianity.

However, this insight does not tell us which aim and which target audience and readers Philo had in mind. It is possible, but not certain, that Philo chose this form or genre in order to comfort and edify Jewish readers.[47] In that case, Philo's intended readers were probably the same as those of the writings of the Hebrew Bible, the books of Maccabees and the other Jewish writings mentioned above.

Another possibility is to interpret Philo's two historical treatises as intended for Roman readers, primarily the new Roman emperor, Claudius, the new imperial prefect in Egypt, Pollio, and other leading roman circles, a hypothesis, which has been advocated in particular by Goodenough in several works.[48]

---

43 Cf. Collins 1983, 104-11, who argues that the *3 Maccabees* also reflects the crisis for the Jews in Alexandria in the years 38-41. Against this interpretation is, e.g., Barclay 1996, 203.

44 Thus also Pelletier 1967, 16-7, who describes this literary genre as an "aretalogy" (16.199, cf. Barclay 1996, 196.

45 In *Ap.* 2.43-144, Josephus describes the fate of the Jew-hater Apion in the same way.

46 Cf. also Bludau 1906, 77-8; Fuchs 1924, 19; Schürer 1973-87, vol. III.1, 543; Borgen 1999, 293, 302-3, 309.

47 Thus, e.g., Krüger 1906, 24, 64; Bludau 1906, 78; Leisegang 1938, 390. Professor Maren Niehoff has orally confirmed that she shares this opinion.

48 Cf. Goodenough 1938, 19-20; 1940, 20, 31, 59-60. Thus also Daniélou 1958, 39, 75; Pelletier 1971,

I am inclined to accept Goodenough's interpretation. On this basis, I tend to argue that both treatises can be understood as having a *political-apologetic* as well as a *theological-apologetic* character.[49] Philo places great emphasis on both features. He emphasises that it will go hard with the ruler who commits ("illegitimate") assaults against the Jewish people. This is a classic theological-apologetic feature (*topos*), which may primarily be intended for internal consumption. Another thing that Philo places great emphasis on is that a Roman ruler's positive ("legitimate") treatment of the Jewish people always used to go hand in hand with a Roman policy, which was also generally for the benefit of Rome itself as well as of the citizens of empire. According to Philo, it is the generally respected Roman Emperors like Caesar, Augustus, Tiberius (and Claudius?) who have been most favourable towards the Jews (cf. *Leg.* 291-320). The moral seems to be that under the reigns of these "good" Emperors, Rome prospered *because* they treated the Jews well.

On the contrary, Philo relates Gaius Caligula's assaults against the Jews to the Emperor's hostile acts against the Roman aristocracy. After that Gaius "had run amok," Philo tells us, he first killed Tiberius' grandson, Tiberius Gemellus (*Leg.* 23-31); then the commander of the Praetorian Guard, the knight Macro (*Leg.* 32-61); besides that Gaius Caligula's own father in law, the senator Silanus (*Leg.* 62-5) and other distinguished Romans (*Leg.* 66-75, 108). Philo thus seems to communicate that the Emperor Caligula, this "mortal enemy" of the Jews, was also an enemy of the Roman aristocracy and the true and healthy Roman traditions. By linking together Caligula's hostile policy towards he Jews with his breach of other Roman traditions, Philo manages very cleverly to agree with the aristocratic critique of this Emperor, which dominates in Roman historiography, e.g., Suetonius (*Calig.* 26-7) and Dio Cassius (*Hist.* 59.24-5).

On this interpretation, Philo's two historical treatises, and in particular the *Embassy to Gaius,* may also be regarded as pieces of effective *political apologetics.* It thus seems as if Philo wished to show Claudius' new government in Rome that the conflict between Caligula and the Jews was part of a policy damaging to Rome itself, whereas the traditional Roman policy towards the Jewish people was an inseparable part of a policy favourable to Rome itself.[50]

---

17. According to Box 1939, LXI, *Against Flaccus* is aimed at both Jewish and pagan readers, whereas Meiser 1999, 426, thinks that this treatise was intended for pagan readers.

49 Krüger calls both treatises "apologetic writings," which, however, do not contain any "coherent, closed apology against all pagan accusations," but relate to specific attacks (1906, 12). Goodenough describes the two treatises as "Philo's two works of apology" (1938, 100). Meiser settles for describing *Against Flaccus*'s aim as "apologetic" (1999, 426-9). Morris, on the other hand, refuses that these two writings should be apologetic, arguing that *Hypothetica* is the only one of Philo's works, "which could be described as apologetic ..." (1987, 867, note 231).

50 This means that Philo's apologetics in the two treatises discussed here is of a different character than the one found in *On the Life of Moses* (de vita Mosis), which emphasises Moses as the founder of culture, and the one found in *The Contemplative Life* (de vita contemplativa), in which Philo maintains that the Jewish ascetics, the so-called "therapists" serve as general religious and moral models (cf. Friedländer 1903, 216, 248-67). Elmgren, however, rightly stresses the connections between these different types of Philonic apologetics (1939, 65-6).

6. Philo's barely disguised menaces against Rome

Behind these pragmatic and rational political apologetics, however, a menacing under-tone may be heard in both *Against Flaccus* and *The Embassy to Gaius*.

Admittedly, both writings are based on the idea that the Jewish people do not defend their rights by force of arms because the Jewish divinity takes care of the nation's needs. And certainly, Philo stresses in *Against Flaccus* that Flaccus' suspicion that the Jews in Alexandria had arms reserves in their houses was unfounded and false (*In Flacc.* 86-96). In spite of a thorough search, the Roman soldiers found no arms, not even kitchen knives (*In Flacc.* 90). Philo is truly outraged about the Roman suspicions, for the Jews have "certainly" never taken up arms; they have never even thought about revolting, and they have always been peacefully disposed towards all people (*In Flacc.* 94).[51]

But at the same time there is a remarkable accentuation in this treatise of the huge number of Jews. Philo tells us that there were no less than a million Jews in Alexandria and Egypt alone (*In Flacc.* 43). According to the same text, the Jews made up one of the two population groups in the country, as Philo generously includes "Greeks" and "Egyptians" in one and the same group. The Jews are also extremely numerous in other cities, Philo records (*In Flacc.* 46). And in the case that non-Jewish population groups in other cities should take inspiration from the events in Alexandria in the summer of 38 and, in the same way, violate their Jewish fellow citizens and ravage their synagogues (*In Flacc.* 47), then, according to Philo, the Jews would react:

> Now the Jews though naturally well-disposed for peace could not be expected to remain quiet whatever happened, not only because with all men the determina-tion to fight for their institutions outweighs even the danger to life, but also be-cause they are the only people under the sun who by loosing their meeting-houses (*proseuchē*) were loosing also what they would have valued as worth dying many thousand deaths, namely their means of showing reverence to their benefactors (the emperors), since they no longer had the sacred buildings where they could set forth their thankfulness (*In Flacc.* 48, translated by Colson 1941, 329).

Also the *Embassy to Gaius* shows this ambiguity. On the one hand, Philo emphasises that the Jewish god alone is the true protector of the Jews (*Leg.* 6-7, 107, 373) and that the Jews are therefore peacefully disposed in both Alexandria and (in particular) Palestine (*Leg.* 225-245). On the other hand, we find statements such as *Leg.* 190: When the five members of the Jewish embassy, who stayed in Puteoli, heard the news about Gaius' project in Palestine, they reacted, Philo records, by saying: "'Let us struggle,' we said, 'to save us from delivering ourselves altogether to fatal acts of lawlessness'" (*agōniasōmen huper to nē eis hapan tais aniatois paronomiais aphethēnai*).[52] This interpretation of *Leg.* 190 is supported by the fact that Philo elsewhere, more or less *incidentally*, tells us that

---

51   Several scholars notice that Philo here exaggerates the peaceful nature of the Jewish people, e.g., Bludau 1906, 71; Bell 1926, 19-20; Barclay 1996, 54; Collins 2005, 12.

52   The translation is from Colson 1962, 97. The same attitude is expressed by Josephus in *Ap.* 2.272.

the Jewish inhabitants in Jamnia pulled down the imperial altar, which the city's non-Jewish citizens had erected in honour of Caligula (*Leg.* 202). This view also seems to be confirmed by Philo's account of Caligula's statue project in Palestine. Philo here writes that Petronius, who was responsible for the accomplishment of the Emperor's project, knew that the Jews in no circumstance would allow that the statue was erected in the Temple of Jerusalem (*Leg.* 209-210). Finally, a little later, Philo again stresses the huge number of Jews assembled to protest against Gaius' project (*Leg.* 214-215, cf. *In Flacc.* 43), their willingness to "die for the law" (cf. *Leg.* 209-210), and the danger that the Jews in this precarious situation might get assistance from the Jews on the other side of the Euphrates (*Leg.* 216).

These menacing features in the two writings, which most scholars do not pay attention to, cannot and should not be explained away. I therefore share Goodenough's interpretation that they are Philo's barely disguised warnings to the Roman élite: If the traditionally positive Roman policy towards the Jewish population is changed to negative, as it happened under the Emperor Caligula, there is a real risk that such a change will provoke armed Jewish resistance of an extent that will cause serious problems to Rome.[53] Over the following almost hundred years, this prophecy was amply fulfilled during the three great Jewish revolts against Rome in 66-70 (74), 115-117 and 132-135.

7. Conclusions

We can now conclude, first, that Philo took an active part in politics, at least for a certain period, especially during the years 38-40, when he led the Alexandrian-Jewish delegation of five representatives on its journey to Italy and Rome, where he pleaded for the Alexandrian Jews with the Emperor Caligula. Goodenough has argued that this political activity of Philo does not contrast with, but is in continuation of his exegetic and philosophical activity. To this can be added that Philo's significant political effort should also be considered in relation to his family background (cf. section 1 above): Philo's brother, Alexander the Alabarch, had close relations with the Roman imperial family (the Julians) as well as with the Herodian royal family in Palestine. These relations also seem to have included Philo, who, according to our two treatises, communicated directly with both Caligula and Agrippa I.

Second, we can conclude that Philo, during and immediately after this critical period, probably in the year 41, wrote the two historical books analysed here, and maybe others of the same kind, which may be lost and which may and should be characterised as both political-apologetic and theological-apologetic writings aimed at Jewish as well as non-Jewish, especially Roman, readers. The theological-apologetic character of these writings places them on the same footing as a great number of earlier and contemporary Jewish writings of the same character, first and foremost the works of Josephus.

---

53   Cf. Goodenough 1938, 6-7, 10-1, 19-20, 101. According to Goodenough, Philo did not give up the Jewish expectation of the coming Messiah, cf. 1938, 115-8. Thus also Geiger 1932, 106-8; Elmgren 1939, 104-18. Against, e.g., Sandmel 1979, 109. More reluctant is Collins 1983, 113-7.

Third, I believe to have demonstrated a contrast in these two writings between Philo's "pacifist" ideology and his barely disguised military threat to Rome. However, I do not find any features in these two treatises that can be interpreted as eschatological and/or messianic (cf., however, the references in footnote 53), which would have brought Philo even closer to the Jews who initiated the later great revolts against Rome.

Finally, I wish to emphasise that, with this interpretation of Philo's two historical writings, I have to place him solidly within the mainstream of Jewish literature in Antiquity.

References

Barclay, J. M. G. 1996 *Jews in the Mediterranean Diaspora. From Alexander to Trajan (323 B.C.E. – 117 C.E.)* Edinburgh: T&T Clark.

Bell, H.I. 1924 *Jews and Christians in Egypt. The Jewish Troubles in Alexandria and the Athanasian Controversey* London: Quaritch (reprinted Westport, Conn.: Greenwood Press 1976).

Bell, H.I. 1926 *Juden und Griechen im römischen Alexandreia. Eine historische Skizze des alexandrinischen Antisemitismus* (Beiheft zum Alten Orient 9) Leipzig: J.C. Hinrischs'sche Buchhandlung.

Bell, H.I. 1941 "Anti-Semitism in Aleaxandria" *Journal of Roman Studies*, 31, 1-18.

Bilde, P. 1983 *Josefus som historieskriver. En undersøgelse af Josefus' fremstilling af Gaius Caligulas konflikt med jøderne i Palæstina (Bell 2,184-203 og Ant 18,261-308) med særligt henblik på forfatterens tendens og historiske pålidelighed* København: C.E.G. Gad.

Bilde, P. 1988 *Josephus between Jerusalem and Rome. His Life, his Works, and their Importance* Sheffield: JSOT Press.

Bilde, P. 2007 "Filon som polemiker og politisk apologet" in: A. Klostergaard Petersen, J. Hyldahl & K. Fuglseth (eds.) *Perspektiver på jødisk apologetik* København: Anis, 155-180.

Bludau, A. 1906 *Juden und Judenverfolgungen im alten Alexandria* Münster: Aschendorff.

Borgen, P. 1997 *Philo of Alexandria. An Exegete for his Time* Leiden-New York-Köln: Brill.

Borgen, P. 1999 "Two Philonic Prayers and Their Contexts: An Analysis of *Who is the Heir of Divine Things (Her.)* 24-29 and *Against Flaccus (Flac.)* 170-175" *New Testament Studies* 45, 291-309.

Box, H. (ed.) 1939 *Philonis Alexandrini In Flaccum.* Edited with Introduction, Translation and Commentary London-New York-Toronto: Oxford University Press.

Collins, J.J. 2005 "Anti-Semitism in Antiquity? The Case of Alexandria" in: C. Bakhos (ed.) *Ancient Judaism in its Hellenistic Context* (Supplements to the Journal for the study of Judaism 95) Leiden: Brill, 9-29.

Collins, J.R. 1983 *Between Athens and Jerusalem. Jewish Identity in the Hellenistic Diaspora* New York: Crossroad.

Colson, F. F. (ed.) 1941 *Philo in Ten Volumes with an English Translation, vol. IX* Cambridge MA: Harvard University Press.

Colson, F.F. (ed.) 1962 *Philo in Ten Volumes with an English Translation, vol. X* Cambridge MA: Harvard University Press.

Daniélou, J. 1958 *Philon d'Alexandrie* Paris: Fayard.

Dyck, J. 2002 "Philo, Alexandria and Empire" in: J.R. Bartlett (ed.) *Jews in the Hellenistic and Roman Cities* London-New York: Routledge, 149-74.

Elmgren, H. 1939 *Philon av Alexandria med särskild hänsyn till hans eskatologiska föreställningar* Stockholm: Svenska Kyrkans Diakonistyrelse.

Feldman, L.H. (ed.) 1965 *Josephus: The Jewish Antiquities, vol. IX* Cambridge, MA: Harvard University Press.

Feldman, L.H. 1993 *Jew and Gentile in the Ancient World. Attitudes and Interactions from Alexander to Justinian* Princeton, NJ: Princeton University Press.

Frick, P. 1999 *Divine Providence in Philo of Alexandria* Tübingen: Mohr Siebeck.

Friedländer, M. 1903 *Geschichte der jüdischen Apologetik als Vorgeschichte des Christentums* Zürich: Schmidt (reprinted Amsterdam: Philo Press 1973).

Fuchs, L. 1924 *Die Juden Ägyptens in ptolemäischer und römischer Zeit* Wien: Rath.

Gambetti S. 2003 *The Alexandrian Riots of 38 C.E. and the Persecution of the Jews. A Historical Assessment* (PhD Dissertation) Berkeley: University of California.

Geiger, F. 1932 *Philon von Alexandreia als sozialer Denker (Teubinger Beiträge zur Altertumswissenschaft 14)* Stuttgart.

Goodenough, E.R. 1938 *The Politics of Philo Judaeus. Practice and Theory. With a General Bibliography of Philo* New Haven: Yale University Press.

Goodenough, E.R. 1940 *An Introduction to Philo Judaeus* New Haven: Yale University Press (reprinted Oxford: Blackwell).

Grant, M. 1973 *The Jews in the Roman World* London: Weidenfeld and Nicolson.

Jones, H.S. 1926 "Claudius and the Jewish Question at Alexandria" *Journal of Roman Studies* 16, 17-35.

Kasher, A. 1985 *The Jews in Hellenistic Egypt. The Struggle for Equal Rights* Tübingen: J.C.B. Mohr (Paul Siebeck).

Krüger, P. 1906 *Philo und Josephus als Apologeten des Judentums* Leipzig: Dürr (reprinted Amsterdam: Philo Press 1973 with Friedländer's work).

Leisegang, H. 1938 "Philons Schrift über die Gesandtschaft der alexandrinischen Juden an den Kaiser Gaius Caligula" *Journal of Biblical Literature* 57, 377-405.

Liddell, H.G., R. Scott & H.S. Jones 1940 *A Greek-English Lexicon* Oxford: Clarendon Press (ninth edition, with a revised supplement 1996).

Meiser, M. 1999 "Gattung. Adressaten und Intention von Philo's 'In Flaccum'" *Journal for the Study of Judaism* 30, 418-430.

Mélèze-Modrzejewski, J.M. 1995 *The Jews of Egypt: From Ramses II to Emperor Hadrian* Philadelphia: The Jewish Publication Society / Edinburgh: T&T Clark.

Mendelsohn, A. 1988 *Philo's Jewish Identity* (Brown Judaic Studies 161) Atlanta: Scholars Press.

Morris, J. 1987 "The Jewish Philosopher Philo" in: Schürer 1973-87, vol. III.2, 809-19.

Nikiprowetzky, V. 1968 "Schadenfreude chez Philon d'Alexandrie? Note sur *In Flaccum* 121ff." *Revue des études juives* 27, 7-19

Pelletier, A. (ed.) 1967 *In Flaccum. Introduction, traduction et notes* Paris: Les Éditions du Cerf.

Pelletier, A. (ed.) 1972 *Legatio ad Gaium. Introduction, traduction et notes* Paris: Les Éditions du Cerf.

Sandmel, S. 1979 *Philo of Alexandria. An Introduction* New York-Oxford: Oxford University Press.

Schürer, E. 1973-87 *The History of the Jewish People in the Age of Jesus Christ (175 B.C.- A.D. 135)* (revised and edited by G. Vermes, F. Millar, M. Goodman, 4 vols.), Edinburgh: T&T Clark.

Schwartz, D.R. 1990 *Agrippa I. The Last King of Judaea* (Texte und Studien zum Antiken Judentum 23) Tübingen: J.C.B. Mohr (Paul Siebeck).

Smallwood, E.M. (ed.) 1961 *Philonis Alexandrini Legatio ad Gaium. Edited with an Introduction, Translation and Commentary* Leiden: Brill.

Smallwood, E.M. 1976 *The Jews under Roman Rule. From Pompey to Diocletian* (Studies in Judaism in late Antiquity 20) Leiden: Brill.

Tcherikover, V.A. 1959 *Hellenistic Civilization and the Jews* Philadelphia: Jewish Publication Society of America (reprinted New York: Atheneum 1970).

Tcherikover, V.A. & Fuks, A. (eds.) 1957-64 *Corpus papyrorum Judaicarum* (3 vols.) Jerusalem: Magness Press / Cambridge, MA: Harvard University Press.

van der Horst, P. W. 2003 *Philo's Flaccus. The First Pogrom* Leiden-Boston: Brill.

Wolfson, H.A. 1944 "Philo on Jewish Citizenship in Alexandria" *Journal of Biblical Literature* 63, 165-168.

CHAPTER 6

Alexandrian Judaism: Rethinking a Problematic Cultural Category[1]

Anders Klostergaard Petersen

Can the aim of freedom of knowledge be the simple inversion of the relation of the oppressor and oppressed, centre and periphery, negative image and positive image? Is our only way out of such dualism the espousal of an implacable oppositionality or the invention of an originary counter-myth of radical purity? Must the project of our liberationist aesthetics be forever part of a totalising Utopian vision of Being and History that seeks to transcend the contradictions and ambivalences that constitute the very structure of human subjectivity and its systems of cultural representations?

Bhabba 2004, 28f.

1. Embarking on the Voyage

On the one hand, the examination of Alexandrian Jewry in antiquity may appear to be a fairly feasible as well as a relatively uncomplicated endeavour. Compared with numerous other locations and particular periods of antiquity, it is not a Herculean task to describe Alexandrian Judaism with a relatively high degree of historical confidence.

[1] It is a small token of gratitude only that I dedicate this essay to professor, Dr. Friedrich Avemarie, Institut für Neues Testament, Philipps-Universität, Marburg. I was enabled to write this contribution during a visit in the summer of 2005 at the Philipps-Universität, Marburg. I am most grateful to the Faculty of Theology, University of Aarhus, for a financial grant enabling my stay in Marburg, and, particularly, to professor Avemarie for so wonderfully organising the practical components of my visit. Additionally, I want to express my gratitude to Avemarie for seminal conversations and inspiration over the past decade. Finally, I want to express my sincere thanks to another friend, John Ranelagh, who not only took upon himself, once again, the arduous task of improving my English language, but also provided me with acute criticism and constructive comments. I am most grateful for this, just as I am indebted to John Ranelagh for having had the opportunity to complete the essay at the Chateau de Moncla of Southern France.

After all, we do find in comparison with so many other epochs and sites of antiquity an abundance of textual records embracing not only writings but also ample epigraphic and papyrological evidence as well as other archaeological remains. On the other hand, the enterprise is not as unproblematic and straightforward as it at first glance may appear. Indeed, a number of complicated and, perhaps, even unsolvable theoretical problems lurk behind the subject matter.

This essay focuses on the theoretical aspects of how to reconstruct past cultural entities and not with the empirical subject matter of Alexandrian Jewry. First, I intend to give a glimpse of some of the most important stages in the history of Alexandrian Jewry. Secondly, I shall discuss Alexandrian Judaism with close attention to a number of theoretical problems that are infrequently mentioned in the predominant strands of scholarship. In this manner, I hope that the examination will, on the one hand, contribute to the continuous research on Alexandrian Jewry. On the other hand, it is primarily intended to increase the scholarly awareness of some fundamental theoretical problems that pertain to the understanding of culture within the academic fields studying antiquity. Hence the essay aspires – compliant with the general theme of this book of Alexandria as a cultural and religious melting pot of antiquity – not only to shed light on some theoretical problems related to how we conceive of Alexandrian Jewry, but also at a more general level to how we shall altogether reconstruct past cultural entities.

I, particularly, want to emphasise two theoretical horns within the studies of antiquity. First, I shall take account of the confined nature of the available sources and discuss the impact of this situation for the scholarly conclusions drawn on the basis of the extant sources. Secondly, I shall pay particular attention to the crux of how to conceive past cultural entities. In conclusion, I hope to be able to illustrate a theoretically viable way of reconstructing ancient cultures in a manner that is simultaneously theoretically adequate to the acknowledgement of the confined nature of the sources, and to current insights within the fields of cultural anthropology and sociology of how to speak and to conceive of culture. Obviously, I realise that the Promethean ambitions of this project are neither realisable within the limits of this contribution nor – in my thinking, at least – have come to anything close to a comprehensive and systematically thoroughly reflected final result. I believe, however, that the potentials of the involved theoretical issues are so suggestive to colleagues working with comparable problems that I venture already at this stage to embark on a voyage steering between the two theoretical cliffs of, on the one hand, acknowledging the restrained character of the source situation and, on the other hand, wrestling with how to conceive of past cultural entities. In this manner, the essay is a prolegomenon to a more comprehensive future study.

I shall develop the argument by first discussing some of the involved theoretical issues that – in my view – have been reflected upon by previous scholarship to a limited extent only.[2] Secondly, I shall present a catalogue of problems extracted from previous scholarship on Alexandrian Jewry that illustrates the involved theoretical moot points.

---

2   In the last phase of writing of this contribution I became aware of the seminal essay by Bohak 2002 with whom I concurrently realised that I share not only many points of agreement but

I shall not exemplify the argument by criticising particular studies. Rather, I prefer to discuss the subject matter at a more general level. Before focusing the lens on ancient Alexandria in general and Jewish Alexandria in particular, I shall attempt to develop a notion of culture that is more adequate to human reality – past and present – than the ones traditionally used by scholarship on Alexandrian Judaism. I shall, then, go on to document the value of this notion by applying it to the history of Jewish Alexandria. Needless to say, I do not pretend to be able to give an exhaustive account of Alexandrian Jewry. That would demand – at least – another comprehensive article, if not an entire monograph, as it is dauntingly evident from some of the previous studies on Alexandrian Judaism.[3]

2. The Cusp of the Dilemma: Reconstruction on the Basis of Confined Sources

Acknowledgedly we do have a large number of remains originating from Alexandrian Jewry. And we are even in the fortuitous situation that we can benefit from numerous non-Jewish texts and archaeological remains that – dating from different periods of the first four centuries of Alexandrian history – pay important witness to the relationship(s) between Alexandrian Jewry and its surrounding Alexandrian community(ies) consisting of a wide plethora of different ethnic, cultural, and social segments.[4] So there is every reason to be appreciative to what history has left us. Focusing on Alexandrian Judaism, we are in a superior situation compared to the ones that challenge so many other scholars of antiquity examining other epochs and other locations.[5]

Before we fall prey to an overconfident historical exaltation or become the victims of scholarly enthusiasm, however, we should be aware of the fly in the ointment. The sources – textual as well as material – are in significant ways confined by their embeddedness in particular situations as well as particular cultural and social strata. They have – most obviously the written sources – been produced under very specific circumstances and are the creations of certain cultural and social contexts. The emphasis on the constraint of the sources, of course, is a triviality, but it does have some wider and

also the common aim to develop more refined cultural models for a theoretically more adequate understanding of ancient Judaism.

3   See for instance Bell 1926; Smallwood 1970; Fraser 1972; Kasher 1985; Mélèze-Modrzejewski 1995; Barclay 1996; Schäfer 1997; Gruen 2002, among whom only a few provide an exhaustive account of the entire history of past Alexandrian Jewry.

4   Cf. the discussion in Fraser 1972, vol. 1, 38-92.

5   Apart from the well-known text corpora of an Alexandrian provenance like the Septuagint, Aristeas, Philo, and possibly Demetrius the Chronographer, Artapanus, Aristobulus, *3 Maccabees*, and presumably *Liber Antiquitatum Biblicarum* and the third book of the Sibylline Oracles, a large number of papyri as well as inscriptions have been preserved from Alexandrian Jewry. See the well-known collections in Frey 1936 and 1952 (= *CIJ*); Tcherikover & Fuks 1957-64 (= *CPJ*); Horbury & Noy 1992 (= *JIGRE*). For an extensive discussion of Alexandrian Jewish literature see Fraser 1972, vol. 1, 687-716. Needless to say, the allegedly Alexandrian provenance of some of the above mentioned texts are contested by other scholars. See, for instance, Collins 1983, 355f.

important implications. Perhaps, we may develop the argument even further. Most of the texts that have been used in classical as well as contemporary scholarship to reconstruct the entity "Alexandrian Jewry" derive from the most intellectual and socially as well as culturally affluent segments of the Alexandrian Jewish population.[6] Additionally, most of these texts stem from situations that are to a very great extent polemical, not to say discursively martial or the remains of belligerent textual battle heroes.[7] Be this as it may. It is the textual basis and, thus, the scholarly presupposition for anyone interested in reconstructing Alexandrian Judaism. This condition is hardly surprising. The banalities of culture and the platitudes of human beings are seldom handed down, probably because they are conspicuously uninteresting. It takes effort to write and to produce meaning.

Since trivialities by their very nature are self-evident, it is most often the oddities, the novelties, the interferences, the discontents with the current state of the art, the attempts to change or to secure the present situation, and the discursive efforts to conquer the cultural battlefield, etc., that are codified in script.[8] Particularly so, when it comes to the aspect of texts preserved or handed down for future generations. The trifles of humanity are frequently left to oblivion, whereas the culturally "extraordinary" and the "surprising" – whatever nature it may be – is preserved for cultural storage. It is a plight intrinsic to human activity. In this manner, we are evidently epistemologically constrained by the vagaries of history and the caprices of fate. Most of what has been culturally transmitted from times past belongs to the category of the exceptional and the anomalous – that is as seen from the perspective of the past cultural context. It may appear a truism to emphasise the need to distinguish between, on the hand, past and distant cultures in their own context (that is, obviously, as we are capable of reconstructing them) and, on the other hand, the past and distant cultures as they have been transmitted to us through their history of reception. Nevertheless, it is of considerable importance to keep the difference between these two aspects in mind since the distinction between them is so often forgotten with fatal consequences for the historical reconstruction of past cultural entities on their own terms.

To make my point clear with regard to Alexandrian Jewry, let me just say that Philo, in my view, however influential his authorship has become through the later history of reception of Alexandrian Jewry, only represented a very particular cultural and social

---

6   Cf. Bohak 2002, 191: "While there is no need to downplay the Jews' unique achievement in developing a 'life-style for diaspora,' it should be noted that many ancient Jews may have been quite ignorant of the intricate blueprints developed by some of their leading intellectuals (and the almost total absence of Judaeo-Greek literature from the papyri of the Egyptian *chora* is quite instructive here)."

7   The social-political impact of Philo's exegesis has been rightly emphasised in a number of works during recent years. See for instance Dawson 1992; Borgen 1997; Niehoff 2001. One example will suffice to illustrate this point. The entire Philonic discussion on the legal status of the Alexandrian Jews should not, as has so often been done by scholarship, be taken at face value, but should rather be seen as fundamental to Philo's rhetorical attempt to change the situation. Cf. Bohak 2002, 182f.

8   For an elaboration of this argument see Petersen 2007a.

segment of past Alexandrian Judaism. Nobody, of course, would contest that Philo played an important role in Alexandrian politics in general at a particularly critical point of the history of the Jewish community and in his own Jewish community in particular,[9] but he certainly did not as is often the impression one gets from Philonic scholarship embody Alexandrian Jewry *in toto*. To speak of Alexandrian Judaism only in terms of the highly intellectual and culturally flourishing traditions handed down to the present in the extant writings of Aristeas, Artapanus, and Philo, is an exaggeration of one particular trajectory of thought, and that is even construed from the present perspective.[10] To base the reconstruction of Alexandrian Judaism on writings like these only, one will envisage a highly distorted picture of past Alexandrian Judaism. Similarly, to build the reconstruction on writings that are closely related to the climaxes of conflict between the Alexandrian Jewish community/ies and their neighbouring cultures is correspondingly to misrepresent the general situation of the Alexandrian Jewish community/ies during most of the period of its/their existence.

One may, of course, contravene that it is a futile task for the historian to defy the nature of the existing sources. He or she should acknowledge the problems, but, then, continue to work on the basis of what history has transferred to the present. That is true, of course, since the character of the sources is an inevitable condition that no mortal can transcend, but that does not exempt the historian from the need to be alert of this epistemological premise and to take account of it in one's reconstructions of distant and past cultures. The problem, however, is that very often the constrained nature of the majority of the extant sources is forgotten, or even worse, not even reflected upon when it comes to the conclusions inferred by wide strands of scholarship, current as well as classical, on Alexandrian Judaism.[11]

3. Thinking and Speaking about Culture

In addition but not entirely unrelated to the previously discussed complex of problems, there is also another bone of contention how to think and to speak about culture. To reconstruct Alexandrian Jewry does also entail the important and theoretically very complex and precarious question how to conceive of culture. Whether or not it is

---

9   For a discussion of Philo's importance in his own day see Borgen 1997 and Bilde's contribution to this volume.

10 In spite of the fact that entries or titles of chapters like *The Alexandrian Jewish Allegorical Tradition* are continuously invoked in encyclopaedias, monographs, and anthologies, that tradition is only one that has been construed on the basis of the later history of reception of various writings. Philo, for instance, does not stand in a direct, causal inter-textual tradition with his alleged "allegorical" predecessors. For this alleged tradition, see, for instance, Dyck 2002, 168, 171-4.

11 Obviously, there are exceptions like the works of Victor Tcherikover on Jewish Alexandria and its literature. It is remarkable how alert Tcherikover in his scholarship was to some of the theoretical problems discussed above. In recent scholarship one may point to Fraser 1972, Gruen, 2002, Niehoff, 2001, and Bohak 2002, who exemplify a type of scholarship that witness an outspoken awareness of the theoretical problems involved in the issues I discuss.

acknowledged by most strands of scholarship on antiquity, an important part of the historian's work entails modes of thinking about culture.[12] Indeed, it is impossible to examine historical entities without a notion as well as a presupposed model of culture. Most frequently, however, scholars do neither discuss nor account for the cultural models they – simply by the fact that they write about cultural entities – take for granted in their studies. For two reasons I consider that to be a problem.

To counter scholarly prejudices and to prevent research from falling prey to thinking in grooves, it is of vital importance to be able to account for the theoretical perspectives involved. For this reason alone, it is crucial to scrutinise the extent to which perceptions and theoretical models of earlier scholarship have set the agenda for contemporary discussion.[13]

Secondly, this effort is all the more important since research on how to think and to speak about culture has developed considerably during recent years (see below). Within the fields studying antiquity, however, the new insights promulgated by the neighbouring disciplines of humanities and social sciences so far have been acknowledged to a limited extent only. The practitioners of the disciplines of antiquity have, to a very great extent, continued to embody notions of culture that on numerous points and on different theoretical levels are moot, not to say seriously flawed by insights of recent scholarship, especially within the disciplines of cultural anthropology and sociology: those fields that are particularly engaged with the study of culture in its manifold form and with the development of refined models for thinking about culture.[14]

4. Catalogue of Problems

If one peruses the scholarly literature on the history of Alexandrian Judaism, it is conspicuous how a few events and a small number of persons have – in the dominant and most prevailing currents of scholarship – been aggrandised to embrace almost the entire history of Alexandrian Jewry. A celestial as well as a tragic series of highlights and downfalls can easily be lined up: the formation of the Septuagint,[15] Aristeas, Aristo-

---

12 For an initial discussion of this subject matter see Petersen, 2002, 51-75, as well as 2003a, 147-64.
13 For an illustration of the importance of this point see Petersen 2004.
14 Among recent works, see, for instance, Swidler 2001; Stolcke 1995; van Beek 2000; 2002; Sewell 1999. In compliance with Swidler I use in this essay the following definition of culture that is based on Hannerz 1969, 184: "that there are social processes of sharing modes of behaviour and outlook within [a] community." Similar with Swidler I also want to underline the Geertzian impact of particular symbolic vehicles (rituals, stories, sayings) in creating and sustaining those modes of behaviour and outlook. Cf. the now classic definition of culture by Geertz 1973, 89, that culture is: "an historically transmitted pattern of meanings embodied in symbols, a system of inherited conceptions expressed in symbolic forms by means of which men communicate, perpetuate, and develop their knowledge about and attitudes toward life."
15 Speaking of the formation of the *LXX* leaves the impression that it was composed at a particular date as one homogeneous body of writings. That is, certainly, not the case as it has been redundantly as well as persuasively emphasised in numerous recent studies. See, for instance, Marcos

bulus, Artapanus, Philo, the Alexandrian "Pogrom" of 38 and its aftermath during the three successive years, the dark chapters subsequent to the Jewish uprising in Palestine in 66 and its repercussions for Alexandrian Jewry, and, finally, the catastrophe of 115-17 from whence Alexandrian Jewry never regained its former high cultural stance and social influence.[16]

In spite of the fact that many scholars – particularly more recent ones – in their introductions to the subject matter emphasise the limited nature of the sources, that limitation often seems to be forgotten as the argument develops. Although it is sometimes poignantly stressed at the beginning of a particular study that the Alexandrian Jewish author in question represents only one particular voice in the chorus of Alexandrian Jews, that acknowledgement is frequently deafened by the triumphant concluding voice that exalts the singular to the status of the general. In this manner, Philo, for instance, is turned into the embodiment of Jewish Alexandrian culture in general. An observation by Victor Tcherikover in his seminal essay on Jewish apologetics makes the point that:

> The aim of the historical approach is to understand Alexandrian literature as a mirror reflecting various opinions within Jewish Alexandrian society, opinions which, in their turn, were influenced by continuously changing political, economic, and social factors. This approach brings movement and development into the somewhat static picture created by the theological scholars.

If one accepts this approach, it is essential to treat with care the implications inferred from such sources. One should as a matter of course turn neither a particular text nor a corpus of texts or a single author into representatives of Alexandrian Jewry in general, but see them as, in fact, particular voices attempting to conquer the discursive battlefield of their respective cultural and social contexts. It is, of course, a truism to claim that texts are composed in particular situations and accordingly – in so far as the aim of the interpretation is of a historical nature – should be interpreted in light of their historical context, that is as it can be construed from the modern point of view. In spite of the trivial nature of this insight, I do not think that we can overestimate its importance. In fact, I believe, that we should push Tcherikover's point even further by arguing that particular writings are not even the creations of homogeneous but composite composers.

What Tcherikover says about particular texts should be extended to apply for particular authors also. Just as an individual text cannot be taken as indicative of an entire culture, nor can a specific author be attributed the status of incarnating a culture in

---

2002; Fabry & Offenhaus 2001; Kreuzer and Lesch 2004; and, particularly, Dines 2004.

16 Evidence exists that a Jewish community of Alexandria re-emerged as a political and religious factor in conflicts with Christianity during the late second and third century, see Smallwood 1976, 516-9. It is beyond the scope of this essay, however, to investigate that period. Since Alexandrian Jewry – to judge from the extant sources – was virtually extinguished at least as a cultural and political factor subsequent to the uprising of 115-7, I shall use that date as a fix point at the one end of the scale for my analysis.

its entirety.[17] It is misleading as it has been pointed out by Verena Stolcke to conceive of persons as "cultural containers" or "carriers" of cultural packages that they share with other members of their culture. Stolcke has designated this hermeneutical manoeuvre *cultural fundamentalism*.[18] A culture that has never existed in reality is by means of an "ontological dumping" turned into reality.[19] Although individuals as "cultural containers" are mutually different they are nevertheless conceived of as identical with regard to particular aspects or central elements. Thus, a group of persons sharing a common cultural background is construed to partake in a common identity. Philo, for instance, is held to embody Judaism *in toto* and, correspondingly, an Alexandrian Greek is thought to incarnate Greekness in its entirety. Similarly, one can think of the examples of Dositheus, the son of Drimylus, the Jewish grand registrar from the last part of the third century BCE who "altered his customs and was alienated from his ancestral beliefs" (μεταβαλὼν τὰ νόμιμα καὶ τῶν πατρίων δογμάτων ἀπηλλοτριωμένος, 3 *Macc.* 1:3), and the nephew of Philo, Tiberius Julius Alexander of the first century CE "who did not remain by his ancestral customs" (τοῖς γὰρ πατρίοις οὐκ ἐνέμεινεν οὗτος ἔθεσιν, Josephus, *AJ* 20.100). In the scholarly literature these two persons are frequently conceived of as the exceptional cultural examples of renegades and apostates to a Jewish faith that by and large succeeded in maintaining its adherents within its fold.[20] But how do we, in fact, know that the diaspora Judaism of Alexandria was such a homogeneous and continuous entity that Dositheus and Tiberius Alexander should be attributed the status of cultural exceptions? Can we also be certain that they did not themselves continue to think of themselves in terms of Judaism? Should we, in fact, take the viewpoint of their adversaries at face value by understanding them as the prototypes of apostasy and the exemplar of renegades par excellence? Attributing to them the status of the culturally exceptional is to a great extent to take their critics at face value and turn their emotionally determined evaluations of them into social reality.[21] By raising these questions my point is not – like much contemporary scholarship within the field of the cognitive sciences – to deny the existence of culture nor to diminish the impact of the cultural level on human action and thinking.[22] On the contrary, but I do want to emphasise some problems that pertain to the traditional way of thinking of culture within the fields of antiquity.

---

17 The substantial part of the argument of this section is also found in Petersen 2003a, 158-60.

18 Stolcke 1995.

19 For the concept of "ontological dumping" to designate the processes by which epistemological relationships are transformed into ontological entities, thus – misunderstandingly – attributing to them the status of empirical entities see Hastrup 2004, 258-61. For the application of this insight to the field of the study of religion see Petersen 2003b.

20 See for instance Fraser 1972 vol. 1, 285; Mélèze-Modrzejewski 1993, 83-5; 1995, 56, 190. Cf. also Tcherikover 1958, 81. See further Barclay 1996, 32, 104-6.

21 Cf. Bohak 2002, 183: "They (*sc.* Dositheus and Tiberius Alexander) are seen as 'upperclass assimilationists,' the precursors of those mediaeval or modern Jews who, for the sake of a secure position in the Church or state, abandoned their Jewish brethren and the Jewish religious identity."

22 See for instance Boyer 2001, 34-36, 152f. and Attran 2002, 234f.

The customary way of interpretation implies a meeting of cultures or religions that are essentially and from their very basis separate and fundamentally different, but internally homogeneous entities. I believe that such a static model gives a distorted picture of the cultural and social reality of human beings, past and present. Culture – and religion as well as part of the cultural construction – should rather be seen as ways of interpreting the world.[23] Culture represents what one does and not what one is.[24] Martijn van Beek has poignantly emphasised this point. He underlines to what a great extent the talk about cultures is itself part of the cultural construction: "The point is not to deny that common features exist in particular fields but to document that the extrapolation from specific similarities and differences to homogenised, cultural and even civilising units is a creative process and not just a mapping of already existing facts."[25] The impact of this argument should be obvious when one thinks not only of, for instance, Philonic scholarship but also on the manner by which the relationships between the different cultural and social entities of ancient Alexandria have been conceived of. I find it rather problematic to note that in prevalent strands of current scholarship on Alexandrian Jewry, it is more or less taken for granted that the entity was from its beginning to its disappearance during the second century CE a consistently static and uniform entity that in so far as it did undergo changes they were due to pressures from the outside world.[26] Is it entirely unthinkable that the alterations Alexandrian Judaism underwent throughout its period of existence mirrored a dialectical process by which it not only changed due to external events but also due to its own creative engagement in the cultural and social processes of the time? To recall an important question raised by Homi Bhabba about the intrinsic tendency in scholarship either to think of different empirical subject matters in terms of dualities, or to place on them a totalising utopian vision of being and history that seeks to transcend the contradictions and ambivalences that constitute the very structure of human subjectivity and its systems of cultural representations.[27]

The aptness of this observation with regard to Alexandrian Jewry is obvious, since a Hellenism–Judaism dichotomy lurks behind so much traditional scholarship on Alexandrian Judaism. On the one hand, different Jewish voices of Alexandria are emphasised as Jewish, that is in contradiction to the neighbouring culturally and socially "ethnic" voices like Greeks, Romans, and Egyptians. On the other hand, the very same Jewish voices are conceived of in terms of an allegedly Hellenistic tone that is derived from an implicit opposition to a normatively perceived Jewish identity corresponding with

---

23 For an extensive discussion along these lines of thought, see Goodman 1978

24 Van Beek 2002, 4.

25 Van Beek 2002, 5f. [my translation]. Cf. the similar point made by Anderson 1996, 163-85.

26 Cf. Bohak 2002, 191: "What I can say, however, with at least some degree of confidence, is that the implicit assumption that the communities of the Jewish diaspora thrived from one generation to the next, always there and always Jewish, flies in the face of what we know about the fate of immigrants of the ancient world — and some of the Jewish evidence as well."

27 Cf. the preamble text of this essay.

a spectre of Judaisms found in the Palestinian geographical area. Philonic scholarship, again, is an illustrious example.

Although scholarly suggestive and on numerous points epoch-making, I find the overall framework of David Dawson's interpretation of Philo problematic by the manner in which Philo is turned into a meta-cultural juggler of Judaism and Hellenism. Summarising a main point in the argument, Dawson claims that: "when the connection between literary revision and social practice is kept in view, it becomes unmistakably clear that for Philo allegorical interpretation is an effort to make Greek culture Jewish rather than to dissolve Jewish identity into Greek culture."[28] Is it really likely that Philo had such a meta-cultural awareness at his disposal that would enable him to do as he liked with the cultural balls he was juggling with?[29] Or should we, rather, see Dawson's description as a reflection of the view modern scholars take of the different traditions that were present during the early Roman era? Only a few scholars would contest the Jewishness of Philo, but the majority is nevertheless keen also to emphasise the Hellenistic nature of his world-view and thinking. Such a categorisation, however, by which Philo's Jewishness to some extent falls short by its enmeshment in a Hellenistic mode of thinking, is meaningful only from the perspective of a preconceived dualism of Hellenism and Judaism.[30] This dualism, however, is theoretically flawed for a number of reasons.

I have already pointed to the problem of misidentifying individual authors with "cultural containers" or aggrandising them to the level of representatives of entire cultures. Additionally, I think that the use of a dualism like the Hellenism–Judaism dichotomy in understanding cultural entities is problematic by the essentialism endorsed by the model.[31] Cultures are by their very nature "messy" or hybrid affairs, which makes it difficult to use notions and concepts like assimilation, diffusion, acculturation, reception, etc. because they – on the basis of the entailed semantics – presuppose the idea of cultural purity or essence. My point is not to deny that such cultural processes exist, but I want to underscore their moot character if they are conceived of in terms of a preconceived idea of cultural purity. At an *etic* level it makes sense to distinguish between Judaism

---

28 Dawson 1992, 74.

29 Cf. the objections to Dawson's interpretation raised by Dyck 2002.

30 Cf. the instructive criticism by Niehoff 2001, 11f: "My emphasis on Philo's individual construction of Jewish Identity and culture furthermore removes the present study from numerous other investigations into his Jewishness. The latter have characteristically taken external criteria as their point of departure. The Hebrew Bible and rabbinic literature served in this context as decisive points of reference. If and to the extent that Philo's views could be interpreted as conforming to these corpuses of Classical Jewish literature, they were identified as proper Jewish concepts. In cases, however, where a departure from them was recognized, the verdict was clear: Philo succumbed to foreign influence. The paramount foreign influence which has been detected in Philo's work is that of Greek culture. Assuming a diametrical and intrinsic opposition between Judaism and Hellenism, modern scholarship from the late 18th century onwards has regularly conceived of Greek culture as an inevitable threat to Philo's Jewishness."

31 Cf. the similar critique in Campany 2003, 288ff.

and Hellenism as conceptual abstractions useful in the taxonomic processing of data. At an *emic* level it also makes sense to the extent that many writings themselves presuppose this distinction, but it is urgent to keep Bateson's point in mind that map is not territory.[32] It is of considerable importance as it has also been sagaciously pointed out by Judith Lieu to distinguish between social and imagined reality.[33] Textual rhetorics should not be taken at face value. They are not a 1:1 reproduction of social reality, but a telic, goal-oriented endeavour. Thus, textual rhetorics attempt to create a reality that has not yet come into existence by aiming at transforming imagined reality into social reality. A number of points underscore the importance of this distinction with regard to the Hellenism—Judaism dichotomy.

First, even the most vehement Jewish antagonist of Greek thinking is culturally as well as socially inevitably enmeshed in what he opposes – just like the most radical Muslim fundamentalists today seems to be rather fond of CocaCola and Western tele- and weapon technology in spite of their stated *totaliter et aliter* war against the West.[34] Secondly, the use of a notion like "Hellenism" is always contextually bound. It relates to particular traits only within the other culture. It is never a comprehensive term that refers to the entire plethora of phenomena of the "other" culture. "Jerusalem" and "Athens" are unfailingly entities that are rhetorically used in particular contexts to refer to specific phenomena. Thirdly, the abstract taxonomic play with terms like Judaism and Hellenism in modern scholarly discourse is very far from their use in antiquity. That, of course, does not invalidate contemporary use, but it certainly should put some restraints on the manner in which they are used.[35] Erich Gruen has succinctly expressed the problems that linger in the inveterate use of the dichotomy in scholarship on antiquity:

---

32 Although originally coined by Korzybski and used by Gregory Bateson within the field of the study of religion this idea has become famous through the now classic essay by Jonathan Z. Smith 1978.

33 For the importance of this distinction in scholarship on antiquity see Lieu 1996.

34 Cf. the acute observation in Bohak 2002, 184: "No reader of the extensive literature of the Second Temple period can fail to note the repeated stress on observing God's commandments and marrying within the fold even in the most adverse conditions, and the recurrent emphasis on one's ability to remain fully Jewish even in distant Gentile lands. And yet, while this ideological structure definitely is impressive, we often cannot tell how widespread it actually was, and how effective in reversing the normal forces of diasporic decay and assimilation into one's host society. On a general level, it might even be claimed that some aspects of this ideology – for example the adoption of Greek and the total neglect of Hebrew and Aramaic – actually made the Jews more vulnerable to Helleniation and assimilation than some of the Phoenician fellow-immigrants, whose inscriptions reveal a much greater adherence to their ancestral language." For a different evaluation see Honigman 1993, 126, who on the basis of anthroponymy argues that: "the study of proper names reveals through the documentary sources of the *chora*... that this vitality and self-awareness (*sc.* the diaspora mentality) were not restricted to an intellectual elite, nor were they limited to Alexandria."

35 See the wide spectrum of views – united in an effort to move beyond the Hellenism-Judaism divide – on this subject matter in Engberg-Pedersen 2001. See further Petersen 2002.

"Judaism" and "Hellenism" were neither competing systems nor incompatible concepts. It would be erroneous to assume that Hellenization entailed encroachment upon Jewish traditions and erosion to Jewish beliefs. Jews did not face a choice of either assimilation or resistance to Greek culture. A different premise serves as starting point here. We avoid the notion of a zero-sum contest in which every gain for Hellenism was a loss for Judaism or vice-versa. The prevailing culture of the Mediterranean could hardly be ignored or dismissed. But adaptation to it need not require compromise of Jewish precepts or practices.[36]

Before leaving these reflections on how to think and to speak of culture, there is one other point – not entirely unrelated to the previous discussion – that I want to emphasise. In spite of the fact that many scholars underline the versatility of and difference between the individual writings of a particular author, they nevertheless tend to presuppose that a single text can be held to represent the author as a whole at the moment he wrote any particular text. That is a moot point, however, which is in many ways comparable to the discussion of cultural entities. Here I shall not venture to open the discussion of the possibility of inferring from a particular text the historical author responsible for its composition. Even if we acknowledge that there is no access to the author behind the text, and that the only authorial instance to which we have access is the one that appears through the text, the problem remains. Writings are neither the Olympic remains of an omniscient instance, nor are they the compositions of homogeneous beings whose thinking and acting necessarily mirror a consistent and uniform response to the world. Rather, texts are particular impacts created by composite individuals who act under specific circumstances with particular situations in mind. What one says in one particular context related to a particular sphere of life is not necessarily what one would say or how one would act in another cultural domain.

Ann Swidler, in a succinct theoretical study on how to speak and think about culture, continuously emphasised that people always act and think according to the particular situations in which they are momentarily situated. Correspondingly, they can simultaneously use sometimes mutually contradictory arguments and understandings. It does not, as most scholarly literature on the subject seems to presuppose, constitute a problem for them. Their ability simultaneously to vacillate between different schemes with mutually different cultural understandings is neither extraordinary nor unusual. Rather, it is typically human. I believe that the study of antiquity should pay attention to the findings of Swidler:

> In the interviews we have examined so far, persons show great complexity in the ways they mobilize culture for practical use. They do not simply express perspectives or values instilled in them by their culture. Instead, they draw from a multiform repertoire of meanings to frame and reframe experience in an open-ended way. In debate, they may be unselective, taking up any arguments

---

36 Gruen 1998, IVX. See also the extensive elaboration of this and parallel points in Petersen 2002.

that seem handy. In other situations, they take up one cultural frame (usually corresponding to an imagined case or situation) until they run up against an unsolvable problem. Undaunted, they usually simply escape the conundrum by jumping outside its boundaries, invoking another situation, another metaphor, another symbolic frame. This frequent shifting among multiple cultural realities is not some anomalous sleight of the hand but the normal way in which ordinary mortals (as distinguished, perhaps, from trained philosophers) operate. People know much more culture than they draw on in any one instance... and they slip frequently between one reality and another, switching the frames within which they understand experience. Geertz has written ... of culture as the defense against meaninglessness, making potentially incoherent experience cohere. Less attention has been paid to the capacity of culture for creating multiple possible meanings, for teaching the imaginative capacity to provide alternative, sometimes competing frames for experience.[37]

The strength of this argument can be demonstrated: Philo the philosopher, for instance, is not necessarily the same as Philo the politician, and even within one particular piece of writing Philo may subscribe to different understandings of reality.[38]

Of course, Swidler's argument is not complete. First, texts and living persons are separate. Texts as mediate responses to the world are often more thought out than the spontaneity of spoken language. Texts, or even passages within a text, are composed in relation to particular "cultural compartments" that may mutually differ from each other in their representation of reality. Thus, we find that texts are produced with the same mix of aims and situations that characterises contemporary debate.

Secondly, it can be objected that a scale exists by which different texts can be graded according to the degree to which they may be constrained by particular cultural and social contexts. Texts differ according to genre and to the extent they reflect responses to particular social and cultural situations. Therefore we customarily distinguish between occasional publications and tractates. It is not particularly difficult to see that Zola's famous *J'accuse* is "more" enmeshed in contextually more constrained social circumstances than is, say, Kant's *Kritik der reinen Vernunft*. On the other hand, it would be foolish to ignore the constraints of time and context even with regard to a philosophical tractate by Kant.

Thirdly, some social historians and historians of intellectual history will object that in speaking about composite individuals, I am projecting an anachronistic concept of personhood back into antiquity. Granted that, we should not speak about individual-

---

37 Swidler 2001, 40. For a discussion of this point with regard to religion, past as well as present, see Petersen 2005.

38 See for instance the passage in *De migratione Abrahami* 89-93. Here Philo opposes the more radical understanding of the allegedly "radical allegorisers". The passage, however, also documents how Philo himself is fluctuating between different understandings of Scripture with correspondingly different understandings of reality, see Petersen 2007b as well as Dyck 2002, 169f.

ity and personhood in a modern sense when we are concerned with antiquity, but we do have the right to analyse persons in antiquity. Additionally, persons in antiquity do not differ from contemporary persons in being composite human beings. With these reservations and reflections in mind, Swidler's point that people can simultaneously act and think in contradictory ways is a proper understanding of the reality of life, present and past, that we need to remember as we progress along our journey into Alexandrian antiquity by raising the question, in what manner can we, in fact, speak of Alexandrian Jewry?

5. Alexandrian Jewry: Historical Reality or Scholarly Phantom?

In the light of these considerations one may, perhaps, be tempted to ask why speak at all monolithically of Alexandrian Jewry/Judaism rather than Alexandrian Judaisms or Jewries as current scholarly jargon would have it?[39] The introduction of the plural has heuristic value, but it is to some extent misleading since it stems from a failing philo-sophical ability to distinguish between a concept and a phenomenon. It is evident that when we speak of early Christianity and ancient Judaism as phenomena they exist in plural forms only. There were many early Christianities just as there were numerous ancient Judaisms – the early Christianities, in fact, being a subclass of ancient Judaism. Nevertheless, the use of terms morphologically characterised by an "ism" never refer to concrete phenomena but are abstract concepts by which social phenomena can be classified. If that is acknowledged, there is no problem in speaking singularly about Al-exandrian Jewry or Judaism, since it is obvious that the concept comprises a plethora of different phenomena. That, however, raises the question of the meaning of the concept of Alexandrian Judaism. Did such a phenomenon ever exist? Or does it have reality within the mind of modern scholarship only?

The question is not as straightforward as it may appear at first glance. On the one hand, it could be argued that Alexandrian Judaism does exist as a modern scholarly phenomenon only. No Jewish citizen of Alexandria would have thought of him- or herself as belonging to the entity of Alexandrian Judaism in the sense promulgated by modern scholarship. On the other hand, it would be wrong to argue that this entity did not exist in antiquity since the concept does, in fact, have a fair *emic* resonance in the primary sources. Once again, therefore, we find ourselves confronted with the challenge of simultaneously operating at different analytical levels as well as different degrees of what Benedict Anderson described as "imagined community." Since Alexandrian Jewry was hardly a community characterised by "the primordial village of face-to-face contact," it does qualify as an imagined community in Anderson's sense in so far as its members constituted a conscious community only because they shared the common frame of reference of being Jews of Alexandria.

---

39 Jacob Neusner has through several writings succeeded in spreading the use of the plural *Judaisms* rather than the singular *Judaism*. See, for instance, Neusner 1987; Segal 1987 and Murphy 1991, 39.

In describing imagined communities with regard to the modern entity of the nation, Anderson enumerates a number of important characteristics that we should pay close attention to when we come to antiquity.[40] First, a community is *imagined* by the fact that "the members of even the smallest nation will never know most of their fellow-members, meet them, or even hear of them, yet in the mind of each lives the image of their communion." Secondly, a community "is imagined as *limited* because even the largest of them, encompassing perhaps a billion living human beings, has finite, if elastic, boundaries, beyond which lie other nations." Thirdly, "it is imagined as a *community*, because, regardless of the actual inequality and exploitation that may prevail in each, the nation is always conceived as a deep, horizontal comradeship. Ultimately it is this fraternity that makes it possible, over the past two centuries, for so many millions of people, not so much to kill, as willingly to die for such limited imaginings."

Whereas the applicability of the first two points to the case of Alexandrian Judaism appears obvious, the relevance of the third point may seem irrelevant to a discussion of Alexandrian Jewry. I believe, however, that it also has an important bearing for the study of Alexandrian Judaism. How should we, for instance, understand Philo's attempts to persuade his countrymen to pay earnest adherence to the common religious as well as cultural and social legacy of the Jewish law? Correspondingly, how should we conceive of *3 Macc.'s* appeals to the importance of the martyrs' willingness to die for the ancestral law – so beautifully expressed in Eleazar's prayer (*3 Macc.* 6.1-15) – were it not for that particular aspect of comradeship in community that Anderson picks out?

We can apply Anderson's concept of community to Alexandria where communities, "are to be distinguished, not by their falsity/genuineness, but by the style in which they are imagined." So, we are left with the arduous question: How should we think of Alexandrian Judaism and conceive of the different analytical levels at which the notion makes sense?

The concept of Alexandrian Judaism does have a bearing on an *etic* as well as an *emic* level. On an *etic* level, it is important to realise that the manner in which contemporary scholarship evokes the notion of Alexandrian Judaism as comprising an entity more or less originating with Alexander's founding of the city and stretching to the virtual annihilation of the Alexandrian Jewish society in the aftermath of 115-17,[41] is something entirely different from the manner in which an Alexandrian Jew of antiquity imagined his or her Jewish community. In current use, the notion designates an abstraction referring to the entire history of Alexandrian Judaism embracing a temporal spectre of almost 450 years, a plethora of different cultural phenomena, and a considerable breadth of different Jewish social segments. Needless to say, no Alexandrian Jew of

---

40 Anderson 1996, 6f. Although Anderson explicitly speaks of nations as imagined communities, I have taken the freedom to apply the notion to a past cultural entity Alexandrian Jewry, whereby I most certainly do not imply that this entity can be conceived in terms of the modern concept of nation. For this reason I have left out of the enumeration those characteristics in Anderson's description that exclusively apply to the modern concept of nation.

41 Cf. Borgen 1992, 1069; Pearson 1992, 153.

antiquity did have such a meta-cultural awareness at his or her disposal. The primary sources, however, do pay witness to a sense of belongingness to the community of Alexandrian Judaism.

6. The *Politeuma* of Alexandrian Judaism

In a severely damaged papyrus from about 5 BCE (*CPJ* II 151) a Jewish petitioner, Helenus, pleads the help of the Roman prefect Gaius Turranius because of a wrong against him by a certain Horus, the public administrator.[42] Helenus presents himself as the son of Trypho, an Alexandrian (Ἀλεξανδρεύς). Although this designation by a later scribe has been crossed out and replaced with the more specific designation "a Jew from Alexandria" (Ἰουδαίου τῶν ἀπὸ Ἀλεξανδρείας), it does tell us that a Jew at the beginning of our era not only understood himself as an Alexandrian, but also expected the Roman authorities to recognise him as such. We do not see in this papyrus an Alexandrian Jew reflecting an awareness of belonging to an imagined community of Alexandrian Judaism. Rather, we see a Jew who thinks of himself in terms of Alexandrian citizenship, whatever that meant at this particular period.[43]

In five[44] inscriptions found at the necropolis of El-Ibrahimiya – situated at the North-Eastern part of Alexandria adjacent to one of the two allegedly Jewish quarters of the city[45] – and originating in the early Ptolemaic period, we find evidence that not only did Jews express themselves in Aramaic and Greek (cf. *JIGRE* nos. 15 and 17), but they were also, although distinctly separated, buried together with other ethnic groups. From an early period on we have inscriptional evidence that testifies to the truth of later sources like Philo claiming that in Alexandria there were many Jewish "houses of worship" (τὰς προσευχάς) in each section of the city.[46] *JIGRE* no. 13, for instance, is an honorific inscription originating from the late Ptolemaic period and found at Gabbary, a Ptolemaic and Roman cemetery site in the South-Western part of the city neighbour-

---

42 For the discussion of the papyrus see *CPJ* II 29-33; Kasher 1985, 200-7; Mélèze-Modrzejewski 1995, Barclay 1996, 50; Schäfer 1997, 155; Gruen 2002, 74.286f.

43 The problem of what Jewish citizenship of Alexandria meant at different periods throughout the history of Alexandrian Judaism probably belongs to the most contested and perplexing question in scholarship on Alexandrian Jewry. There is hardly a monograph or an article published on the subject of Alexandrian Judaism that does not wrestle with this Gordian question. In my view, the most persuasive description, in so far as it is possible to provide a fairly accurate account of the legal status enjoyed by Alexandrian Jews during the period, is found in Gruen 2002, 73-8. Cf. the extensive discussion in Smallwood 1976, and Kasher 1985.

44 *JIGRE* nos. 3-8. It may be doubted whether no. 8 (Ψύλλας) is of a Jewish provenance or not, since the only argument for this interpretation is its finding place in the proximity of definitely Jewish burials.

45 Not to be mistaken with the so-called Delta-quarter D, see below.

46 *Leg* 132; 134. See also *Flacc* 41; 45; 53; Josephus *AJ* 13.65f. See Levine 2000, 84-9, and for the whole discussion of the meaning of *proseuchē*, Runesson 2001, 437-59.

ing the Delta-quarter.[47] It states that "Alypus on behalf of the queen and the king made the *proseuchē* for the great God who listens to prayer, in the 15th year, Mecheir…" Apparently, Alypus did not have any trouble with the fact of being both Jew and a loyal subject to the Ptolemaic kingdom. Correspondingly, we find evidence in other dedicatory inscriptions of Jewish prayer houses that were made in the name of an entire Jewish community, although not from Alexandria but from nearby Schedia,[48] that Jews – or at least some – did not altogether think it a problem to be both Jews and citizens of the Ptolemaic kingdom. In fact, this perception is not at all likely to have occurred to the people responsible for the inscriptions.[49] On the basis of the inscriptional data we do not find an awareness of being Jewish that implies a correspondingly negative sense of being non-Ptolemaic or non-Alexandrian. On the contrary, the extant inscriptional data underline that the fact of being simultaneously Jewish and Ptolemaic was a natural condition that was neither questioned nor turned into a problem.[50]

At this point, we need to raise the complementary question of the judicial nature of past Alexandrian Jewry at its different historical stages. At the outset, however, it should be acknowledged that when it comes to the understanding of the legal status of Jews during the Ptolemaic period we have no contemporary statement of principle pertaining to their judicial position.[51] In so far as we can reconstruct an approximate account of their legal status in the late Ptolemaic period, it is built on conjectures primarily made on the basis of sources stemming from the Roman period. Two exceptions, however, do exist: *3 Macc.* and the *Letter to Aristeas*. On the basis of *3 Macc.* and other later writings, it is evident that the Greek citizens of Alexandria enjoyed a judicially better status than Jews (*3 Macc.* 2.30; 3.21). They were regular citizens of Alexandria. We can also surmise from the sources that Jews were, in fact, reckoned as citizens of a fairly high position, otherwise it would be hard to understand the seriousness of the threat posed by king Ptolemy in *3 Macc.* 2:28 that all the Jews should be required to register (εἰς λαογραφίαν) and be reduced to the status of slaves if they did not participate in the sacrifices of the state cult. In the *Letter to Aristeas* – the dating of which, however, is very uncertain but presumably from sometime during the first century BCE[52] – it is claimed that upon the completion of the Greek translation of the Hebrew Bible that: "As the books were read, the priests stood up together with the elders from among the translators (οἱ πρεσβύτεροι τῶν ἑρμηνεύων) and of those from the community (καὶ τῶν ἀπὸ τοῦ πολιτεύματος) that is the leaders of the people (οἵ τε ἡγούμενοι τοῦ πλήθους οἵ τε

---

47 See Fraser 1972, vol. 1, 27 as well as note 186, 34 with notes 259f.

48 *JIGRE* nos. 22 and 25.

49 For an understanding of the dedicatory inscriptions and their close parallelism with pagan comparanda see Fraser 1972, vol. 1, 282-4.

50 Cf. Fraser 1972, vol. 1, 286.

51 Tcherikover 1959, 320-8; Fraser 1972, vol. 1, 54.

52 See Fraser 1972, vol. 2, 970-2; and Gruen 1998, 210f.

ἡγούμενοι τοῦ πλήθους)" (310).[53] It is a moot point what is meant by πολίτευμα.[54] Be that as it may. Whatever the exact meaning of the term is, we can infer with some confidence that Alexandrian Jews during the last part of the Ptolemaic period enjoyed a certain degree of political freedom as well as distinct religious autonomy.

Were this not so, later sources from the Roman period that ascribe a certain sense of political autonomy to the Jewish community of Alexandria along with religious rights to abide by their ancestral customs, would be hard to explain. There is no reason for Augustus to suddenly bestow the Jewish community of Alexandria with the judicial status of semi-political autonomy, had the community not already enjoyed this privilege during the late Ptolemaic period. However, in projecting the legal status of the Jewish community of Alexandria – enjoyed during the first part of the Roman era – back to the late Ptolemaic period, I do not mean to say that Jews – in compliance with Josephus' account[55] – had been granted this civic status by Alexander the Great at the foundation of the city.

The geographer Strabo – a contemporary of Josephus – is quoted by him as saying that the Jews had a particular as well as a great part of Alexandria allotted to them. They had their own *ethnarch* to govern them, to decide disputes between them, and to supervise contracts and ordinances. In exercising this administrative and judicial power the ethnarch was like "the head of an independent city" (ὡς ἂν πολιτείας ἄρχων αὐτοτελοῦς) (*AJ* 14.117).[56] Similarly, Philo speaks of the Jewish *gerousia* which may

---

53   The syntax of this sentence is not entirely evident due to the uncertainties of the precise relationship between οἱ πρεσβύτεροι and οἵ τε ἡγούμενοι τὸ καὶ τῶν ἀπὸ τοῦ πολιτεύματος, and the relationship between τῶν ἀπὸ τοῦ πολιτεύματος and οἵ τε ἡγούμενοι τοῦ πλήθους. I am inclined with Fraser 1972, vol. 2, 139, to make οἱ πρεσβύτεροι govern τῶν ἑρμηνεύων only, and to understand the οἵ τε ἡγούμενοι τοῦ πλήθους as an epexegetical construction that further explains the τῶν ἀπὸ τοῦ πολιτεύματος.

54   See the discussion in Gruen 2002, 74f.

55   According to Josephus – creating an honourable ancient pedigree for Alexandrian Jewry – it was Alexander the Great himself who in return for the valour and faithfulness of the Jews (*Ap.* 2.42) settled them in Alexandria in their own quarter and gave them equal civic rights with the Macedonians (*Ap.* 2.35 ἴσης παρὰ τοῖς Μακεδόσι τιμῆς ἐπέτυχον). In *BJ* 2.487 it is also said that Alexander due to the support of the Jews against the Egyptians as a reward for their assistance granted them equal rights (ἐξ ἰσομοιρίας/ἰσοτιμίας) to stay in the city with the Greeks. In this passage, however, the assignment of a particular quarter of the city to the Jews is attributed to the Ptolemies and not Alexander himself. In *AJ* 12.8, however, the establishment of Alexandrian Jews as citizens on equal terms with the Macedonians (ἰσοπολῖται) is altogether attributed to Ptolemy I Soter. Finally, the account given in *AJ* 19.281 of Claudius' edict entails that the Jews from the very earliest times were fellow-colonisers with the Alexandrians and had been granted equal civic rights (ἴσης πολιτείας τετευχότας) by the Ptolemaic kings. The divergent versions found in different works by Josephus clearly document his interest in creating a true mythic past for Alexandrian Jewry.

56   In *Flacc.* 74 Philo speaks of a genarch, but that title is most likely synonymous with the ethnarch mentioned by Strabo *apud* Josephus. See also *Corpus papyrorum Judaicarum* 2.143 that speaks of a specific notarial office of the Jews (τὸ Ἰουδαϊκὸν ἀρχεῖον) and Josephus, *AJ* 19.283.

already have existed in the Ptolemaic period, but certainly from the time of Augustus' late principate it became the prime organ for exercising administrative and judicial power over the Alexandrian Jews.[57] Thus, Jews not only enjoyed great religious freedom but apparently had also been granted particular political rights although not amounting to full and independent political autonomy.[58] It is not entirely unthinkable that it is the ambivalent nature of this status that Josephus has in mind when he uses the term of "the same citizenship" and the "same fate" as the Macedonians (*AJ* 19.281 ἴση πολιτεία, and *BJ* 2.487 ἐξ ἰσομοιρίας).[59] We can probably not come closer to a fair description of the political situation of the Jews of Alexandria by the beginning of the first century CE than the concise statement formulated by Erich Gruen:

> The Jews plainly had some institutional organization of their own, a political structure and not simply a religious one, with a chief official who held sway—but a structure whose status was something less than full autonomy. This evidently means that Jews governed their internal affairs but were also part of a larger Alexandrian entity to which they owed allegiance.[60]

From the famous letter of the emperor Claudius from 41 to the city of Alexandria (*CPJ* II no. 153) – attempting once and for all to settle the disputes between the different ethnic groups of the Alexandrian populace – it also appears that the Alexandrian Jews, "should enjoy what is their own and – albeit in a foreign city (ἐν ἀλλοτρία πόλει) – possess an abundance of benefits (περιουσίας ἀπθόνων ἀγαθῶν)" (Col. V 94f.). It is conspicuous that the Jews after more than probably 350 years of residency in Alexandria were seen by the emperor as foreign inhabitants, but it is also clear that they were acknowledged as having rights too. And whatever the precise nature of the changes that occurred following the death of the Jewish *ethnarch* in the latter part of Augustus' principate (*Flacc.* 74; *AJ* 19.283), the Jews enjoyed a semi-autonomous control over their internal affairs – whether that power had been entirely handed over to the assembly of

---

57 *Flacc.* 74. Cf. Smallwood 1976, 227.

58 We are often inclined to think stereotypically of the rights of Greek Alexandrians as if these rights included all Greek citizens of Alexandria. That, however, is not very likely. In the Letter from emperor Claudius to the city of Alexandria, for instance, it is made perfectly clear that the privileges and benefits entailed in Alexandrian citizenship should include only *ephebes*: "To all those who have been registered as *epheboi* up to the time of my principate I guarantee and confirm their Alexandrian citizenship (τὴν Ἀλεξανδρέων πολιτείαν) with all the privileges and benefits enjoyed by the city, with the exception of any who, though born of slave-parents, have made their way into your ephebate" (*CPJ* II no. 153, col. III 53-7). Certainly not all Hellenes made their way into the ephebate that was predominantly reserved those of wealth or of a noble family.

59 See Gruen 2002, 71, 285.

60 Gruen 2002, 71. Cf. the discussion in Kasher 1985, 233-61, and Smallwood 1976, 230: "They (sc. the Jews) occupied an intermediate position between the Greek citizens of Alexandria and the wholly unprivileged Egyptians, who lacked any sort of franchise. They enjoyed the political rights of residence and organized civic life, but they were not an integral part of the Greek body politic."

the elders, or was exercised by the *gerousia* in company with a newly appointed *ethnarch*, remains unknown. The exception to this was the horrendous – and for the Jewish community – devastating experience of the "pogrom" of 38 CE and for three successive years afterwards. Overall, we are left with a clear impression that throughout the late Ptolemaic as well as the Roman period, unlike indigenous Egyptians, but parallel with the Greek population, the Jews did, in fact, enjoy wide civil privileges as well as freedom to practice their religion. [61]

It may well be that the Jewish stratum of the Alexandrian population for a great part and throughout most of the period of its existence thought of itself as an ethnic as well as a religious enclave among the inhabitants of Alexandria, but, once again, we need to underscore the constrained nature of the existing sources just as we need to emphasise the difference between map and territory. Whatever the exact nature and the judicial rights of the *ethnarch* and, at a later time, the *gerousia*, it is remarkable to note that in the surviving papyri dealing with legal matters in which Jews were involved we find no traces of Jewish jurisprudence.[62] On the contrary, these papyri testify to Jews using the *synchōrēsis*, a documentary type that had emerged under the legal conditions of Ptolemaic Alexandria.[63] The existence of these *synchōrēsis*-documents is an important reminder that we should be careful not to aggrandise the references in elite sources to the extent that a Jewish *politeuma* in Alexandria entailing an *ethnarch* and a *gerousia* handled all social aspects of Alexandrian Jewry. In fact, the social reality of Alexandrian Jewry as it appears on the basis of these papyri is rather far away from the political and social map echoed in Josephus and Philo. Correspondingly, we do not know whether all Jews remained members of the Jewish *politeuma* of Alexandria for generations, nor do we have clear insights into the social composition of the Jewish *politeuma*. Were all Jew, for instance, members of this political and religious body regardless of their social standing? Did all new Jewish immigrants to Alexandria automatically belong to the Jewish *politeuma*? Did they all conceive of the religious components of Jewry in the same exclusive manner as, for instance, Philo and Josephus? Puzzling as the questions are, we do not know their answers, and, therefore, should abstain from drawing conclusions inferred *e silentio*. We should, however, also be wary of turning the map drawn by Philo, Josephus and other elite writers into social territory. Their continuous emphasis on the exclusive character of Jewish faith indicates a certain discrepancy between their ideal religious map and actual social territory. Indeed, this divergence was greater than they wished.

The sources, however, also testify to the fact that Jews conceived of themselves in terms of Alexandrian citizenship. Philo, for instance, unhesitatingly speaks of "our Alexandria" (κατὰ τὴν ἡμετέραν Ἀλεξάνδρειαν *Leg.* 150), and Josephus bears testimony – in his

---

61 Cf. the apologetic remark put in the mouth of Flaccus in Philo's *Flacc.* 172: "I cast on them the slur that they were foreigners without civic rights, though they were inhabitants with full franchise (ἵν᾽ ἡσθῶσιν οἱ ἀντίπαλοι), just to please their adversaries." Transl. by F. H. Colson (Loeb). Cf. the discussion in Gruen 2002, 71-83.

62 See *CPJ* II, nos. 142-9.151-2.

63 *CPJ* II, 4.

transmission of the Claudian edict – to the fact that the Jews of Alexandria were called by the name of Alexandrians (*AJ* 19.281; cf. *Ap.* 2.38). On the basis of existing sources, it is impossible to judge to what extent the entire Jewish population perceived itself in terms of cultural hybrids or Jewish Alexandrians. And most likely it is – as already noted – historically misleading at the *emic* level to use categories like hybridisation or cultural creolisation with regard to Alexandrian Jewry, since we thereby attribute to Alexandrian Jews an awareness of being multiculturally composite beings. Erich Gruen's characterisation of the situation as one of symbiosis rather than syncretism feels right.[64]

Although anachronistically formulated, the situation of Alexandrian Jews may be compared to the culturally "messy" conditions of contemporary Europeans who also – unconsciously and often unknowingly – vacillate between traditions that originate in quite different contexts. The traditions, however, are not experienced in the manner of their origin. They are simply eclectically used in particular situations with particular aims in mind. Thus, Muslim immigrants may be apparently integrated in modern Germany, but may also live in communities of their own, practicing religious and social customs separate from the surrounding population, and be technically foreign and thus without particular rights that EU citizens may have. Similarly, Philo, for instance, can speak quite frankly of Jewish citizenship (πολιτεία) as well as of Jewish political rights (πολιτικὰ δικαῖα),[65] thereby endorsing a strong Jewish feeling and sense of group identity, but simultaneously he can emphasise Jewish Alexandrian citizenry. Apparently, he did not conceive of the two entities as alternative or exclusive to each other.

Rather than construing Alexandrian Jewry in terms of an exceptional melting pot existence, this condition is, in fact, widespread. Dependent on the cultural context and the social circumstances of time and place, the cultural situation in question may be of a more or less "messy" nature, but cultural "messiness" is not a description of a particular state. It is a fact of human culture.

7. Different Stages in the History of Alexandrian Judaism

We have already noted how Josephus endorses a mythic pedigree for Alexandrian Jewry dating it back to the time of Alexander's foundation of the city. Although this honourable lineage is rather dubious and should be explained as intrinsic to Josephus' desire to create a noble ancestry for Alexandrian Jewry, there is evidence that Jews settled in Alexandria from an early period on. That, of course, should not be surprising. There were always close relations as well as exchanges of many different sorts between Palestine and Egypt. While the figure of 100.000 Jewish captives is almost certainly exaggerated for dramatic purposes in the *Letter to Aristeas*,[66] it is not unlikely that gross numbers of

---

64 Gruen 2002, 70.

65 *Flacc.* 47, 53; *Leg.* 193f. et al.

66 According to the *Letter of Aristeas* 12-27, 37, 100.000 Jewish captives were taken as spoils of war to Egypt. 30.000 prisoners were placed in fortresses and the remaining part, consisting of old men and children, were given by the king to his soldiers as slaves.

Jews were taken as captives to Egypt in different rashes from 320 to 301 BCE by Ptolemy I Soter. Additionally, a flourishing and growing city like Alexandria is likely to have attracted traders and artisans as well as people of all other occupations. Papyri document that Jews were from an early period active in the military as well as in agriculture.[67] They also show that Ptolemy VI Philomotor and his wife Cleopatra appointed Jews as military commanders and civil servants, and admitted Jews to the royal court. It is also possible that Alexandrian Jews were regularly attached to the Macedonian garrison guarding the city.[68]

During the second century BCE we find the first evidence testifying to a Jewish presence in Alexandria, although it is likely to have occurred earlier at the beginning of the third century as can be inferred from the second century Jewish literature of a high standard that was created in Alexandria. It is also from this period that a number of dedicatory inscriptions celebrating the building of different *proseuchē* in the vicinity of Alexandria originate. *JIGRE* no. 9, in fact, offers evidence of a dedication of a *proseuchē* in Alexandria itself, thus paving the way for the later situation described by Philo that in Alexandria there were many *proseuchē* scattered over the different quarters of the city (see note 6). Similarly, there is funerary evidence from the same period of inscriptions written in Aramaic and Greek and stemming from the necropolis of El-Ibrahimiya in the North-Eastern part of Alexandria (see above). We can also gather from the extant Jewish literature of a presumably Alexandrian provenance (see note 5) that the Jewish community(ies) of Alexandria from early in the second century had developed to a considerable size and had – at least as some strands were concerned – reached a cultural and social level that enabled Jews to create literature fully comparable with parallel Greek efforts. Needless to say, the translation initiated most probably during the late third century BCE of the Hebrew Scriptures into Greek known as the Septuagint – whatever the precise form and whatever the precise circumstances of the translation(s) were – does mark a decisive culminating point of Alexandrian Jewish culture.[69] Correspondingly, there are already in the third century BCE traces of the literary anti-Judaic tradition that became more pronounced later on.[70] The existence of this tradition testifies to the increasing cultural and social influence not only of Alexandrian Jewry but of Jews in Egypt in general. An increase in the Jewish population of Egypt, probably including Alexandria, is likely to have occurred during the years surrounding the outbreak of the Maccabean revolt. As tensions increased not only between the reigning Seleucids of Palestine and the indigenous population, but also between the different influential families of Jerusalem, Jews in large numbers fled to Egypt – the most notable among them being the high priest Onias III (*AJ* 13.62; see, however, *BJ* 1.33; 7.423 for an alternative account). It was at this time the Jewish temple and settlement at Leontopolis was erected.

---

67 Borgen 1992, 1064; see *CPJ* I, nos. 48-55.
68 Tcherikover 1958, 80.
69 See footnote 5. The later Jewish traditions eulogising the creation of the Septuagint are of a predominantly mythic character, see *Letter to Aristeas*; *Mos.* 2.25-44; *AJ* 12.12-118.
70 Schäfer 1997, 17-21.

Although Josephus would like us to think – at least in *Ap.* 2.42 – that the Jews had been assigned a particular quarter in Alexandria by Alexander the Great, we do not know from which time the relationship between Alexandrian Jewry and the so-called Delta-quarter Δ in Alexandria originates (cf. *BJ* 2.495).[71] In *Flacc.* 55 Philo claims that Alexandria was divided into five quarters named after the first letters of the alphabet, of which two were described as Jewish because of their predominantly Jewish populations. Additionally, Philo claims that not a few Jews were also scattered in the remaining sections of the city. During the "pogrom" of 38 and the Jewish uprising in 66, however, it appears that the Jews were forced into the Delta quarter, functioning as "the first known ghetto in the world."[72]

In the standard literature on Alexandrian Jewry the transfer from the Ptolemaic to the Roman period is described as one of decline entailing Jewish losses of privileges.[73] We do not know of "pogroms" with complementary Jewish uprisings before the Roman era, but we should be careful, as has convincingly been argued by Erich Gruen, not to drive in a wedge between the late Ptolemaic and the Roman era. However atrocious the events of 38 CE were,[74] they should not be taken as a characteristic of the Jewish situation during the first part of the Roman period. In fact, by reconfirming the civic privileges enjoyed by the Jewish community prior to the "pogrom" the emperor Claudius' letter to the city of Alexandria substantiates the picture of a "generally prosperous and successful Jewish community in Alexandria."[75] That situation, however, drastically changed after the First Jewish War. As early as 66 at least parts of the Jewish community in Alexandria were suffering (*BJ* 2.487-98 is the only source we have of the events).[76]

We do not know the exact reasons why the citizenry of Alexandria decided to send a delegation to Nero in Rome. When the meeting convened at Alexandria's amphitheatre to endorse the initiative, some Jews, apparently, felt threatened by what was proposed and "sneaked" into the meeting. In the eyes of the Greek Alexandrians they were – not altogether surprisingly – seen as intruders. A mob formed crying "enemies" and "spies" at Jews and three were burned to death (*BJ* 2.490f.). In retaliation for this gruesome assault, the Jews – stereotypically conceived of as one group by Josephus – set about stoning Greeks and tried to set the amphitheatre on fire. The Roman prefect, Philo's nephew

---

71 For the location of these quarters see Adriani 1966, vol. 1, 239f; Pearson 1992, 154-5. Cf. *Ap.* 2.33-6; *BJ* 2.488.
72 Smallwood 1976, 240.
73 Tcherikover 1961, 311-28; 1963, 3; Smallwood 1976, 230-5; Mélèze-Modrzejewski 1995, 163f. See, however, Barclay 1996, 48-51, and Gruen 2002, 70-82.
74 It is beyond the limits of this essay to go into the complex subject matter of the "pogrom" of 38 and its repercussions during the successive years. Of the vast literature on the topic, see Gruen 2002 for a balanced view.
75 Gruen 2002, 82. Cf. 83: "In short, the dreadful pogrom of 38 in no way defines or exemplifies the history of Jews in Alexandria. It exploded suddenly and unexpectedly, the product of special circumstances – the peculiar combination of a shaken Roman prefect, the perverse ambitions of certain civic leaders, and the bitterness of the indigenous population."
76 For the subsequent period see Smallwood 1976, 364-8; Barclay 1996, 72-7.

Tiberius Julius Alexander, together with the leading members of the Jewish community, sought to calm down the mobbing Jews by talking them out of their self-destructive frenzy, but did not succeed. On the contrary, the Jews in question mocked the governor with the result that the attempt to obtain peace in a non-violent manner completely failed. Tiberius Alexander, then, ordered the Roman legions to restore order. Although the figure of 50.000 Jews that according to Josephus at this occasion were massacred is doubtless an exaggeration, there can be no doubt that the Jewish community of Alexandria suffered severely from this blow. Not only was the community diminished by the loss of numerous Jews killed by Roman soldiers, but Alexandrian Jewry also suffered a severe loss of credibility in the eyes of the Roman authorities as well as of the Greek citizens of Alexandria. Josephus claims that subsequent to the Jewish War Alexandrian citizens appealed to the Roman emperor Vespasian to remove the remaining privileges of the Jews. It was a token of magnanimity – that is in the eyes of Josephus – that Vespasian did not comply with this wish, but, on the contrary, confirmed Jewish rights (*AJ* 12.121-4). Correspondingly, it must have been a shock of tremendous dimensions for Alexandrian Jewry, the impact of which is hardly conceivable today, to cope with the fact of the destruction of the Temple in Jerusalem and the defeat of the Jewish revolt in Palestine. The humiliation was pressed home by Vespasian who, upon the destruction of the Temple, transformed the annual Temple tax into the *fiscus Judaicus*, a tax that after 70 CE was levied, "On all Jews, wheresoever resident he imposed a poll-tax to be paid annually into the Capitol as formerly contributed by them to the temple of Jerusalem" (*BJ* 7.218).[77] Tcherikover's is probably a fair portrayal of the shame experienced by Jews after this tax was imposed: "the Jews were now put to shame not only in the eyes of the Greeks but in the eyes of the Egyptian villagers as well. The payment of the Jewish tax acquired something of the significance of the 'yellow spot' on Jews' clothes in the Middle Ages; it marked the Jews as a dangerous and seditious people."[78]

Suspicions and mutual fear set the agenda for the years subsequent to the Jewish revolt of 66-70 CE culminating in the Alexandrian Jewish revolt of 115-17.[79] The uprising was part of a greater current of partly related insurgencies that from 115-17 swept across Egypt, Cyrenaica, Cyprus and Mesopotamia. Eusebius, our main source about these insurgencies, is frustratingly late and removed from the uprising experience.[80] A few years prior to the outbreak of the Alexandrian revolt, papyrological evidence testifies to the continuous strife between Greek and Jewish Alexandrians over the rights of the Jews.[81] Whatever the

---

77 Transl. by Thackeray (Loeb).

78 *CPJ* I, 82.

79 See Smallwood 1976, 389-412.

80 Eusebius *Hist. Eccles.* 4.2f. Scarce references are found in Dio Cass. 68.32; 69.8; Oros. 7.12 (dependent on Euseb., however); App., *B Civ* 2.90; SHA, *Hadr.* 5; *CPJ* II nos. 435-50.

81 See *CPJ* II no. 157 and *P Oxy.* 1242: *Acta Hermaisci*. The latter is of an entirely fictional nature, but it is important since it reflects pro-Jewish sentiments and testifies to the ongoing ethnic conflicts between the different ethnic segments of Alexandria, here in the form of a rivalry between Greeks and Jews. For an understanding of the text see Musurillo 1954, 161-72.

precise background for the insurgency was, Jews in a relatively great number attacked the Greek population in 115 CE in Alexandria, the *chōra*, and in Cyrenaica. Thereafter, Greeks in great number came to Alexandria, where they successfully and full of vengeance struck back at the Jewish population.[82] A certain Lucuas, leading the Cyrenaican Jews, subsequently joined forces with Egyptian Jews plundering and pillaging their way through Egypt. The Romans were now put in a position where they could no longer ignore the development of the events. Not only was Egypt the great granary of the Roman Empire, but Lucuas' aspirations appeared to be of a profoundly messianic character venturing a full war against the Empire.[83] The renowned Q. Marcius Turbo was called in from the East, where he was engaged in war against the Parthians, to bring the revolt to a halt. The impact and the gravity of the uprising is evident both from the fact that Turbo was put in charge of the army and that he had to fight the Jews with a combined land and naval force, as well as from the fact that it took him a considerable span of time and several battles to finish the "work". In Alexandria the "Great Synagogue" was burned down, other synagogues were demolished, the Jewish quarters were looted, and Jewish property confiscated. From this time on we hardly find any more testimony about Alexandrian Jewry before a Jewish community reappears at the end of the second century and early third century engaged in theological strife with a new player on the scene: Alexandrian Christianity. Alexandrian Jewry, however, never regained the flourishing cultural level and the affluent social standards that had characterised at least particular strands of it during the Ptolemaic and first part of the Roman period.

8. A Brief Conclusion

The constrained nature of the sources should not only be acknowledged but also paid close heed to in the conclusions drawn from them. Philo, for instance, most certainly did not embody Alexandrian Judaism in its cultural and social breadth as is often the impression one gets from studies on Alexandrian Jewry; nor should he be thought of as a homogeneous, uniform thinker always subscribing to the same understanding of reality. Like other writers, Philo's writings should be interpreted as the creations of a composite being who under particular circumstances and with particular aims and situations in mind attempts to conquer the cultural battlefield of his time. That, of course, applies to all other ancient writers as well.

Correspondingly, although we have several sources that speak of the Jewish *politeuma* of Alexandria entailing the existence of a Jewish *ethnarch* as well as a *gerousia*, we should be careful not to exaggerate the impact of these institutions on the judicial and social life of Alexandrian Jews as also *CPJ* II nos.142-9.151-2 cause us to remember.

---

82 *CPJ* III no. 435 does throw some light on the conflict by emphasising the rivalry between Jewish and Greek Alexandrian citizens as an important component behind the events. See Smallwood 1976, 395f. See also the *Acta Pauli et Antonini* of the *Acta Alexandrinorum* (*CPJ* II no. 158α, β) in Musurillo 1954, 49-58, with subsequent commentary 179-94, and Smallwood 1976, 406-9.

83 On this enigmatic figure see Hengel 1983.

It is rather remarkable to note than in the surviving papyri dealing with legal matters in which Jews were involved we find no traces of Jewish jurisprudence. Similarly, it is crucial to keep in mind that we are not in a position on the basis of the sources to make inferences about the lower social segments of Alexandrian Jewry. We should, in fact, not fall prey to the illusion that we have anything but a very particular glimpse into elite strands of Alexandrian Jewry. The surviving inscriptions as well as the papyri only give us an impression of the more affluent segments. There were many forms of Alexandrian Judaism that we shall never be able to catch a glimpse of or an insight into. It is an important premise that should be acknowledged in any study on Alexandrian Jewry, however trivial it may sound.

It is also evident from this study that we should be careful in presupposing the relevance of cultural dualisms like the Hellenism-Judaism dichotomy that has so frequently been projected onto the sources, thereby frequently leading to the confusion of map with territory. In so far as the dichotomy has a bearing on the primary sources and is not exclusively the reflection of the taxonomising practices of modern scholarship, it is urgent to distinguish between actual ancient social reality and its imagined reality. However much an Alexandrian Jew belonging to the elite strands of Alexandrian Jewry rhetorically attempts to distance himself from the surrounding neighbouring cultures, he is, in fact, by his very endeavour decisively influenced by those cultures, the impacts of which he allegedly does not acknowledge or seeks to evade. Although it would be anachronistically wrong to ascribe to Alexandrian Jews a meta-cultural awareness of being the hybrids or the creolisations of Jewish, Greek, Egyptian and other traditions circulating in ancient Alexandria, we can see that this was the case. In that sense Alexandrian Jewry does not only testify to the cultural and social conditions of a melting pot existence, but is strong testimony to the "messy" nature of human culture in general. However perplexed and confounded we may be as a result of engagement with cultural "messiness," the great intellectual challenge for future studies not only on past Alexandrian Jewry, but on ancient cultural entities in general, will be to take the "messiness" of human cultural and social affairs profoundly seriously.

References

Adriani, A. 1966 *Repertorio d'Arte dell'Egitto Greco-Romano*, Serie C vol. 1 (Testo) and vol. 2 (Tavole) Palermo: Fondazione "Ignazio Mormino" Banco di Sicilia.

Anderson, B. 1996 *Imagined Communities. Reflections on the Origin and Spread of Nationalism* London and New York: Verso.

Attran, S. 2002 *In Gods We Trust. The Evolutionary Landscape of Religion* Oxford: Oxford University Press.

Barclay, J. M. G. 1996 *Jews in the Mediterranean Diaspora. From Alexander to Trajan (323 BCE – 117 CE)* Edinburgh: T&T Clark.

Beek, M. van 2000 "Beyond Identity Fetishism: 'Communal' Conflict in Ladakh and the Limits of Autonomy" *Current Anthropology* 15/4, 525-69.

Beek, M. van 2002 "Identiteternes møde, civilisationernes sammenstød?" *Religionsvidenskabeligt Tidsskrift* 40, 1-11.

Bell, H. I. 1926 *Juden und Griechen im Römischen Alexandreia. Eine historische Skizze des alexandrinischen Antisemitismus* (Beiheft zum Alten Orient 9) Leipzig: J. C. Hinrischs'sche Buchhandlung.

Bhabba, H. K. 2004 *The Location of Culture* London-New York: Routledge.

Bohak, G. 2002 "Ethnic Continuity in the Jewish Diaspora in Antiquity" in: J. R. Bartlett (ed.) *Jews in the Hellenistic and Roman Cities* London-New York: Routledge, 175-92.

Borgen, P. 1992 "Judaism in Egypt" in: D. N. Freedman (ed.) *The Anchor Bible Dictionary* (vol. 3) New York-London-Toronto-Sydney-Auckland: Doubleday, 1061-72.

Borgen, P. 1997 *Philo of Alexandria. An Exegete for His Time* (Suppl. NT 86) Leiden: Brill.

Boyer, P. 2001 *Religion Explained. The Evolutionary Origins of Religious Thought* New York: Basic Books.

Campany, R.F. 2003 "On the very Idea of Religions (in the Modern West in and Early Medieval China)" *History of Religions* 42:4, 287-319.

Collins, J. J. 1983 "Sibylline Oracles (Second Century B.C. – Seventh Century A.D.)" in J. H. Charlesworth (ed.) *The Old Testament Pseudepigrapha. Volume 1. Apocalyptic Literature and Testaments* New York-London-Toronto-Sydney-Auckland: Doubleday, 317-472.

Collins, N. L. 2000 *The Library in Alexandria and the Bible in Greek* (Supplements to Vetus Testamentum 82) Leiden-Boston-Köln: Brill.

Dawson, D. 1992 *Allegorical Readers and Cultural Revision in Ancient Alexandria* Berkeley-Los Angeles-Oxford: University of California Press.

Dines, J.F. 2004, *The Septuagint* (Undersdtanding the Bible and its World) London-New York: T&T Clark.

Dyck, J. 2002 "Philo, Alexandria and Empire. The politics of allegorical interpretation" in J. R. Bartlett (ed.) *Jews in the Hellenistic and Roman Cities* London-New York: Routledge, 149-74.

Engberg-Pedersen, T. (ed.) 2001 *Paul Beyond the Judaism/Hellenism Divide* Louisville-London-Leiden: Westminster John Knox Press.

Fabry, H.-J. and Offerhaus, U. (eds.) 2001 *Im Brennpunkt: Die Septuaginta. Studien zur Entstehung und Bedeutung der Griechischen Bibel* (Beiträge zur Wissenschaft vom Alten und Neuen Testament, Achte Folge) Stuttgart: Kohlhammer.

Fraser, P. M. 1972 *Ptolemaic Alexandria* (3 vols.) Oxford: Oxford University Press.

Frey, J.-B. 1936 *Corpus inscriptionum Iudaicarum* (vol. 1) Rome: Pontifical Institute; revised by B. Lifshitz, New York: Ktav 1975).

Frey, J.-B. 1952 *Corpus inscriptionum Iudaicarum* (vol. 2) Rome: Pontifical Institute.

Geertz, C. 1973 "Religion as a Cultural System" in: *Interpretation of Cultures* New York: Basic Books.

Goodman, N. 1978 *Ways of Worldmaking* (Harvester Studies in Philosophy) Sussex: Harvester Press.

Gruen, E.S. 1998 *Heritage and Hellenism. The Reinvention of Jewish Tradition* Berkeley-Los Angeles-London: University of California Press.

Gruen, E. S. 2002 *Diaspora. Jews amidst Greeks and Romans*, Cambridge, MA.-London: Harvard University Press.

Hannerz, U. 1969 *Soulside: Inquiries into Ghetto Culture and Community* New York: Columbia University Press.

Hastrup, K. 2004 "Religion in Context. A Discussion of Ontological Dumping, in: P. Antes, A.W. Geertz & R.W. Warne (eds.) *New Approaches to the Study of Religion. Volume 1: Regional, Critical, and Historical Approaches* Berlin-New York: De Gruyter, 253-70.

Hengel, M. 1983 "Messianische Hoffnung und politischer 'Radikalismus' in der 'jüdisch- hellenistischen Diaspora'" in: D. Hellholm (ed.) *Apocalypticism in the Mediterranean World and the Near East* Tübingen: Mohr-Siebeck, 655-86.

Honigman, S. 1993 "The Birth of a Diaspora: The Emergence of a Jewish Self-Definition in Ptolemaic Egypt in the Light of Onomastics" in: S.J.D. Cohen & E.S. Frerichs (eds.) *Diasporas in Antiquity* (Brown Judaic Studies 288) Atlanta, GA: Scholars Press, 93-126.

Horbury, W. & Noy, D. 1992 *Jewish Inscriptions of Graeco-Roman Egypt* Cambridge: Cambridge University Press.

Kasher, A. 1985 *The Jews in Hellenistic and Roman Egypt: The Struggle for Equal Rights* Tübingen: Mohr-Siebeck.

Kreuzer, S. & Lesch, J. P. (eds.) 2004 *Im Brennpunkt: Die Septuaginta* (Studien zur Entstehung und Bedeutung der griechischen Bibel. Band 2, Beiträge zur Wissenschaft vom Alten und Neuen Testament, Neunte Folge) Stuttgart: Kohlhammer.

Levine, L. I. 2000 *The Ancient Synagogue: The First Thousand Years* New Haven: Yale University Press.

Lieu, J. M. 1996 *Image and Reality. The Jews in the World of the Christians in the Second Century* Edinburgh: T&T Clark.

Marcos, N. F. 2000 *The Septuagint in Context: Introduction to the Greek Versions of the Bible* Leiden: Brill.

Mélèze-Modrzejewski, J. M. 1993 "How to be a Jew in Hellenistic Egypt?" in: S.J.D. Cohen and E. S. Frerichs (eds.) *Diasporas in Antiquity* (Brown Judaic Studies 288) Atlanta, GA: Scholars Press, 65-92.

Mélèze-Modrzejewski, J.M. 1995 *The Jews of Egypt: From Ramses II to Emperor Hadrian* Philadelphia: The Jewish Publication Society / Edinburgh: T&T Clark.

Murphy, J.F. 1991 *The Religious World of Jesus: An Introduction to Second Temple Palestinian Judaism* Nashville: Abingdon Press.

Musurillo, H.A. 1954 *The Acts of the Pagan Martyrs. Acta Alexandrinorum* Oxford: Clarendon Press.

Neusner, J., Green, W.S., & Frerichs, E. S. (eds.) 1987 *Judaisms and their Messiahs at the Turn of the Christian Era* Cambridge: Cambridge University Press.

Niehoff, M. 2001 *Philo on Jewish Identity and Culture* (Texte und Studien zum Antiken Judentum 86) Tübingen: Mohr-Siebeck.

Pearson, B. 1992 "Alexandria" in: D.N. Freedman (ed.) *The Anchor Bible Dictionary*, New York/London/Toronto/Sydney/Auckland: Doubleday vol. 3, 152-7.

Petersen, A. Klostergaard 1998 "Skellet går, hvor skellet sættes" *Præsteforeningens Blad* 18, 398-407.

Petersen, A. Klostergaard 2002 "Hellenisme og kristendom – en skæbnesvanger konstruktion" *Religionsvidenskabeligt Tidsskrift* 41, 51-75.

Petersen, A. Klostergaard 2003a "Between Old and New: The Problem of Acculturation Illustrated by the Early Christian Use of the Phoenix Motif" in: F. Garzía Martínez & G.P. Luttikhuizen (eds.) *Jerusalem, Alexandria, Rome: Studies in Ancient Interaction in Honour of A. Hilhorst* (Supplements to the Journal for the study of Judaism 82) Leiden-Boston: Brill, 147-64.

Petersen, A. Klostergaard 2003b "The Notion of Demon. Open Questions to a Diffuse Concept" in: A. Lange, H. Lichtenberger & K.F. Römheld (eds.) *Die Dämonen. Demons. Die Dämonologie der israelitisch-jüdischen und frühchristlichen Litteratur im Kontext ihrer Umwelt. The Demonology of Israelite-Jewish and Early Christian Literature in Context of their Environment* Tübingen: Mohr-Siebeck, 23-41.

Petersen, A. Klostergaard 2004 "Paraenesis in Pauline Scholarship and in Paul – an Intricate Relationship" in: T. Engberg-Pedersen and J. Starr (eds.) *Early Christian Paraenesis in Context* (Beihefte zur Zeitschrift für die neutestamentliche Wissenschaft und die Kunde der älteren Kirche 125) Berlin-New York: De Gruyter, 267-95.

Petersen, A. Klostergaard 2005 "Fra skizofreni til balkanisering – troen som en blandt andre virkelighedsverdener" *Fønix*, 112-31.

Petersen, A. Klostergaard 2007a "Makkabæerbogslitteraturen i et apologetisk perspektiv – Historieskrivning, filosofi og apologetik" in: A. Klostergaard Petersen, K. Fuglseth & J. Hyldahl (eds.) *Perspektiver på jødisk apologetik* (Kristendommen og antikken 3) København: Forlaget Anis, 115-53.

Petersen, A. Klostergaard 2007b "Filon som apologet: en læsning af *De migratione Abrahami*" in A. Klostergaard Petersen, K. Fuglseth & J. Hyldahl (eds.) *Perspektiver på jødisk apologetik* (Kristendommen og antikken 3) København: Forlaget Anis, 233-61.

Runesson, A. 2001 *The Origins of the Synagogue. A Socio-Historical Study* (Coniectanea biblica. New Testament series 37) Stockholm: Almqvist & Wiksell.

Schäfer, P. 1997 *Judeophobia. Attitudes toward the Jews in the Ancient World* Cambridge, MA-London: Harvard University Press.

Segal, A. F. 1987 *The Other Judaisms of Late Antiquity* Atlanta: Scholars Press.

Sewell, W. H. Jr. 1999 "The Concept(s) of Culture" in: V.E. Bonnell & L. Hunt (eds.) *Beyond the Cultural Turn: New Directions in the Study of Society and Culture* Berkeley: University of California Press, 35-61.

Smallwood, E. M. 1976 *The Jews under Roman Rule. From Pompey to Diocletian* (Studies in Judaism in late Antiquity 20) Leiden: Brill.

Smith, J.Z. 1978 "Map is not Territory" in: *Map is not Territory. Studies in the History of Religion* (Studies in Judaism in Late Antiquity 23) Leiden: Brill, 289-309.

Stolcke, V. 1995 "Talking Culture: New Boundaries, New Rhetorics of Exclusion in Europe" *Current Anthropology* 36, 1-13.

Swidler, A. 2001 *Talk Love. How Culture Matters* Chicago-London: Chicago University Press.

Tcherikover, V.A. 1956 "Jewish Apologetic Literature Reconsidered" *Eos* 48, 169-93.

Tcherikover, V.A. 1958 "The Ideology of the Letter of Aristeas" *Harvard Theological Review* 51, 59-85.

Tcherikover, V.A. 1961 *Hellenistic Civilization and the Jews* (transl. by S. Applebaum) Philadelphia: Jewish Publication Society of America / Jerusalem: Magness Press.

Tcherikover, V.A. 1963 "The Decline and Fall of the Jewish Diaspora in Egypt in the Roman Period" *Journal of Jewish Studies* 14, 1-32.

Tcherikover, V.A. & Fuks, A. 1957-64 *Corpus papyrorum Judaicarum* (3 vols.) Jerusalem: Magness Press / Cambridge, MA: Harvard University Press.

CHAPTER 7

From School to Patriarchate: Aspects on the Christianisation of Alexandria

Samuel Rubenson

1. Introduction

In the transformation of the classical heritage into an early medieval Christian culture the city of Alexandria played a decisive role. In the long process forming the relations between the Church and the political authorities, Rome and Constantinople were finally to become the most important arenas, and in the slow formation of Christian cult the developments in Jerusalem and Antioch were perhaps more influential. But from the late third century until the mid-fifth century Alexandria was the most important city in early Christianity. It was only the combined efforts of the emperor and the bishops of Rome and Constantinople that finally ended Alexandrian ecclesiastical power by means of the council of Chalcedon in 451. And as far as the formation of Christian teaching and theology and its reworking of classical philosophy is concerned no city rivals Alexandria. In the development of Christian hermeneutics and Bible interpretation no teacher in the early Church can match Origen of Alexandria. In the battle for a Christian understanding of God as trinity as well as in the defence of the freedom of the Church to define its basic dogma no bishop was more influential than Athanasius of Alexandria, and in the struggle to find a solution to how Jesus Christ could be understood as being both man and God no theologian has been as important as Cyril of Alexandria. It is on the basis of the work of them that most of the theological achievements of others like Augustine, the Cappadocians, Maximus the Confessor or John of Damascus rest.

In spite of this, the development of Christianity in Alexandria and the Christianisation of the city is poorly documented and analysed. The basic reason for this is the sparcity of archaeological and documentary evidence. It is only with the writings of Athanasius in the mid-fourth century and his famous successors on the patriarchal throne that we have substantial primary sources. Archaeological excavations have been very limited and seldom focused on the developments of Christianity and due to the climate no papyrological sources can be safely connected with Alexandria.[1] We are thus much better informed about life in the minor towns of Egypt and in the rural areas, including some of the oases, in the period of Christianisation than developments in Alexandria.[2] As has often been stated, there is almost no information in any sources about Christianity in Alexandria until the end of the second century A.D. This fact even constituted the main basis for Bauer's famous thesis about orthodoxy and heresy in early Christianity in his *Rechtgläubigkeit und Ketzerei im frühesten Christentum*.[3] According to him the reason for the lack of any sources about the establishment of a Christian tradition and the emergence of the Church in Alexandria lies in the fact that until the end of the second century Alexandrian Christianity was dominated by a plurality of heterodox gnostic interpretations which were later suppressed by emerging Christian orthodoxy. Although Bauer's thesis has received substantial criticism, especially in relation to developments in Egypt in general,[4] the lack of substantial evidence for Alexandria makes it virtually impossible to prove anything about the developments of Christianity prior to the end of the second century.

In contrast to Bauer and others who have mainly seen the early developments of Christianity in Alexandria as a matter of doctrinal change I will here suggest that we should look at the changes from a social point of view. My suggestion is that the significant move is not from Gnostic heterodoxy to Ecclesial orthodoxy but from a vigorous school of philosophy to a powerful communal institution supplanting traditional forms of imperial as well as local power.

2. The Christian School in Alexandria

Our first solid information about Christianity in Alexandria is related to a school traditionally, but rather misleadingly, known as the catechetical school, and to its Christian teachers.[5] In his Ecclesiastical history Eusebius of Caesarea writes about Pantaenus, a famous teacher who is said to have been directing the school of the believers in Alexandria when Commodus became emperor in 180 CE.[6] According to Eusebius the school,

---

1   For a survey of archaeological results see Empereur 1998. A basic reference work is Adriani 1961-66. The significance of the polish excavations of Kom el-Dikka for early Christianity is discussed in Haas 1997, 189-206. For the excavations see: Alexandria: Tomasz Derda, Tomasz Markiewicz and Ewa Wipszycka (eds.), *Auditoria of Kom el-Dikka and Late Antique Education*, Warsaw. Journal of Juristic Papyrology, Supplements 2007.

2   For Egypt in general see Bagnall 1993. For the early development in Alexandria see Griggs 1990, and Pearson & Goehring 1986. See also Roger S. Bangnall (ed.), *Egypt in the Byzantine World 300-700*, Cambridge: Cambridge University Press 2007.

3   Bauer 1934.

4   For the most thorough refutation of Bauer see Roberts 1979.

5   For a thorough discussion and evaluation of earlier literature on early Christian teachers in Alexandria and the beginnings of a Christian school see Neymeyr 1989, 40-105. For the issue of the "catechetical" school see also Scholten 1995.

6   Euseb., *Hist. eccl.* 5.10.

still known in his own time, *i.e.* around 320 for its high philosophical and theological standards had existed in Alexandria "from ancient time'. Pantaenus is described as a very learned man, originally from the school of the Stoics. He is said to have travelled widely in the East before settling in Alexandria where he apparently taught Christian philosophy. According to Eusebius, Pantaenus was the teacher and predecessor of Clement of Alexandria and a friend of Alexander, who was bishop first in Cappadocia and then in Jerusalem.[7] A possible predecessor of Pantaenus was Athenagoras of Athens, who, according to recent studies, moved to Alexandria in the 170's and wrote his apology addressed to Marcus Aurelius there. His name actually appears as the first in a list of the heads of the Christian school of Alexandria belonging to the lost church history by Philip of Side, a historian of the early fifth century.[8]

But already before the beginnings of the so called catechetical school there had been Christian teachers in the intellectual milieu of Alexandria. Although our sources are very vague at least three Christian teachers, later denounced as Gnostics, are associated with Alexandria in the first half of the second century. Our knowledge about Carpocrates, Basilides and Valentinus and their teachings comes, however, from the writings of their opponents, who were more interested in describing their teaching than informing us about their lives. Carpocrates is said to have been an Alexandrian, living in the time of emperor Hadrian (117-138), Basilides is thought to have studied in Egypt, and perhaps also taught there, and Valentinus studied in Alexandria, and perhaps also taught there before settling in Rome ca. 136 A.D.. The fact that Clement of Alexandria spends much time on refuting them suggests their continued influence in Alexandria in his days.[9]

There are consequently good reasons to assume that Christianity in Alexandria in the second century was dominated by one or several, probably small schools of Christian philosophy.[10] These schools were all engaged in attempts to integrate the Biblical tradition and the gospel about Jesus Christ as saviour with elements of Greek philosophy. A likely background is the tradition of Jewish philosophy in Alexandria in the first century made famous through the writings of Philo. The connection between Jewish centres of learning in Alexandria and Christianity is actually hinted at in the description of Apollo, a learned Jew from Alexandria who had embraced Christianity already around 50 A.D.[11] Some early Christian writings like the Letter of Barnabas are also traditionally related to Christian centres of study in Alexandria in the first part of the second century.

It is, however, only with the writings of Clement of Alexandria in the last decade of the second century that we have more substantial evidence for the Christian com-

---

7   Euseb., *Hist. eccl.* 5.11, 6.6, 6.13, 6.14.
8   For an in-depth discussion of the testimony of Philip of Side and the possible role of Athenagoras as teacher in Alexandria see Pouderon 1997.
9   For details see Griggs 1990, 47-56.
10 It has even been suggested that the Christian community in Alexandria until the early third century consisted solely in a loosely interconnected group of small schools represented by their teachers. See Hornschuh 1960. For a discussion see Neymeyr 1989, 86-93.
11 *Acts of the Apostles* 18.24-25.

munity in Alexandria. From his writings we can presume that Clement taught pagan converts and catechumens as well as Christians looking for more profound knowledge. His philosophical background is Stoic in matters of ethics and Middle Platonic in theology and his main writings are an attempt to show that Christianity is not a religion for the ignorant. Christ as Logos is the teacher of man and the goal is assimilation to God. Clement does not seem to have belonged to any ordained clergy, but anxious to defend the orthodoxy of his co-religionists. The tradition he claimed to belong to and wanted to hand on was the *paradosis* of the Church, which he primarily thought of as a school. In spite of a clear distinction between Christians with profound knowledge, Gnostics, and simple believers, Clement emphasises the unity of the Church.[12]

The academic and also wealthy setting of at least important parts of Alexandrian Christianity is, moreover, evident in the description of the youth of Clement's most famous pupil, Origen. His father, Leonides, was according to Eusebius a rich man who eagerly supervised his child's education, both in Greek science and holy wisdom.[13] When Leonides was martyred in the persecutions under Septimius Severus, probably in 202, the wealth of the family was confiscated, but a rich Christian lady undertook to support not only his higher education, but also that of other scholars. Already at the age of 18 Origen was able to earn his living by teaching, probably as a grammarian, and after Clement's departure from Alexandria he became the head of the school of the Christians. The new task gave little room for other teaching activities and Origen decided to sell his private library of classical authors, earning him enough money to support his life as a true independent philosopher.

The traditional designation of the school of Pantaenus, Clement and Origen as a catechetical school is misleading. First the idea that there was a school in which Pantaenus, Clement and Origen succeeded each other as formal heads is a construct by Eusebius, who evidently was not particularly well informed about the situation in Alexandria 100 years earlier. Secondly its is clear from Eusebius account, as well as from the writings of Clement and Origen, and the farewell address to Origen by one of his pupils in Caesarea, that their school was not a church institution caring for candidates for baptism, but financially independent and open to pagans and Christians alike. Its curriculum, moreover, included both pagan and Christian traditions.[14]

3. Teachers and Bishops

Although it is clear not only that Christianity was established in Alexandria long before the third century, but also that it had prominent representatives in the intellectual

---

12 For a short survey of Clement as a teacher see Neymeyr 1989, 45-95. Recent work on Clement includes Buell 1999 and Eric Osborn, *Clement of Alexandria*, Cambridge: Cambridtege University Press 2008.

13 Euseb., *Hist. eccl.* 6.2.8, 15. Literature on Origen is vast. In addition to Trigg and Crouzel and the article by Hornschuh 1960 a survey of Origen as teacher is given in Neymeyr 1989, 95-102.

14 The issue of attendance and curriculum of the school is discussed in detail by Scholten 1995.

milieu, the first decisive steps in the establishment of a more organised and centralised Church in Alexandria seem to have been related to the persecutions of Christians under Septimius Severus in the early years of the third century. The persecutions, based on the emperor's prohibition of conversion to Christianity, were primarily directed against Christian teachers and their students. The fact that they hit Alexandria rather harshly indicates that the spread of Christianity in the intellectual circles was fairly successful and that the Christian teachers were gaining influence. During the persecutions Clement and probably other teachers left the city and the father of Origen was executed.[15] Although Eusebius, who is our only source on the events in Alexandria, is writing in defence of Origen, there is no reason to doubt his description of the interest for Christian teaching as well as the problem for the authorities to stop popular teachers and punish their students. The official endorsement of Origen's teaching activity by the Alexandrian bishop Demetrius (189-232), mentioned by Eusebius, was probably a result of a need created by the persecution of the teachers to strengthen their ties to the official representatives of the Christian community.[16]

Demetrius, who is the first bishop of Alexandria of whom we know more than a mere name, seem to have had some kind of recognition in the city itself, and as such also a responsibility for the Christian teachers. This does not, however, mean that they were in any way employed by the church or that their teaching was controlled by the bishop. When Origen was invited to teach in Arabia, the invitation was sent to the governor as well as to the bishop, who both acted in approving the trip.[17] When Origen in 215 left Alexandria on account of the riots and violent retributions during the visit of Caracalla, and on the invitation of the bishops of Palestine began teaching in Caesarea, the Alexandrian bishop reacted against this with the argument that a layman should not preach in the church in front of bishops.[18] The issue seems to have been if someone not ordained should be allowed to preach in the Church in connection with the episcopal liturgy on Sunday. Their arguments that this was established custom are not entirely convincing, as is also evident from their later ordination of Origen as presbyter in connection with his next visit to Caesarea. Origen was called back and returned to Alexandria. The fame of Origen as teacher was spreading, and he was invited to the imperial court in Antioch, and later sent to Athens on an important ecclesiastical mission.[19] When Origen on his trip to Athens was ordained a presbyter by the bishops of Caesarea and Jerusalem as an approval of his teaching in the church, and probably in an attempt to settle him in Palestine, the bishop of Alexandria acted by accusing him of castrating himself in his youth and the Palestinian bishops of thus ordaining someone not fit to be ordained.[20] According to Eusebius it was the fame of Origen that gradually had become a problem

---

15 Euseb., *Hist. eccl.* 6.2-3.

16 Euseb., *Hist. eccl.* 6.3.8.

17 Euseb., *Hist. eccl.* 6.19.15.

18 Euseb., *Hist. eccl.* 6.19.16-9.

19 Euseb., *Hist. eccl.* 6.21.3-4 (Antioch), 6.23.4 (Athens).

20 Euseb., *Hist. eccl.* 6.8.4.

for bishop Demetrius, who was overtaken with jealousy.[21] Although it is evident that Eusebius is biased in favour of Origen it is likely that there had been a growing conflict between Demetrius and Origen. But it is less obvious whether this conflict was mainly personal or it also included doctrinal aspects. There is, however, little evidence that it in fact was part of a more general struggle between an academic Christian tradition and a developing ecclesiastical institution. When Origen as a result of the accusations decided to move to Caesarea, and Demetrius died soon after, the tensions seem to have disappeared.

In contrast to previous tensions the following period witnesses a very close relation between school and bishopric. In Alexandria Origen's former student and close associate, Heraclas took over the leadership of the school. According to Eusebius, Heraclas had originally been a student of pagan philosophy, who had been attracted by Origen and later hired by him to teach on an elementary level.[22] When Origen left in 231 A.D. Heraclas had been attached to the school for several decades, and was probably responsible for much of the teaching taking Origen's frequent travels into account. Unlike Origen Heraclas had been ordained presbyter in Alexandria and thus more formally attached to the bishopric of the city.[23] When Demetrius died soon after Origen's departure it was Heraclas who became bishop of the city and another pupil of Origen, Dionysius became the head of the school. When Heraclas died in 248 his successor at the school became bishop.

With Demetrius' successors Heraclas and Dionysius we thus have bishops of Alexandria who seem to have controlled the Christian community including the school tradition and have been recognised as leaders both by the Church at large and by local secular authorities. Both were educated in the tradition represented by Origen and according to him Heraclas encountered the same criticism as he himself for his interest in pagan philosophy. Heraclas is even said to have continued to wear the garb of the philosophers after he was ordained a presbyter of the Church.[24] As well educated teachers Heraclas and Dionysius, probably in contrast to Demetrius, were able to unite the Christian academic tradition and the emerging ecclesiastical institution. Dionysius, who personally faced persecutions under both Decian and Valerian, is known both for his contribution to church regulations on baptism and admittance of heretics and those who lapsed in the persecutions, as well as his refutations of Epicureanism and his critical biblical scholarship.[25] It is also in the time of Dionysius that we have the first evidence for a responsibility on the part of the Alexandrian bishop for other bishops in the region, i.e. Egypt and Cyrenaica.[26]

The real challenge to the academic tradition of the Alexandrian school of Christianity

---

21 Euseb., *Hist. eccl.* 6.8.3-4.

22 Euseb., *Hist. eccl.* 6.15.

23 The precise meaning of the term presbyter in the Alexandrian church in the first half of the third century is a matter of debate. See Koch 1921, 43-8, Hornschuh1960; Mees 1984, 114-26; Neymeyr 1989, 47-9, 86-93.

24 Euseb., *Hist. eccl.* 6.19.14

25 For Dionysius see Bienert 1978.

26 Euseb., *Hist. eccl.* 7.24.1-9.

and its position in the church was throughout the third century not the bishop, but the so called *simpliciores*. Already Clement had pointed out a difference between simple believers and Christians with deeper understanding (*gnosis*) and in Origen's writings this distinction is fundamental.[27] It was against the faith of these simple Christian believers that the pagan critics directed their writings. The fact that not only Origen, but also Heraclas and Dionysius had to defend themselves against accusations of being too closely connected with pagans and heretics shows that the simpliciores were probably not unimportant within the Christian community. But even if Origen was officially deposed and he as well as Dionysius was later criticised on dogmatic grounds, there is no evidence that the school tradition disappeared after them. Although little is known about the school in the latter part of the third century, some important teachers and authors like Theognostus and Pierius, are known to us through the much later academic tradition of the monks of the Egyptian desert.[28]

4. Persecution and Schism

The most important and dramatic shift in the early development of Christianity in Alexandria came as a result of the severe persecutions of the Christians under Diocletian. In contrast to earlier persecutions, which had been sporadic and had centred upon a few prominent members of the Christian community, the persecutions under Diocletian were well organised and aimed at eradicating the church, which in cities like Alexandria had grown into a strong institution. When the persecutions hit Alexandria, the Alexandrian archbishop, Peter, went into hiding.[29] Other ecclesiastical leaders, including several Egyptian bishops were detained, and some later killed, severely maimed or exiled. Some, however, decided to accept the imperial edict and renounce their Christian allegiance. Melitius, who was appointed bishop of Lycopolis to replace one of the lapsed bishops, became an itinerant bishop rather than taking up the dangerous position in Upper Egypt. Accusing the leaders in exile or hiding for not doing their job he took upon himself to take care of the ordinations of presbyters and bishops for the vacated churches, thus usurping the position of the archbishop of Alexandria.[30] His acts were, however, not accepted by the majority, who remained faithful to Peter, and thus a schism between rival hierarchies was established.

The most prominent teacher in Alexandria, Pierius, was apparently not arrested, but free to leave for Rome, a move that later caused accusations against him for earning his freedom by yielding to the authorities. It is quite likely that it was now easier for Christian teachers than for the ordained clergy to escape persecution. As lay persons

---

27   See Hällström 1984.

28   See Radford 1908. For Pierius in Egyptian monasticism see Rubenson 1995, pp. 179-82.

29   On Peter of Alexandria see Vivian 1988. Peter must have left Alexandria sometime in 305, but we cannot establish firmly for how long he was absent from the city. He had most probably been back for some time when he was martyred in 311.

30   For a discussion of the developments and the conflicting sources see Williams 2001, 32-6.

they did not represent the institution and they could either just keep quiet or leave the cities. Even if there are earlier examples of Christian ascetics living outside the civic centres, there are good reasons to believe that the emergence of the monastic tradition in the early fourth century is partly linked to teachers of Alexandrian tradition settling down on the fringes of the desert as a result of the persecutions. The image of Antony as a pioneer of the movement, emerging from a comparison of his letters and the biographical account, the *Vita Antonii,* suggests, for example, that Antony was educated in an Alexandrian tradition in the latter part of the third century.[31] The first episode in the *Vita* which connects Antony to any known historical facts actually depicts him as appearing as a Christian apologist in Alexandria during the persecutions. Denied martyrdom he decides at the end of the persecutions to live an ascetic life in the inner desert "in daily martyrdom."[32]

When the persecutions finally ended Alexandrian Christianity had lost many of its most prominent members. Even if lay teachers seem to have been less harshly treated than clerics, the persecutions dealt a heavy blow to the tradition of accommodation between pagan and Christian philosophy. Except for Didymus the blind we do not hear about any Christian independent teacher in Alexandria in the fourth century. Considering the abundance of Alexandrian sources for the century, especially in comparison with the previous centuries, this is remarkable. In contrast not only to the Alexandrian bishops of the third century, but also to bishops in other parts of the Empire none of the fourth-century bishops of Alexandria seems to have had a background in Greek philosophy. It is, moreover, not in Alexandria, but in the desert that we find the teachers cherishing the writings of Origen and his disciples.[33] By the end of the century they are even singled out as a major problem for archbishop Theophilus of Alexandria, who decides to send them into exile in what is generally called the first Origenist controversy.

In Alexandria itself the persecution ended in bitter conflicts, which came to dominate much of the fourth century. In addition to the Melitian schism with its rival hierarchy, a popular preacher and theologian, the presbyter Arius refused to be silenced when he was accused of heresy and sentenced by his bishop Alexander.[34] As argued by Williams the conflict between Arius and the archbishops must partly be understood as a conflict between Christian intellectuals preserving a philosophical and rather conservative tradition and the archbishops trying to establish a social institution centred upon the liturgy and social work, and those responsible for this, i.e. the ordained ministers of the Church. Both the Melitian and Arian schisms were taken up at the great council gathered at Nicaea in 325 to celebrate Constantine's complete victory and the establishment of a concord between the emperor and the entire Church represented by all its bishops. The decisions of the council were, however, not easily implemented, and certainly not in Alexandria. The stubborn refusal of Athanasius, bishop from 328 to

31 For a detailed discussion of the texts and a comparison see Rubenson 1995, 126-44.
32 *Vita Antonii* 46-47.
33 See Rubenson 1999.
34 On the career of Arius see Williams 2001, 44-81.

372, to compromise led to his being exiled five times and on several occasions the army had to be called in in support of him or his opponents. At stake were not only pivotal dogmatic issues partly related to basic philosophical presuppositions, but also questions about the social and political role of the bishop, and more specifically in what sense the bishop was subordinate to the emperor.[35]

5. Archbishop and Emperor

With the decision of Constantine to make the Church an established and in certain respects privileged institution of the empire there was a need to make sure how and by whom the church was governed. Thus the council of Nicaea, summoned by the emperor, who also attended some of its sessions, had among other issues to decide on rules for participation in church communion, rules for ordination of clergy and geographical areas of jurisdiction for bishops on various levels. In general the secular administrative structure became decisive also for the church, but on account of their importance Alexandria, Antioch and Rome were singled out as having more universal jurisdictions in their respective areas. The bishops of these cities and some other important capitals o provinces were consequently designated archbishops. In the sixth century, after Jerusalem and Constantinople had been added to the list, the bishops of these cities were called patriarchs. Their prerogative was to ordain and if necessary depose the metropolitan bishops, who were responsible for the churches in their province, and to hear appeals from their judgements.

In the case of Alexandria there seems to have been a tradition already earlier that all bishops in Egypt and Libya had to be approved of and ordained directly by the bishop of Alexandria, probably since there were originally no provinces in Egypt and thus no metropolitans. With the recognition of the church and the privileges given to its representatives, the bishop of Alexandria became a very powerful man. Given the importance of Alexandria for the empire and especially for the delivery of wheat to the new capital, Constantinople, and the recurrent waves of upheavals in the city, the archbishop of Alexandria turned out to be a key figure of the imperial administration. At a council in Tyre in 335, archbishop Athanasius of Alexandria was accused of having threatened to halt the fleet of corn going to the capital, an accusation that led to one of his periods of exile.[36]

At the end of his long reign as archbishop of Alexandria Athanasius had secured not only his victory over both Melitians and Arians, but also a position for his office that could not be neglected by any emperor or council. Twice the emperors had tried to appoint their own choices to replace him, but in both cases Athanasius prevailed. Supported by on the one hand many other bishops, primarily the bishop of Rome, and on the other by the local Church and with it parts of the population in Alexandria, any new emperor preferred to attempt reconciliation and recalled the archbishop from his exile.

---

35 The conflict between the emperors and Athanasius is vividly depicted in Barnes 1993.
36 On the early career of Athanasius and the accusations against him at the synod of Tyre see Arnold 1991, 103-73.

When Athanasius died the position as archbishop of Alexandria had become a centre of political and economic power of its own. As a consequence succession became a matter of major concern to the institution itself. Successors were thus either selected from the closest associates of the previous archbishop, or in the case of Cyril and Dioscorus in fifth century even from the family of the archbishop.

Although the percentage of actual baptised members of the Church was still fairly low in Alexandria at the end of the fourth century, the changes in imperial policy towards pagan cult, made it possible for the Christians to confront the representatives of classical tradition in the city. The attempts in the 380's of the envoy of Emperor Theodosius, to enforce decisions on the closure of temples and the prohibition of sacrifice had already engaged the defenders of the traditions, primarily teachers of Neo-Pythagorean and Neo-Platonic schools. The subsequent violent conflicts seem to have been largely between pagan and Christian students and to have centred on the practice of pagan cult. As in the case of the destruction of the Serapeum in 391 triumphant Christian students desecrating pagan cult objects enraged pagan students and teachers of philosophy resulting in violence. Without the support of the authorities the representatives of the pagan cults could not defend their shrines.[37]

It would, however, be misleading to think that the violent actions against the pagan tradition in the city were part of an ecclesiastical policy. Both Theophilus and his successor Cyril were eager to keep good relations with the largely pagan elite of the city as well as with the imperial administration, whose main interest was to avoid violent clashes in the city. Recent studies on the career of Hypatia, the famous female philosopher of the city in the first decade of the fifth century, show that many of her students were Christians. Of these several became bishops which did not prevent them from staying in close contact with her.[38] The descriptions of student life in Alexandria in the late fifth century, moreover, proves that the tradition of pagan schools and even pagan cult was still very much alive.

The main problem for archbishops like Theophilus and Cyril was not the continued presence of pagan schools and shrines. In addition to recurring street violence which often included attacks on Christian students by Jews or pagans enraged by imperial support for Christianity, their main concern was with various forms of opposition within their own ranks, an opposition often based in intellectual circles. Theophilus was throughout his career as archbishop accused by his associates as well as by monastic teachers, for various forms of corruption and a fondness for being more interested in buildings than in people. When his opponents turned to the archbishop in Constantinople, John Chrysostom, he sided with his rivals opponents, including members of the imperial household, and in 403 he was able to have John deposed. When Theophilus died a violent conflict erupted between Cyril, his nephew, who had most probably been singled out by him to be his successor, and the archdeacon Timothy. It was only through the intervention of the au-

---

37 On the destruction of the Serapeum see Haas 1997, 159-69.
38 For Hypatia and her Christian students see Dzielska 1995, 27-46.

thorities that Cyril could be installed.[39] Cyril was soon to be engaged in a bitter fight with the highest secular authority in Alexandria, the prefect Orestes. Although the sources are conflicting on the reasons and development of the conflict, it seems clear that the issue was the question of the supreme authority of the archbishop in the religious affairs of the city, and especially in relation to Christian opponents and to the Jewish community.[40] As is evident from the story of Hypatia, the pagan philosopher with Christian students, the Christians were strongly divided on the issue of how to deal with the pagan tradition. Although probably not implicated in the riot against and murder of Hypatia, Cyril sided with the anti-pagan forces, probably knowing the the emperor would support him against the local pagan elite. In the subsequent conflicts between the Antiochene and Alexandrian churches, Cyril was likewise able to gain the support of the emperor and in 431 have several of his critics, including the archbishop of the capital deposed. In 449 his successor Dioscorus was entrusted to chair a new ecumenical council at which a third archbishop of Constantinople was deposed.

Thus by the middle of the fifth century it seemed as if the archbishops of Alexandria were not only holding power in Alexandria itself, but among the most powerful persons in the empire. In Constantinople they had their own agents and the support of monastic institutions, and throughout the provinces there were bishops who had their background in Alexandria. With the death of Theodosius II and the promotion of Marcian, a general, to imperial power in 450, things changed. The archbishop of Alexandria, Dioscorus had already offended Rome at the council of 449 and when the new emperor invited all bishops to a new council at Chalcedon nothing was done to secure support for the Alexandrian archbishop. On the contrary, Dioscorus was deposed, not for any dogmatic reason, but for his conduct, and a new dogmatic definition, based on a letter from Rome and unacceptable to the church in Egypt and much of the East, was promulgated. Except for a minority in Alexandria the entire church in Egypt stood by their deposed patriarch, and a permanent schism between the imperial and the Alexandrian church was a fact. The anti-Chalcedonians did not accept the deposition of their man, and when he died in exile they elected their own successor, uninterred by the lack of imperial recognition.

6. Monks and Bishops

A major factor in the development of Christianity in Alexandria and the role played by the bishops of the great city was the emergence of the monastic tradition. Asceticism was deeply rooted in the Christian tradition, and especially in the philosophical school tradition. With the growing importance of Neo-Pythagoreanism and Neo-Platonism in the third century asceticism of some kind became a necessary part of philosophy. For Origen asceticism and renunciation of the material world was necessary to gain

---

39 Our main source is the Church historian Socrates. See his *Hist. eccl.* 7.7. For a critical examination of his account see Wessel 2004, 15-7.

40 See Wessel 2004, 17-22, 45 for an examination of the issues.

spiritual knowledge and communion with the divine. As recent studies have gradually shown Egyptian monastic tradition owns much of its ideals and teachings to him and his disciples.[41]

A new interpretation of the sources, as well as recent studies of the papyri that document the first monastic centres, show that the first monks were not at all as illiterate and asocial as has been claimed. They were clearly involved in economic and political affairs and had both the intellectual and material resources to communicate with prominent people in the cities and have an influence there.[42] The letters of St. Antony, written in the desert in the 330's make it likely that he had studied in a school of Christian philosophy dependent on the heritage of Origen.[43] Others who left the cities, including Alexandria in the first decades of the fourth century had much of the same background. Others, like Didymus stayed in Alexandria as a teacher of Christian philosophy, but in addition kept a cell in the desert.

Between the emerging monastic centres in the desert south of Alexandria and in the desert along the Nile, and the established churches with their bishops there was a certain tension. The monks persisted on their own independence and their own spiritual formation and were often critical of the people of the cities, including bishops. The bishops, on the other hand, feared that the monks would support their opponents and undermine their position. From papyri found in the desert we know of at least two monastic communities that sided with the Melitian opposition to Athanasius.[44] Other monks and monasteries were reluctant to become involved in the conflicts of the bishops.

In order to gain the support of the monks and to have them involved in the responsibilities of the church institution Athanasius tried hard to have loyal monks ordained as bishops, but many refused, preferring the solitude and independence of the monastic teacher and philosopher of the desert. Only gradually was the archbishop able to make his influence felt inside the monastic tradition, as is clear from his festal letters, and for instance define what literature was to be read as canonical by the monks. Athanasius' success in finally gaining almost a universal support of the monastic tradition speaks loudly about his abilities and his willingness to accommodate to the demands and views of the monks. In return he gained the probably strongest support he could find in his staunch opposition to the demands of the emperors.[45]

Athanasius' successors continued his policy of looking for monastic support and of ordaining prominent monks as bishops. But the rapid growth of the monastic establishments south of Alexandria, and the steady flow of intellectuals into the monastic retreats, tended to increase the tension. Monks enlisted in ecclesiastical service were

41 See Rubenson 1999.
42 See Wipszycka 1994.
43 See Rubenson 1995, 59-88.
44 See the discussion of the Meletian papyri in Bell 1924 and of the Nephoros archive in Krämer & Shelton 1987.
45 On Athanasius and the monks see Brakke 1995.

not always servile, and Theophilus became harshly criticised by his monastic associates for his way of handling the money entrusted to him. Leading monastic intellectuals refused to be ordained by him and treated him with contempt. The fact that Origen and several of his disciples were read and highly regarded by the leading monks, while criticism of Origen's teaching was gaining ground in other ecclesiastical centres, gave Theophilus a possibility to act against his most vocal monastic opponents.[46] Origen was condemned by a synod in Alexandria in 400, and the monastic centres were raided for their support of Origen. The intellectual leaders of the centres of Cellia and Nitria, not far from Alexandria, were sent into exile, and the archbishop made it entirely clear that monks were to obey the bishops. The successors of Theophilus, realised the importance of the monasteries for ecclesiastical politics. In the ensuing conflicts with the pagan elite of Alexandria the monks became an important factor as is shown both in the case of Cyril's attack on pagan cult and the struggle between Christian and pagan students in Alexandria the late fifth century.[47]

Conclusion

The early phase of Christianity in Alexandria is primarily known to us through the presence of a number of Christian teachers during the second century. They established a tradition of Christian schools and some of them became prominent philosophers gaining recognition both in the city and in the wider Christian community. Their success as teachers resulted in the growth of a Christian community which in the third century was led by a series of Christian philosophers. The severe and prolonged persecutions of the Christian leadership of Alexandria in 303-311 resulted in schisms as well as a rift between the leadership of the church and the school. The recognition of the position of the bishop of Alexandria by Emperor Constantine and his successors gave the bishops of the fourth century a completely new official position and responsibility. In their efforts to unite the Christians under their control they encountered opposition from groups of intellectuals who had settled on the fringes of the desert. With support from the local authorities the bishops were able to defeat the opposition and with the support of the imperial power they could unite the Christians against the continued pagan tradition of parts of the Alexandrian elite.

46 For the controversy between Theophilus and the monks see Clark 1992 and Rubenson 333-7.
47 For these conflicts we have an excellent source in the biography over Severus of Antioch by Zacharaias Scholasticus. For an analysis see Trombley 1993-94, vol. 1, 1-28 and Haas 1997, 326-30.

References

Adriani, A. 1961-66 *Repertorio d'arte dell'Egitto greco-romano* (series C, vols. 1-3) Palermo: Fondazione "Ignazio Mormino" del Banco di Sicilia.

Arnold, D. 1991 *The Early Episcopal Career of Athanasius of Alexandria* Notre Dame-London: University of Notre Dame Press.

Bagnall, R. 1993 *Egypt in Late Antiquity* Princeton: Princeton University Press.

Barnes, T. 1993 *Athanasius and Constantius: Theology and Politics in the Constantinian Empire* Cambridge, MA: Harvard University Press.

Bauer, W. 1934 *Rechtgläubigkeit und Ketzerei im frühesten Christentum* Tübingen: Mohr.

Bell, H.I. 1924 *Jews and Christians in Egypt. The Jewish Troubles in Alexandria and the Athanasian Controversy* London: Quaritch (reprinted Westport, Co.: Greenwood Press 1976).

Bienert, W. 1978 *Dionysius von Alexandrien* (Patristische Texte und Studien 21) Berlin-New York: Walter de Gruyter.

Brakke, D. 1995 *Athanasius and Asceticism* Oxford-New York: Oxford University Press.

Buell, D.K. 1999 *Making Christians: Clement of Alexandria and the Rhetoric of Legitimacy* Princeton: Princeton University Press.

Clark, Elizabeth 1992 *The Origenist Controversy* Princeton: Princeton University Press.

Dzielska, M. 1995 *Hypatia of Alexandria* Cambridge, MA-London: Harvard University Press.

Empereur, J.-Y. 1998 *Alexandria Rediscovered* London: British Museum Press.

Griggs, C.W. 1990 *Early Egyptian Christianity. From its Origins to 451 C.E.* Leiden: Brill.

Haas, C. 1997 *Alexandria in Late Antiquity. Topography and Social Conflict* Baltimore-London: The John Hopkins University Press.

Hällström, G. af 1984 *Fides simpliciorum according to Origen of Alexandria* (Commentationes humanarum litterarum 76) Helsinki: Societas Scientiarium Fennica.

Hornschuh, M. 1960 "Das Leben des Origenes und die Entstehung der alexandrinischen Schule" *Zeitschrift für Kirchengeschichte* 71, 193-203.

Koch, H. 1921 "War Clemens von Alexandrien Priester?" *Zeitschrift für neutestamentliche Wissenschaft* 20, 43-8

Krämer, B. & Shelton, J. (eds.) 1987 *Das Archiv des Nepheros und verwandte Texte* (Aegyptiaca Treverensia IV) Mainz: Philipp von Zabern.

Mees, M. 1984 "Die frühe Christengemeinde von Alexandrien und die Theologie des Klemens von Alexandrien" *Lat.* 50, 114-126.

Neymeyr, U. 1989 *Die christlichen Lehrer im zweiten Jahrhundert* (Supplements to Vigiliae Christianae 4) Leiden: Brill.

Pearson, B. & Goehring, J. (eds.) 1986 *The Roots of Egyptian Christianity* Philadelphia: Fortress Press.

Pouderon, B. 1997 *D'Athènes à Alexandrie. Études sur Athénagore et les origines de la philosophie chrétienne* (Bibliothèque Copte de Nag Hammadi, Études 4) Québec-Louvain-Paris:Édition Peeters.

Radford, L.B. 1908 *Three Teachers of Alexandria: Theognostus, Pierius and Peter* Cambridge: Cambridge University Press.

Roberts, C. 1979 *Manuscript, Society and Belief in early Christian Egypt* London-New York: Oxford University Press.

Rubenson, S. 1995 *The Letters of St. Antony* Minneapolis: Fortress Press.

Rubenson, S. 1999 "Origen in the Egyptian Monastic Tradition of the Fourth Century" in: W.A. Bienert & U. Kühneweg (eds.) *Origeniana Septima* Leuven: Peeters, 319-37.

Scholten, C. 1995 "Die alexandrinische Katechetenschule" *Jahrbuch für Antike und Christentum* 38, 16-37.

Trombley, F. 1993-94 *Hellenic Religion and Christianization, c. 370-529* (2 vols.) (Religions in the Greco-Roman World 115:2) Leiden: Brill.

Vivian, T. 1988 *St. Peter of Alexandria: Bishop and Martyr* Philadelphia: Fortress Press.

Wessel, S. 2004 *Cyril of Alexandria and the Nestorian Controversy* Oxford: Oxford University Press.

Williams, R. 2001 *Arius. Heresy and Tradition* London: SCM Press (second edition).

Wipszycka, E. 1994 "Le monachisme égyptien et les villes" *Travaux et mémoires* 12, 1-44.

CHAPTER 8

Religious Conflict in Late Antique Alexandria: Christian Responses to "Pagan" Statues in the Fourth and Fifth Centuries CE

Troels Myrup Kristensen

1. Introduction

At several points in its history, the city of Alexandria witnessed tension between different social, ethnic and religious groups that occasionally erupted into violence. The fourth and fifth centuries CE, a time of religious and social change across the Mediterranean, were no exception. As such, the rise and ultimate "triumph" of Christianity took place within an already complex social, religious and political setting in the Egyptian metropolis.[1] Religious violence as the outcome of local tensions between Christian and pagan groups is furthermore observable in both the historical and archaeological record for Late Antique Alexandria.

Pagan statues came to play a significant role in these conflicts, most notably in the closing of Alexandria's famous Serapeum in 392 CE.[2] In the Classical world, statues were an important component of civic and religious life in all urban centres, Alexandria included.[3] Christian responses to pagan statues demonstrate both continuity and change, and the destruction of the Serapeum's cult statue only represents one extreme.

---

[1] On Alexandria in Late Antiquity see Haas 1997; Heinen 1991; 1998; McKenzie 2003, 58-61; 2007, 229-60; Hahn 2004, 15-120; Watts 2006a, 143-231; Kiss 2007. On Christianisation and its consequences in Alexandria see Kaegi 1966; Bernand 1966, 79; Bagnall 1993, 278-89; Trombley 1993-94, vol. 2, 1-51; Frankfurter 1998, *passim*. On religious conflict in Late Antiquity see Croke & Harries 1982; Beatrice 1990; Brown 1998; Gaddis 2005; Whitby 2006.

[2] Such statues are at present more frequently referred to as "mythological," "allegorical" or *Idealplastik*, thus downplaying the religious significance that they could have had to some viewers. Note the discussion in Stirling 2005, 22-8.

[3] On classical cities as "cities of sculpture" see Beard & Henderson 2001, 83.

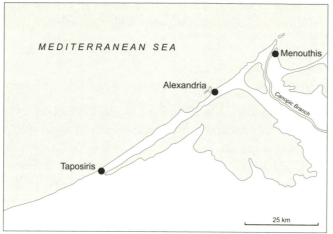

Map of Alexandria and hinterland (based on Bagnall & Rathbone 2004, 74).

Fig. 1

In this paper, I review the literary and archaeological evidence for these responses and what they reveal about early Christian attitudes towards the past.

Using Alexandria and its hinterland (Fig. 1) as a case study offers both opportunities and challenges. We possess a large number of literary sources to the history of the city in Late Antiquity, especially by Christian church historians, but the triumphal nature of these inevitably leads to doubts over their accuracy and value. At the same time, the archaeological remains we have from Late Antique Alexandria are scant and often difficult to interpret. However, recent years have seen an increase in our understanding of the city's topography in Late Antiquity as well as a growth in comparative material, and this allows us to moderate the often one-sided views expressed in the triumphant Christian literary tradition. The historical and archaeological evidence from Late Antique Alexandria thus provides a testing ground to show the range of Christian response to pagan sculpture that existed in one single city.[4]

The religious conflicts in Late Antique Alexandria are primarily rooted in a specifically local context, but they are also part of a larger picture, particularly that of the Christianisation of the Roman world and how this process came to shape social interaction and religious expression in cities across the Mediterranean. It is thus important to contextualise them within the broader phenomena of religious conflict and change in the Late Antique world. In his account of the events around 392 CE, Theodoret dryly notes that after the Serapeum's destruction, "all over the world the shrines of the idols were destroyed."[5] To an extent this comment can be disregarded as little more than one Christian's fantasy of fanaticism, but it also reminds us that the religious conflicts in Alexandria were not isolated from the rest of the world. To

---

4   For a (more or less) complete catalogue of statuary from Alexandria see Tkaczow 1993, 230-42 (Pharaonic), 183-98 (Ptolemaic), 243-60 (Roman), 285-92 (Late Roman/Byzantine), 309-19 (uncertain date).

5   Theodoret, *Hist. eccl.* 5.22, trans. Schaff & Wace.

contextualise the evidence from Alexandria, it is therefore necessary first to see what early Christian writers reveal about attitudes towards pagan sculpture and how these changed over time.

2. Early Christians and Pagan Statues

With its roots in the Judaic tradition and the Mosaic prohibition against idolatry, early Christianity had a seemingly troubled relationship to images, especially those with a pagan subject matter. However, Jewish attitudes towards images were by no means static or uniform. This is for example seen in the *Abodah Zarah* that discusses the complexities of the religious prohibition against idols in an immensely detailed fashion.[6] The prescribed responses to sculpture in the round range from destruction by pulverisation to rituals of nullification through only superficially destructive means, but also more accepting attitudes of, for example, fragments of statuary. Regardless of this ambiguity in the Jewish tradition, vocal attacks on the practices of idolatry became a regular fixture in several Christian writings in the second and third centuries CE. Damning critique of idolatry is thus a core component of Clement of Alexandria's *Exhortation to the Greeks*.[7] The point raised time and time again by theological commentators such as Clement and his peer Tertullian is that images were manmade, lifeless and thus could be destroyed just like any other material object. The attitude and wording of these Church fathers is, as we shall see, mirrored in the descriptions of iconoclasm in Late Antique authors.

The view that early Christian authors argued so fiercely against was that images had powers of their own and in that sense were alive. Concepts of living images and divine presence in representations have been important aspects of "popular" religion in many societies.[8] Concern over the supernatural agency of images is also expressed in the eighth-century *Parastaseis syntomoi chronikai* that warns its readers to "…take care when you look at old statues, especially pagan ones."[9] Exposed in this view are not only the potentialities of representation but also how the power of images could advocate both positive and negative responses.[10] Much of Clement's text argues against these popular beliefs, and he tauntingly proclaims that "even monkeys know better than this."[11] Nonetheless, demonic (rather than divine) presences in images are frequently evoked in Christian hagiographies of Late Antiquity. Unlike theological writers, these texts are less concerned with what idols *are* than what they *do*. By emphasising their demonic

---

6   On the complexities of art and Judaism see Fine 2005. See Kelley 1994; Levine 2000, 336-44 for discussions of art and iconoclasm in synagogues. On the biblical prohibition of idolatry see Besançon 2000, 63-108.

7   Clem. Al., *Protr.*, esp. book 4.

8   On "living images" see Dodds 1947, 63-4; Frontisi-Ducroux 1975; Caviness 2003; Maniura & Shepherd 2006.

9   *Parastaseis Syntomoi Chronikai* 28, trans. Av. Cameron & J. Herrin (1984). On the *Parastaseis* and its view of pagan monuments see also James 1996; Donkow 2002.

10 On the history of responses to images see Freedberg 1989; Gamboni 1997.

11 Clem. Al., *Protr.* 4.51, trans. Butterworth.

powers, the images became worthy but ultimately futile opponents of the saints whose lives were being written up.

Aside from the theological discussions of idolatry, pagan images do not appear to have been a crucial concern during the fourth and fifth centuries, when Christianity became the dominant religion of the Roman Empire.[12] The edicts preserved in the Theodosian Code are rarely concerned with sculpture, and when they are, it occurs in the context of worship and sacrifice which is condemned repeatedly and punished severely.[13] The art of the early Christian period is furthermore characterised by its ability to draw on earlier traditions including the iconography of pagan divinities, and display of both old and new statues continued in both the public and private spheres.[14] The new capital of Constantinople was thus adorned with statuary from pagan sanctuaries across the Mediterranean.[15] Reinterpretation of images and imagery was crucial to the construction of early Christian society.

Yet this view of continuity in attitudes towards sculpture is paralleled by a different tradition that emphasises Christian violence and destruction. This tradition draws mainly on literary sources that inform us of the iconoclastic tendencies of bishops, monks and Christian mobs. Their attacks on images were occasionally carried out in spite of the official stand of ecclesiastical and secular authorities.[16] In recent years, a number of scholars have begun to investigate the archaeological evidence for the Christian destruction of statuary in Late Antiquity.[17] This development is partly led by an archaeological interest in understanding the fragmentary state of many sculptures that survive to this day. The causes of fragmentation may of course be many and difficult to establish firmly. When destruction and mutilation of sculpture took place, it may have had political or other non-religious significance. We must also keep in mind that seemingly destructive acts could have had other meanings than exclusively negative ones.[18] However, it is possible to convincingly argue that Christian violence was involved in a number of cases. Both literary and archaeological sources thus make it clear that some Christian groups and individuals in the fourth and fifth centuries were hostile to pagan sculpture, even

---

12 See especially the discussions in Stirling 2005, 156-63.

13 *Cod. Theod.* 16.10, *passim*. Iconophobia is here directly evoked: "if any person … should suddenly fear the effigies which he himself has formed … [he/she] shall be punished by the forfeiture of that house or landholding in which it is proved that he served a pagan superstition" (16.10.12.2, trans. Pharr).

14 On sculpture in Late Antiquity see Hannestad 1994; 1999; 2007; Stirling 2005; Bauer & Witschel 2007.

15 On collections of statuary in Late Antique Constantinople see Mango 1963; Bassett 2004.

16 An edict issued in 423 thus condemns Christian violence against pagans (*Cod. Theod.* 16.10.24).

17 On the destruction and mutilation of statues in Late Antiquity see Stewart 1999; 2003, 290-298; Rothaus 2000, 105-25; Hannestad 2001; Sauer 2003; Kristensen in prep.

18 See for example Croxford 2003 for an interpretation of the fragmentation of sculpture in a (late) Romano-British context. Note also *Thesaurus Cultus et Rituum Antiquorum* vol. 2, 501-7.

Fig. 2

The site of the Alexandrian Serapeum as it appears today. Photo: author.

if attitudes changed over time and never were uniformly held by all members of the Christian community.[19]

In recent years, it has been emphasised by several scholars that statuary with pagan motifs continued to be on display in domestic setting, at least into the fifth century.[20] The find of a perfectly preserved cache of statuary from a suburban villa in Sidi Bishr offers evidence of this continuity in an Alexandrian context.[21] However, this cache also raises important issues given the fact that it was intentionally hidden, presumably as a means of safekeeping. The case of the destruction of the Serapeum and its sculptures may give us an idea of what possible dangers the Sidi Bishr cache had been hidden from.

3. The Destruction of the Serapeum and its Statuary

The destruction of Alexandria's Serapeum in 392 CE is alongside the murder of the philosopher Hypatia among the best known cases of religious violence in Late Antiquity (Fig. 2-3). The background and sequence of events leading up to its destruction have been discussed extensively elsewhere,[22] and I will here focus on the fate of the temple's

---

19 Mango 1963; Thornton 1986.

20 On the continuity of sculptural embellishment of houses in Late Antiquity see Hannestad 1994, 105-49; 2007; Stirling 2005. However, sculpture in domestic contexts was occasionally destroyed by Christians, for example by Shenoute in the case of Gesios (Besa, *Life of Shenoute,* 125-26), and the bishop Porphyrius in Gaza breaking into houses after the destruction of the Marneion (Mark the Deacon, *Life of Porphyrius,* 71). Only one edict in *Cod. Theod.* is concerned with domestic sculpture, but only in the context of sacrifice (16.10.12.2).

21 The cache included 13 sculptures, several of which are now on display in the Antiquities Museum of the Bibliotheca Alexandrina. On this group see Gassowska 1977; Hannestad 1994, 123-6; 2007, 292-3; Kiss 2007, 195-6.

22 On the Serapeum see now the fundamental work of Sabottka 2008 as well as the historical syn-

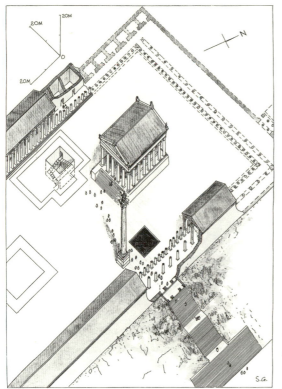

Reconstruction drawing of the Sera-   **Fig. 3**
peum in its latest phase, after 298
CE. Drawing by Sheila Gibson (from
McKenzie, Gibson & Reyes 2004, pl. I).

sculptural decoration that is known from a number of literary sources. It is important to note, however, that the attack on the Serapeum was not the first example of religious conflict in Alexandria known from historical sources that centred on pagan sculpture. Already in 325 CE, the patriarch Alexander was involved in a controversy over the local cult of Cronus and its cult statue. In the end, the temple was rededicated as the church of Theonas, and the wooden cult statue was broken into pieces that were re-carved in the shape of a cross.[23]

The Serapeum, in the neighbourhood of Rhakotis on the south-eastern outskirts of the city, had been founded in the early Ptolemaic period and was famous for its admirable collection of life-like sculpture.[24] The chryselephantine cult statue of Serapis is described

---

thesis in Hahn 2004, 78-97; 2006. Hahn argues that the year of the destruction was early 392. The history of the Serapeum is also discussed in O'Leary 1938, 52-3; Schwartz 1966; Haas 1997, 159-68; McKenzie 2003, 50-7; McKenzie, Gibson & Reyes 2004, 107-10.

23 Haas 1997, 209-10. This is the earliest temple conversion known from Alexandria, although admittedly the source for the event is very late (tenth-century).

24 Amm. Marc. 22.16.12 describes the statues of the Serapeum as "almost breathing." On the sculptural decoration of the Serapeum see McKenzie, Gibson & Reyes 2004, 79-81; 100-1. Individual pieces from the Serapeum are collected in Tkaczow 1993.

in great detail by Clement, who informs us that it was made by Bryaxis, although there is no consensus which sculptor by that name he refers to.[25] Some of the statue's intricate devices to "deceive" pagan worshippers and to turn it into a "living image" are described by Rufinus.[26] However, the most important aspect of the cult statue as conceptualised by the inhabitants of Alexandria was the very persistent idea that its destruction would lead to the end of the world.[27] The fourth-century bishops of Alexandria were keen to prove that this was not the case, and their attempts to intervene in the activities at the Serapeum led to several episodes of violent conflict, including one that cost the Patriarch George his life after he had vowed to destroy the sanctuary.[28] The attack in 392 CE thus represented the final outcome of a long-going struggle between pagans and Christians in Alexandria.

The event that ultimately led to the destruction of the Serapeum and its cult statue also involved pagan statuary. During renovation work at a Christian basilica that had been constructed on the remains of either a Mithraeum or a temple of Dionysus,[29] pagan cult objects were retrieved from an underground chamber. These objects included a number of "ridiculous" statues that were taken in an impromptu procession to the city's Agora. Interestingly, the inclusion in the parade of images of *phalli* evokes memories (at least to the modern reader) of a similar golden specimen carried in procession during the festival of Ptolemaeia centuries before and described by Callixinus of Rhodes.[30] The procession and desecration of the images provoked the pagans to the degree that they after an initial attack on the Christians barricaded themselves in the Serapeum.

Theophilus finally succeeded in closing the temple by imperial intervention after a particularly violent stand-off between the pagans inside the Serapeum and the Christians outside. The fate of the cult statue of Serapis is known from several sources, of which Rufinus represents the earliest and most comprehensive. A number of the sources present detailed narratives of the destruction of the cult statue, carefully designed to persuade their readers that the centuries-old image did not hold supernatural powers. While some sources focus on Theophilus as the protagonist behind the destruction of the temple, others give us a more direct picture of the events as they unfolded on the ground. We are thus told that it was a Christian soldier who attacked the statue, mockingly referred to as "the Old Man," with his double-edged axe:

---

25   On the cult statue of Serapis see Bernand 1966, 128-9; McKenzie, Gibson & Reyes 2004, 79-81. On the iconography on Serapis see *LIMC* 7.1, 666-92. A reminiscence of the statue may be seen in a wooden statue of Serapis preserved from the Fayyum (Alexandria Greco-Roman Museum, inv. 23352).

26   Rufinus, *Hist. eccl.* 11.23.

27   Rufinus, *Hist. eccl.* 11.23.

28   A similar fate came upon Dracontius, the superintendent of Alexandria's mint who had destroyed an altar (of Juno Moneta?) in the Caesareum, cf. Haas 1997, 288, 292-3; Kiss 2007, 191-2.

29   Mithraeum: Socrates, *Hist. eccl.* 5.16. Temple of Dionysus: Sozom., *Hist. eccl.* 7.15.

30   Rice 1983: 21.

Thus with repeated strokes he felled the smoke-grimed deity of rotten wood, which upon being thrown down burned as easily as dry wood when it was kindled. After this the head was wrenched from the neck, the bushel having been taken down, and dragged off; then the feet and other members were chopped off with axes and dragged apart with ropes attached, and piece by piece, each in a different place, the decrepit dotard was burned to ashes before the eyes of the Alexandria which had worshiped him. Last of all the torso which was left was put to the torch in the amphitheatre.[31]

The triumphal strain of the narrative comes through very clearly in this passage when Rufinus informs us how the severed limbs of the powerless idol were distributed across Alexandria and burnt for citizens in all parts of the city to see. Disconcerting but also revelatory of Christian concepts of images is the fact that the murder of Hypatia was followed by similar treatment, as her body was first disarticulated and then burnt.[32]

The burning of the cult statue partly served to publicly signify the Christian victory over the cult of Serapis, but just as importantly, it very literally demonstrated for the superstitious inhabitants of Alexandria that the statue really was powerless, just as Christian polemicists had preached for centuries. A number of other Christian *topoi* on idols can be observed in the church historians that describe the destruction of Serapeum. In his version of the story, Theodoret for example mocks the cult statue, calling it a "lifeless block" and "a dwelling place for mice."[33] The successful attack on the cult statue thus revealed once and for all the weakness of their former patron god to the citizens of Alexandria. A similar point is made in a marginal illustration in the Papyrus Goleniščev, an illustrated manuscript made in Alexandria and now in Moscow.[34] In one often-reproduced illustration, the cult statue of Serapis with its *modius* is clearly visible inside the temple that is shown with a triumphant Theophilus on top. The far from subtle implication is that between Serapis and Theophilus, the latter was the most powerful.

A closer look at the literary sources for the destruction of the Serapeum reveals a variety of fates for the remainder of the temple's sculptural decoration. According to Socrates, the bronze statues were melted down to be recast as pots and other utensils in the city's churches.[35] However, one statue was kept with the explicitly stated purpose

---

31 Rufinus, *Hist. eccl.* 2.23, trans. Amidan.

32 On Hypatia see Dzielska 1995; Watts 2006b. John of Nikiu explicitly links Hypatia and idolatry (*Chronicle* 84.103).

33 Theodoret, *Hist. eccl.* 5.22, trans. Schaff & Wace.

34 The original publication of the Papyrus Goleniščev with excellent colour plates is Bauer & Strzygowski 1906. Theophilus and the Serapeum are shown on folio VI verso. The accompanying fragment of monks throwing rocks is folio VI verso A. Suggestions for the date of the papyrus range from early fifth to the eighth century. See also Elsner 1998, 256-7; Haas 1997, 179-80; Kiss 2007, 193-4.

35 Socrates, *Hist. eccl.* 5.16. This also seems to be the common fate of the "adornments of the temples" mentioned by Firm. Mat., *Err. prof. rel.* 28.6. See also *Anth. Pal.* 9.773 on the irony of the transformation of statues into frying-pans *et alia*.

of displaying it for mockery in a public space.³⁶ Reinterpretation of images and other pagan objects can also be observed. The most noteworthy episode in this regard was the interpretation by Christians roaming the temple ruins of a number of hieroglyphs as being prophetic representations of crosses.³⁷ This may be disregarded as a wishful misunderstanding, but it is difficult to blame the Christians at this time since knowledge of the meaning of hieroglyphs was dwindling, as clearly revealed by some of the misguided readings in Horapollon's *Hieroglyphica*, written during the same period.

Archaeological excavations at the site of the Serapeum from the late eighteenth century onwards have uncovered the fragmentary remains of buildings dating to the Ptolemaic, Roman and later periods (Figs. 2-3).³⁸ The majority of the sculpture from the site, ranging in date from the Pharaonic to the Roman period, was unearthed in early excavations and unfortunately comes with very little contextual information.³⁹ However, it is clear that far from all the statuary from the Serapis was destroyed or burnt as described in the literary sources. Excavations in 1905-6 thus unearthed a polychrome head of Serapis that shows very little damage other than from what appears to be accidental breakage.⁴⁰

The defining feature of the Serapeum site today is the so-called "Pompey's Pillar," raised by Diocletian in 298 after his victory over the usurper Domitius Domitianus. Similar to other columns of this type, it originally held a statue on top, most likely a portrait of Diocletian himself. Various cuttings and other features to support such a statue have been located on top of the column.⁴¹ These suggest that the statue was of colossal size. A number of porphyry fragments, found in the late eighteenth century and now missing, may come from this statue, given that some of them were found in the immediate vicinity of the Pillar.⁴² However, the history of the discovery of these fragments and their subsequent disappearance make it impossible to establish whether they in fact had fallen from the top of the column, and if so, when and why. Of course, a number of other causes than Christian violence could have been responsible for such an event, even if it is interesting to note the thirteenth-century mosaics in Venice's San Marco that show pagan statues being pulled down from similar columns.⁴³

Concerning the end of the Alexandrian Serapeum and its sculptures, we thus depend almost entirely on a strongly biased Christian literary tradition. The archaeological evidence confirms the church historians' view that the temple was razed to the ground.⁴⁴ However, it is also clear that the responses to the pagan images in the sanctuary were rather more diverse, ranging from destruction to reinterpretation. The archaeology

36 Such was the fate in later times of a nude statue of Venus placed for mockery and stoning outside a church in Trier see Gramaccini 1996, 41, abb. 10.

37 Socrates, *Hist. eccl.* 5.17.

38 For a thorough history of the excavations of the Serapeum see Sabottka 2008, 3-29.

39 Tkaczow 1993, 233-8; 244-7; 285-6; 335-6.

40 Alexandria Graeco-Roman Museum, inv. no. 3912 see Tkaczow 1993, 245, no. 160.

41 See Fraser 1972, vol. 2, 85-9, § 4, with further references.

42 Delbrueck 1932, 100-1; Tkaczow 1993, 285-286, nos. 269-269A; Kiss 2007, 187.

43 See Gramaccini 1996, 30, abb. 3-4; Sauer 2003, 65.

44 McKenzie, Gibson & Reyes 2004, 107.

demonstrates a similar range of responses, and a number of the statues that survive to this day may simply have been ignored or forgotten because they were of little interest or concern to the Christians. Some statues were moved, either for mockery as we saw in one case, or simply knocked over and since forgotten. Palladas describes one such statue of Heracles in one of his epigrams, but similar to what Olympius and other pagans argued after the attack on the Serapeum, the downfall of their representations did not impair the powers of the gods.[45] As Heracles himself states in the words of Palladas: "Even though I am a god I have learnt to serve the times."[46]

4. Further Christian Responses to Pagan Statues in Alexandria

A number of other sculptures from Alexandria provide further evidence of Christian responses to pagan images. Some of these can be included in a larger group of sculptures that have been furnished with a secondary carving of a Christian cross sometime during Late Antiquity.[47] The most prominent example of this kind of response is found on an over-life-size, cuirassed statue of a young Marcus Aurelius (Fig. 4).[48] On the lower part of the cuirass, the original relief decoration has been removed and a cross has been carved in its place. Two further examples of secondary carvings of crosses on sculpture, a male and a female portrait, are also known from Alexandria.[49] The location of the secondary crosses on these sculptures is on the head. Very little is known about the archaeological context of these sculptures, and it is impossible to date when they were furnished with crosses.

The carving of crosses on statuary can be interpreted in both positive and negative ways. It may be understood as a reaction against the iconophobia inherent in early Christian literature dealing with images, as a way of "neutralising" the powers believed to be inherent in the image, perhaps even as exorcism. Yet, it may also be seen in a more positive light as part of a ritual act of baptism or as a means of accepting the pagan image into a Christian life.[50] The practice seems to be entirely limited to the eastern part of the Mediterranean, and the Alexandrian examples do not help us to solve the matter

---

45 *Anth. Pal.* 9.441.

46 *Anth. Pal.* 9.441, trans. Paton.

47 This phenomenon is often referred to as *sphragis* see Delivorrias 1991; Hjort 1993; Marinescu 1996.

48 Alexandria Greco-Roman Museum, inv. 3250 see Graindor 1939, 58-61. The statue was found during construction works in the Zizinia neighbourhood of Alexandria. See also Bergmann 1978, 20-1, abb. 22; Kiss 1984, 64; Tkaczow 1993, 248-9, no. 169 (note incorrect inv. no.).

49 Male portrait: Alexandria Greco-Roman Museum, inv. 22186 see Graindor 1939, 27, note 111; Delivorrias 1991, 113, note 31; Marinescu 1996, 289, cat. no. 13. Female portrait: Alexandria Greco-Roman Museum, inv. 3607 see Graindor 1939, 59; Delivorrias 1991, 113, note 31; Marinescu 1996, 289, cat. no. 12.

50 Hjort 1993, 111. The use of the cross as a means of "purifying" a formerly pagan place or monument is commonly attested (e.g. in *Cod. Theod.* 16.10.25), also in the literary sources concerning Alexandria. Rufinus informs us that after the destruction of the Serapeum, busts of Serapis in public and private spaces were defaced and then replaced by crosses (*Hist. eccl.* 2.29).

of their interpretation. The statue of Marcus Aurelius was found alongside a number of other sculptures, none of which were furnished with a cross, and it is difficult to know why exactly this particular representation was singled out for this response, although its monumental size (2.15 m in height) may have been a factor.[51]

Literary sources suggest that some sculptures from pagan temples in Alexandria survived intact in their original setting until the seventh century and the Arab conquest of Egypt. A group of statues in the Tychaeum that included representations of both gods and men are thus mentioned by the Byzantine historian Theophylact Simocatta as still standing on their pedestals.[52] This may suggest that the statues had been reinterpreted as Christian figures as happened in a number of other cases, most notably in the case of Marcus Aurelius' equestrian statue on Campidoglio.

The archaeological material from Alexandria at large confirms the complex nature of responses to pagan statues during Late Antiquity. The sculpture unearthed by the Polish excavations at Kom el-Dikka demonstrates this point.[53] Finds include sculpture in the round dating to the sixth century and with Christian motifs, and although a large part of the material is heavily fragmented there is little to suggest that systematic destruction or mutilation took place.[54] Some finds raise questions, however. Fragments of a life-size chryselephantine statue that apparently had been hacked into pieces and then deliberately burnt were found in a mid-fifth-century destruction layer west of the imperial baths.[55] The identity of the statue has been suggested as Serapis or Isis, and its original location may have been in a nearby sanctuary. Alongside the chryselephantine fragments were found two headless busts of Serapis, both blackened by fire.[56] These also appear to have been mutilated before disposal. Although the date of the deposition and burning of these objects is slightly later, the find is intriguing given the historical evidence quoted above that images of Serapis were burnt after the destruction of the Serapeum. It can be difficult to establish the cause of such fire damage, even if in other cases it has been connected to Christian violence.[57] This cache of burnt sculptures may

51 The statue was found sometime around 1872 during construction work on Horeya Street at the site of the former Zizinia Theatre. It was found together with a nude torso (Tkaczow 1993, 248, no. 168), an Isis-Tyche (Tkaczow 1993, 249, no. 170) and a possible portrait of Alexander the Great, also over-life-size (Tkaczow 1993, 313, no. 342, now missing).

52 Theophylact Simocatta, *History* 8.13.10. On the Tychaeum and its sculptures see Fraser 1972, vol. 1, 242; vol. 2, 392-3 n. 417.

53 The sculptures from the Polish excavations at Kom el-Dikka (in both public and private contexts) have been published in Kiss 1988.

54 Fragments are numerous, see e.g. Kiss 1988 figs. 84-130. A statuette of Hygieia was found face-down, reused as a paving stone, presumably in the late fourth century, in House H, but it is difficult to see this kind of reuse as decidedly destructive, see Daszewski 1991.

55 Rodziewicz 1992; Lapatin 2001, 150-1, no. 51; *Thesaurus Cultus et Rituum Antiquorum* II, 506, no. 765.

56 Rodziewicz 1992, 320, 324, fig. 7.

57 Christian agency has been suggested as responsible for the fire damage at a number of temples (with statuary) in Cyrene, cf. Goodchild, Reynolds & Herington 1958: 40.

Cuirassed statue of Marcus Aurelius with inscribed cross, Alexan- **Fig. 4**
dria Greco-Roman Museum (from Kiss 1984).

be one of the best archaeological cases from Alexandria of Christian mutilation and destruction of pagan statues.

5. Responses to Pagan Statues in Alexandria's Hinterland

Adopting the larger perspective of the immediate hinterland of Alexandria, a number of other sites inform us of the Christian responses to pagan images, both through literary and archaeological sources. Many of these cases are slightly later in date than those known from Alexandria and suggest the continuity of pagan practices in the countryside into the fifth century.

The most well-known case involving statuary occurred in the 480s at the site of Menouthis, east of Alexandria.[58] Here, the Patriarch Peter located a large collection of idols hidden behind a double wall in a Temple of Isis. The worst atrocity, however, was not the presence of the statues themselves, but the fact that the patriarch and his entourage found clear evidence of sacrifice and worship. Thus, both incense and sacrificial cakes were found, and an altar was covered in blood.[59] These are the criteria to establish that a pagan cult is active according to the Theodosian Code, and are thus important

---

58 See Kaegi 1966; Trombley 1993-94, vol. 2, 219-25; Hahn 2004, 101-5.
59 Zachariah of Mytilene, *Life of Severus* 27-9.

for what followed.[60] The idols were loaded onto twenty camels and taken to a public "trial" in which Peter presided, held in the centre of Alexandria:[61]

> "When he [Peter] had sat down with them [the city's officials], he had the priest of the idols brought forth and ordered him to remain standing in a certain elevated place. Then, after the idols had been exhibited, he began to interrogate him. He asked what this idolatry meant which was used on lifeless matter, ordered him to give the name of all the demons and to tell what was the cause and the form of each of them. At that moment all of the people already had come to see. He listened to what was said and then mocked the infamous actions of the pagan gods which the priest revealed. When the altar of bronze had arrived together with the wooden serpent, the priest confessed the sacrifices which he had dared to complete, and declared that the wooden serpent was the one which had deceived Eve … It was then delivered to the flames, along with the other idols."[62]

This vivid account tells us in great detail of the public aspect of the destruction of pagan images at a time when the population of Alexandria was almost entirely Christian. The public "trial" bears all the bureaucratic traits that the Theodosian Code assigned; inventories were made before the idols were transported to the city, and the legality of the action is emphasised by the presence of not only the patriarch but what is portrayed as the entire city, including all of its highest officials. The response of the Christian authorities is once again deeply embedded in local politics. At the same time, as Frank Trombley has suggested, the inventory made of the statues suggests pecuniary motives, and it was clearly only the worthless wooden idols that were burnt.[63]

A contrast to the fate of the statuary from Menouthis is observable at the site of Ras el-Soda, immediately east of Alexandria. Excavations in 1936 revealed the well-preserved remains of an Isis temple with its cache of five cult statues in perfect condition and still *in situ* on a podium in the cella (Fig. 5).[64] The details of how this particular sanctuary went out of use are not known, but it seems that it was completely forgotten and simply covered by sand.

Recent Hungarian excavations inside the Sanctuary of Osiris at Taposiris Magna, located on the Mediterranean coast west of Alexandria, demonstrate some of the difficulties of interpreting sculpture in secondary contexts.[65] Similar to a number of other Egyptian sanctuaries that shared the same fort-like structure, the temple at Taposiris was converted into a Roman fortress in the second or third century. Later again, it

---

60 *Cod. Theod.* 16.10.12.2.

61 The statuary collected did apparently not all originate from the Menouthis temple, as some had been transported there from Memphis, cf. Zachariah of Mytilene, *Life of Severus* 29.

62 Zachariah of Mytilene, *Life of Severus* 29-35, quoted from Kaegi 1966, 252f.

63 Trombley 1993-94, vol. 2, 223-4.

64 Adriani 1940; Naerebout 2007.

65 Vörös 2004.

The statues of the Ras el-Soda **Fig. 5**
temple shortly after their dis-
covery (from Adriani 1940, pl.
LIX, fig. 1).

came to serve as a Coptic monastery. During the excavations, three fragments of a basalt half-life-size statue of Isis were found at several different locations within the sanctuary.[66] In spite of its small size, the excavators have suggested that this was the temple's cult statue. The well-preserved head was found in the temple courtyard, and two fragments of the torso had been reused as pivot stones in the south gate, dating to the early Byzantine period. Close to the pivot stones, a cross had been carved on the pavement. The excavators have suggested that the statue had been hidden by the last pagans at the site, similar to a number of cult vessels also found at Taposiris, and then later uncovered by iconoclastic monks. There is no evidence of this, and it is to very difficult to interpret the fragmented state of the statue. Looking at the individual pieces, the head is very well-preserved, and although cut off from the torso, the cause of this break is difficult to establish. The other pieces are very fragmented, but have also been shaped into a convenient size for architectural reuse. We do not know if the statue had been mutilated before parts of it were reused as pivot stones. Was this reuse purposefully demeaning or simply pragmatic? Would the fragments even have been recognised as being from an idol? Similar issues are raised in studies of spoliation, and too little has so far been published about the archaeological context of the Taposiris statue to establish the motifs behind its fragmentation and later reuse.

6. Conclusion

In spite of interpretive problems, the archaeological and literary sources from Late Antique Alexandria and its hinterland suggest a wide spectrum of Christian responses to pagan sculpture, including full-scale destruction in the case of the cult statue of Serapis,

---

66 Vörös 2004, 128-39. Other interesting finds from the excavations that may be suggestive of the religious climate during the period of Christianisation include a fragment of a life-size male portrait in black granite (*ibid.*, 60) and the temple's inventory of metal vessels, hidden in the corner of a small room (*ibid.*, 94-125).

rituals of exorcism or "neutralisation" such as the three examples of Alexandrian statues with secondary carvings of crosses, pragmatic reuse seen at both Taposiris, the Serapeum and the temple of Cronus, public display and mockery of idols (again in the case of the Serapeum), and finally reinterpretation of which the Tychaeum sculptures may be examples of. We also see an example from Sidi Bishr of the deliberate deposition of sculpture as a means of safekeeping, presumably from Christian violence, although this kind of deposition of statuary has been a hotly debated topic.[67] In the case of Ras el-Soda, the temple and its cult statues seem to simply have been forgotten. This spectrum of responses has implications for how we understand Late Antique religious conflict and violence, and suggests an inherent Christian ambivalence towards pagan statues. When destruction took place, it usually carried social, symbolic or political significance (perhaps even economic in the case of Menouthis) rather than strictly religious. Christian responses to pagan sculpture thus cannot be studied in isolation.

In histories of Late Antique social and religious transformation, Alexandria is often presented as a place where religious conflict and violence was rampant. There is ample literary evidence to suggest this. This violence may be seen as the result of the "brutalisa-tion of local politics" or "progressive Christianisation,"[68] and may have little to do with the edicts issued by the imperial government. Regardless of the cause of the violence, its limits are clearly seen in both the literary and archaeological sources as nowhere is systematic destruction or mutilation of pagan sculpture evident. It seems that even in Alexandria, undisputed evidence for the Christian destruction of images can be hard to come by, although there are a number of potentially suggestive cases, especially the find of the burnt statues at Kom el-Dikka.

For studying religious conflict in Late Antique Alexandria, the historical and archaeological sources both have their weaknesses and strength. The bias of the Christian literature concerning the "end" of pagan cult at Alexandria makes it difficult to accept them at face value. The archaeological evidence is notoriously difficult to interpret and often poorly documented. Yet the two compliment each other in suggesting that even in a place where religious conflict was seemingly rampant in Late Antiquity, it is still possible to locate a very broad range of Christian responses to the pagan past.

---

67 See e.g. the discussion over the deposition of sculpture in House C (also known as the Omega House) at the Athenian Agora in Frantz 1986, 90 (deposition as reverence) and Rothaus 2000, 117 (deposition as exorcism or ritual burial).

68 "Brutalisation": Mitchell 2007, 320; "progressive Christianisation": Haas 1997, 179.

References

Adriani, A. 1940 "Sanctuaire de l'époque romaine a Ras el Soda" *Annuaire du Musée Gréco-Romain* 2, 136-48.

Bagnall, R.S. 1993 *Egypt in Late Antiquity* Princeton: Princeton University Press.

Bassett, S. 2004 *The Urban Image of Late Antique Constantinople* Cambridge: Cambridge University Press.

Bauer, A. & Strzygowski, J. 1906 *Eine alexandrinische Weltchronik. Text und Miniaturen eines griechischen Papyrus der Sammlung W. Goleniščev* (Denkschriften der kaiserlichen Akademie der Wissenschaften. Philosophisch-historische Klasse, Band 51) Wien: Gerold.

Bauer, F.A. & Witschel, C. (eds.) 2007 *Stauen in der Spätantike* Wiesbaden: Reichert Verlag.

Beard, M. & Henderson, J. 2001 *Classical Art from Greece to Rome* Oxford: Oxford University Press.

Beatrice, P.F. (ed.) 1990 *L'intolleranza cristiana nei confronti dei pagani* Bologna: Centro Editoriale Dehoniano.

Bergmann, M. 1978 *Marc Aurel* (Monographie 2) Frankfurt: Liebighaus.

Bernand, A. 1966 *Alexandrie la Grande* Paris: Arthaud.

Besançon, A. 2000 *The Forbidden Image. An Intellectual History of Iconoclasm* Chicago: University of Chicago Press.

Brown, P. 1998 "Christianization and Religious Conflict" in: *Cambridge Ancient History* vol. 13, Cambridge: Cambridge University Press 632-64 (second edition).

Cameron, A. & Herrin, J. (eds.) 1984 *Constantinople in the Early Eighth Century: The Parastaseis Syntomoi Chronikai* Leiden: Brill.

Caviness, M.H. 2003 "Iconoclasm and Iconophobia: Four Historical Case Studies" *Diogenes* 50:3, 99-114.

Croke, B. & Harries, J. 1982 *Religious Conflict in Fourth-Century Rome. A Documentary Study* Sydney: Sydney University Press.

Croxford, B. 2003 "Iconoclasm in Roman Britain?" *Britannia* 34, 81-95.

Daszewski, W.A. 1991 "A Statuette of Hygieia from Kam el-Dikka in Alexandria", Mitteilungen des Deutschen Archäologischen Instituts, Abteilung Kairo 47, 61-66.

Delbrueck, R. 1932 *Antike Porphyrwerke* (2 vols.) Berlin: Walter de Gruyter.

Delivorrias, A. 1991 "Interpretatio Christiana. Γύρω απο τα όρια του Παγανιστικού και Χριρτιανικού Κόσμου" in: *Ευφρόσυνον. Αφιέρωμα στον Μανόλη Χατζηδάκη* (vol. 1) Athens: Archaeological Society of Athens, 107-23.

Dodds, E.R. 1947 "Theurgy and its Relationship to Neoplatonism" *Journal of Roman Studies* 37, 55-69.

Donkow, I. 2002 "Byzantine Attitudes towards Ancient Remains as expressed in *Parastaseis syntomoi chronikai*" = *http://www.srii.org/ IzabellaDonkow.pdf* (accessed 1 August 2007).

Dzielska, M. 1995 *Hypatia of Alexandria* Cambridge, MA: Harvard University Press.

Elsner, J. 1998 *Imperial Rome and Christian Triumph* Oxford: Oxford University Press.

Fine, S. 2005 *Art and Judaism in the Greco-Roman World: Toward a new Jewish Archaeology* Cambridge: Cambridge University Press.

Frankfurter, D. 1998 *Religion in Roman Egypt. Assimilation and Resistance* Princeton, NJ: Princeton University Press.

Frantz, A. 1988 *The Athenian Agora XXIV. Late Antiquity: A.D. 267-700* Princeton, NJ: American School of Classical Studies at Athens.

Fraser, P.M. 1972 *Ptolematic Alexandria* (3 vols.) Oxford: Clarendon Press.

Freedberg, D. 1989 *The Power of Images: Studies in the History and Theory of Response* Chicago: University of Chicago Press.

Frontisi-Ducroux, F. 1975 "Statues vivantes" in: F. Frontisi-Ducroux & P. Vidal-Naquet (eds.) *Dédale. Mythologie de l'artisan en Grèce ancienne* Paris: François Maspero, 95-117.

Gaddis, M. 2005 *"There Is No Crime For Those Who Have Christ": Religious Violence in the Christian Roman Empire* Berkeley: University of California Press.

Gamboni, D. 1997 *The Destruction of Art. Iconoclasm and Vandalism since the French Revolution* London: Reaktion Books.

Gassowska, B. 1977 "Depozyt rzeźb z Sidi Bishr w Aleksandrii" in: M.L. Bernhard (ed.) *Starożytna Aleksandria w badaniach polskich* Warsaw: PWN, 99-118.

Goodchild, R.G., Reynolds, J.M. & Herington, C.J. 1958 "The Temple of Zeus in Cyrene: Studies and Discoveries in 1954-1957" *Papers of the British School at Rome* 26, 30-62.

Graindor, P. 1939 *Bustes et statues-portraits d'Égypte romaine* Le Caire: Imprimerie P. Barbey.

Gramaccini, N. 1996 *Mirabilia. Das Nachleben antiker Statuen vor der Renaissance* Mainz: Philipp von Zabern.

Haas, C. 1997 *Alexandria in Late Antiquity. Topography and Social Conflict* Baltimore: The Johns Hopkins University Press.

Hahn, J. 2004 *Gewalt und religiöser Konflikt. Studien zu den Auseinandersetzungen zwischen Christen, Heiden und Juden im Osten des Römischen Reiches (von Konstantin bis Theodosius II.)* Berlin: Akademie Verlag.

Hahn, J. 2006 "*Vetustus error extinctus est* – Wann wurde das Sarapeion von Alexandria zerstört?" *Historia* 55:3, 368-83.

Hannestad, N. 1994 *Tradition in Late Antique Sculpture. Conservation, Modernization, Production* Aarhus: Aarhus University Press.

Hannestad, N. 1999 "How did rising Christianity cope with Pagan Sculpture?" in: E. Chrysos & I.Wood (eds.) *East and West: Modes of Communication. Proceedings of the First Plenary Conference at Merida* Leiden: Brill, 173-204.

Hannestad, N. 2001 "Castration in the Baths" in: N. Birkle, I. Domes, S. Fähndrich, A. Nießner, T. Reiß & A. Zschätzsch (eds.) *Macellum. Culinaria Archaeologica. Robert Fleischer zum 60. Geburtstag von Kollegen, Freunden und Schülern* Mainz: Nicole Birkle, 66-77.

Hannestad, N. 2007 "Late Antique Mythological Sculpture – In Search of a Chronology" in: Bauer & Witschel (eds.) *Statuen in der Spätantike* Wiesbaden: Reichert Verlag, 273-305.

Heinen, H. 1991 "Alexandria in Late Antiquity" *Coptic Encyclopedia* 1, 99-100.

Heinen, H. 1998 "Das spätantike Alexandrien" in: M. Krause (ed.) *Ägypten in spätantik-christlicher Zeit. Einführung in die koptische Kultur* Wiesbaden: Dr. Ludwig Reichert Verlag, 57-79.

Hjort, Ø. 1993 "Augustus Christianus – Livia Christiana: *Sphragis* and Roman Portrait Sculpture" in: Rydén & Rosenqvist (eds.) *Aspects of Late Antiquity and Early Byzantium* (Transactions 4) Stockholm: Swedish Research Institute in Istanbul, 99-112.

James, L. 1996 ""Pray Not to Fall into Temptation and Be on Your Guard": Pagan Statues in Christian Constantinople" *Gesta* 35:1 12-20.

Kaegi, W.E. 1966 "The Fifth-century Twilight of Byzantine Paganism" *Classica & Medievalia* 27, 243- 275.

Kelley, C.P. 1994 "Who did the Iconoclasm in the Dura Synagogue?" *Bulletin of the American Schools of Oriental Research* 295, 57-72.

Kiss, Z. 1988 *Alexandrie IV. Sculptures des fouilles polonaises à Kôm el-Dikka 1960-1982* Warsaw: PNW – Éditions Scientifiques de Pologne.

Kiss, Z. 1984 *Études sur le portrait impérial romain en Egypte* Warsaw: PNW – Editions Scientifiques de Pologne.

Kiss, Z. 2007 "Alexandria in the fourth to seventh centuries" in: R.S. Bagnall (ed.) *Egypt in the Byzantine World, 300-700* Cambridge: Cambridge University Press, 187-206.

Kristensen, T.M. in prep. *Archaeologies of Response: Christian Destruction, Mutilation and Transformation of Sculpture in Late Antiquity* (PhD dissertation) University of Aarhus.

Lapatin, K.D.S. 2001 *Chryselephantine Statuary in the Ancient Mediterranean World* Oxford: Oxford University Press.

Levine, L.I. 2000 *The Ancient Synagogue. The First Thousand Years* New Haven: Yale University Press.

Mango, C. 1963 "Antique Statuary and the Byzantine Beholder" *Dumbarton Oaks Papers* 17, 55-75.

Maniura, R. & Shepherd, R. 2006 *Presence. The Inherence of the Prototype within Images and Other Objects* Aldershot: Ashgate.

McKenzie, J. 2003 "Glimpsing Alexandria through Archaeological Evidence" *Journal of Roman Archaeology* 16, 35-61.

McKenzie, J. 2007 *The Architecture of Alexandria and Egypt c. 300 BC to AD 700* New Haven: Yale University Press.

McKenzie, J., Gibson, S. & Reyes, A.T. 2004 "Reconstructing the Serapeum in Alexandria from the Archaeological Evidence" *Journal of Roman Studies* 94, 73-121.

Marinescu, C.A. 1996 "Transformations: Classical Objects and their Re-Use during Late Antiquity" in: R.W. Mathisen & H.S. Sivan (eds.) *Shifting Frontiers in Late Antiquity* Aldershot: Ashgate, 285-98.

Mitchell, S. 2007 *A History of the Later Roman Empire, AD 284-641. The Transformation of the Ancient World* Malden, MA: Blackwell.

Naerebout, F.G. 2007 "The Temple at Ras el-Soda. Is it an Isis temple? Is it Greek, Roman, Egyptian, or neither? And so what?" in: L. Bricault, M.J. Versluys & P.G.P. Meyboom (eds.) *Nile into Tiber. Egypt in the Roman World* Leiden: Brill, 506-54.

O'Leary, D.L. 1938 "The Destruction of Temples in Egypt" *Bulletin de la Société d'Archéologie Copte* 4, 51-7.

Rice, E.E. 1983 *The Grand Procession of Ptolemy Philadelphus* Oxford: Oxford University Press.

Rodziewicz, E. 1992 "Remarks on Chryselephantine Statue from Alexandria" in: G.P. Carratelli, *et al.* (eds.) *Roma e l'Egitto nell'Antichità Classica. Cairo, 6-9 Febbraio 1989. Atti del I Congresso Internazionale Italo-Egiziano* Roma: Istituto Poligrafico e Zecca dello Stato, 317-28.

Rothaus, R. 2000 *Corinth: The First City of Greece. An Urban History of Late Antique Cult and Religion* Leiden: Brill.

Sabottka, M. 2008 *Das Serapeum in Alexandria* Le Caire: Institut français d'archéologie orientale.

Sauer, E. 2003 *The Archaeology of Religious Hatred in the Roman and Early Medieval World* Stroud: Tempus.

Schwartz, J. 1966 "La fin du Sérapeum d'Alexandrie" *American Studies in Papyrology* 1, 97-111.

Stewart, P. 1999 "The destruction of statues in late antiquity" in: R. Miles (ed.) *Constructing Identities in Late Antiquity* London: Routledge, 159-89.

Stewart, P. 2003 *Statues in Roman Society* Cambridge: Cambridge University Press.

Stirling, L.M. 2005 *The Learned Collector. Mythological Statuettes and Classical Taste in Late Antique Gaul* Ann Arbor: The University of Michigan Press.

Thornton, T.C.G. 1986 "The Destruction of Idols – Sinful or Meritorious?" Journal of Theological Studies 37: 121-9.

Tkaczow, B. 1993 *Topography of Ancient Alexandria. An Archaeological Map* Warsaw: Centré d'Archéologie Méditerranéenne de l'Academie Polonaise des Sciences.

Trombley, F. 1993-94 *Hellenic Religion and Christianization, c. 370-529* (2 vols.) (Religions in the Greco-Roman World 115:2) Leiden: Brill.

Vörös, G. 2004 *Taposiris Magna 1998-2004. Alexandriai Magyar Ásatások* Budapest: Egypt Excavation Society of Hungary.

Watts, E. 2006a *City and School in Late Antique Athens and Alexandria* Berkeley, CA: University of California Press.

Watts, E. 2006b "The Murder of Hypatia: Acceptable or Unacceptable Violence?" in: H. Drake (ed.) *Violence in Late Antiquity. Perceptions and Practices* Aldershot: Ashgate, 333-42.

Whitby, M. 2006 "Factions, Bishops, Violence and Urban Decline" in: J.-U. Krause & C. Witschel (eds.) *Die Stadt in der Spätantike – Niedergang oder Wandel?* Stuttgart: Franz Steiner Verlag, 441-61.

Professor emeritus Per Bilde
Independent Scholar in Religious Studies
Himmelbjergvej 116, Laven
8600 Silkeborg, Denmark
pb@ballebo.dk

Associate Professor George Hinge
Department of Language, Literatur
and Culture
Classical Philology
University of Aarhus
Victor Albecks Vej 2, 8000 Aarhus C
Denmark
george.hinge@hum.au.dk

Professor Emerita Minna Skafte Jensen
University of Southern Denmark
Campusvej 55, 5230 Odense M
Denmark
minna.s.j@gmail.com

Associate Professor Jens A. Krasilnikoff
Department of History and Area Studies
Victor Albecks Vej 2, 8000 Aarhus C
Denmark
hisjk@hum.au.dk

PhD student Troels Myrup Kristensen
Department of Archaeology,
Anthropology and Linguistics
University of Aarhus
Victor Albecks Vej 2, 8000 Aarhus C
Denmark
klatmk@hum.au.dk

Associate Professor Anders Klostergaard
Petersen
Department of the Study of Religion
University of Aarhus
Tåsingegade 3, 8000 Århus C, Denmark
akp@teo.au.dk

Professor Samuel Rubenson
Centrum för Teologi och
Religionsvetenskap, Hs 36
University of Lund
Sweden
Samuel.Rubenson@teol.lu.se

Professor Marjorie Susan Venit
Department of Art History
and Archaeology
University of Maryland
College Park, MD 20742-1335, USA
venit@umd.edu